Sierra Hotel

Sierra Hotel

Flying Air Force Fighters in the Decade after Vietnam

By

C. R. Anderegg

GOVERNMENT REPRINTS PRESS
Washington, D.C.

© Ross & Perry, Inc. 2001 All rights reserved.

No claim to U.S. government work contained throughout this book.

Protected under the Berne Convention. Published 2001

Printed in The United States of America
Ross & Perry, Inc. Publishers
717 Second St., N.E., Suite 200
Washington, D.C. 20002
Telephone (202) 675-8300
Facsimile (202) 675-8400
info@RossPerry.com

SAN 253-8555

Government Reprints Press Edition 2001

Government Reprints Press is an Imprint of Ross & Perry, Inc.

Library of Congress Control Number: 2001095687
http://www.GPOreprints.com

ISBN 1-931839-04-2

Image on cover provided by www.af.mil

⊗ The paper used in this publication meets the requirements for permanence established by
the American National Standard for Information Sciences "Permanence of Paper for Printed
Library Materials" (ANSI Z39.48-1984).

Foreword

In February 1999, only a few weeks before the U.S. Air Force spearheaded NATO's Allied Force air campaign against Serbia, Col. C. R. Anderegg, USAF (Ret.), visited the commander of the U.S. Air Forces in Europe. Colonel Anderegg had known Gen. John Jumper since they had served together as jet forward air controllers in Southeast Asia nearly thirty years earlier. From the vantage point of 1999, they looked back to the day in February 1970, when they first controlled a laser-guided bomb strike. In this book Anderegg takes us from "glimmers of hope" like that one through other major improvements in the Air Force that came between the Vietnam War and the Gulf War.

Always central in Anderegg's account of those changes are the people who made them. This is a very personal book by an officer who participated in the transformation he describes so vividly. Much of his story revolves around the Fighter Weapons School at Nellis Air Force Base (AFB), Nevada, where he served two tours as an instructor pilot specializing in guided munitions. But he also takes a look at other "Fighter Mafia" outposts in the Pentagon and elsewhere. Readers meet young Mafiosi like John Jumper, Larry Keith, Ron Keys, Joe Bob Phillips, Earl Henderson, Moody Suter, John Corder, Jim Brown, John Vickery, Jack Lefforge, Jack Ihle, Stump Bowen, Dave Dellwardt, Tommy Dyches, John Madden, and Dick Myers.

As one might expect to find in a fighter pilot story, there is a lot of fun along the way. For a distilled example, consult the appendix on "Jeremiah Weed" (replete with instructions for drinking "afterburners"). Colonel Anderegg's book is likely to please anyone with an interest in fighter pilots and how they molded today's Air Force.

RICHARD P. HALLION
Air Force Historian

Contents

Part I: The Vietnam School of Hard Knocks

Part II: Changing of the Guard

Part III: The Training Revolution

Part IV: Killing the Target

Part V: Reticles to HUDs—The New Fighters

Illustrations
Figures

Photographs

Introduction

During the time I was hard at work on my first book, *The Ash Warriors,* about the explosion of Mount Pinatubo and the actions at Clark Air Base, the Philippines, Lt. Gen. Marv Esmond, USAF, approached me at a gathering hosted by a mutual friend. Esmond, whom I knew only through his reputation as a superb fighter pilot and respected leader, asked me how my book was going. When I replied that it was a good story and easy to tell, he said, "Good. I've got one I want you to write." When I hesitated by pointing out that I was pretty busy with *The Ash Warriors*, he laughed and said, "Well, you can do two at the same time, can't you?" This was a typical fighter pilot challenge. He might have said, "Can't you walk and chew gum at the same time?" and it would have meant the same thing. He knew that because I was a fighter pilot as well, I would not, could not, pass up the challenge.

He wanted me to tell how the fighter force evolved in the decade after the end of the Vietnam War. During those ten years, fighter pilots fundamentally changed the way they trained, how they employed weapons, even how they thought about themselves. Essentially, they built a new culture and the anvil upon which the success of Desert Storm would be forged another decade later.

Those old enough to remember the decade after Vietnam will recall those years as exciting but difficult ones to be a fighter pilot. Struggling to come to terms with poor performance by U.S. forces in Vietnam, we seemed to have the wrong jets, unreliable weapons, and inadequate training. On top of this we faced the specter of the next war coming in Europe against the Warsaw Pact, which out-numbered us two to one. We called the Soviet and Soviet-trained pilots Ivan, and sometimes Ivan seemed ten feet tall.

We should have had an edge with our force of combat veterans. However, within five years after Vietnam, the number of experienced combat fighter pilots dropped precipitously as many disgruntled aviators left the Air Force for the greener pastures of commercial aviation. For the ones who stayed it was no consolation to know that combat experience always evaporates after every war. All they could see was men who knew how to fight laying down their arms and retiring from the field.

The ones who stayed struggled mightily, and this is their story. I did not focus this book on the generals and legislators who worked hard to improve the fighter force. Rather, this book is about the young officers, the line pilots, and weapons systems operators (WSOs), whose innovations, devotion to duty, intelligence, flying skills, and sheer determination made indelible marks on combat capability. Of course, generals made a difference, and nothing could have happened without the leadership and support of some, like the former commanders of Tactical Air Command (TAC), Lieutenant Generals Robert J. Dixon, William W. Momyer, and Wilbur Creech. Some of the stories I relate include them, but the thrust is toward the "blighters in the trenches." Most worked long, usually thankless hours in an environment where the cynics among them stated that the reward for excellence was no punishment.

History is at once educational and fickle. After reading this, a young officer, pilot or not, will have a better understanding of how the fighter force developed. Nonetheless, much of the information herein comes from interviews, and memories dim over the decades. An old joke: What is the difference between a fairy tale and a fighter pilot's war story? Answer: None, except the fairy tale starts out, "Once upon a time…" whereas the fighter pilot story starts out, "There I was…" That said, the information from the interviewees is the best available. All of them were in the hunt during those years, flying the jets, teaching the younger pilots, and striving for excellence. No one knows more about the era.

Throughout the book I have attributed credit where it is due. However, many statements in the book are my own. For example, in the last chapter I write that the F–16 is a better day, visual dogfighter than the F–15. F–15 pilots who read that statement will howl with anger. Sorry, Eagle pilots, but I flew the F–15 for over ten years, and that's the way I see it. (Fighter pilots are not happy unless they are stirring the pot.)

Discerning readers may wonder why I wrote about particular areas and omitted others. The emphasis in the first two-thirds of the book is on the F–4, even though the Air Force had other wonderful fighters at the time. However, the F–4 was the main fighter deployed worldwide. In Europe alone there were eleven F–4 bases. There were tactical innovations in other jets during this period, and they also improved performance. However, the F–4 was the big dog on the porch. Also, some will notice that the book says little about electronic countermeasures (ECM). Although it is vital in modern combat, ECM was hated by fighter pilots in the 1970s. Invisible electrons shot back and forth, and the pilot never knew how he was doing. Let us just say that ECM is a big field, better left to a book all its own.

It was an exciting decade, and I count myself fortunate to have watched it unfold firsthand. It should come as no surprise that most of the action in this book took place at the Fighter Weapons School, Nellis Air Force Base, Nevada. Nellis is the center for weapons and tactics development, so much of what starts in the tactical forces has its genesis at Nellis, "Home of the Fighter Pilot."

Many thanks are in order to the legion of people who have helped me. First and foremost is Col. Tom Griffith, an old friend and young historian, who edited my first drafts into a readable form. Bob Tone in Las Vegas, a retired fighter pilot whose judgment is spot-on, arranged many meetings and interviews for me. Joe Mike Pyle, editor of the *USAF Weapons Review*, guided me through their archives. Yvonne Kinkaid at the Air Force History Support Office library was invaluable, and I thank her for pulling hours of microfilm out of the vault for me.

I am deeply grateful to those who spent hours and hours telling me their stories: Ron Iverson, Randy O'Neill, Roger Wells, John Vickery, Jim Brown, Bill Kirk, Larry Keith, Hugh Moreland, Tim Kinnan, John Jumper, Dick Myers, John Madden, Buzz Buzze, Kevin McElvain, Steve Hanes, John Corder, Tom Hall, Earl Henderson, Ron Keys, Don Peterson, Mike Mateyka, Wally Moorhead, Jack Lefforge, Tom Owens, R. T. Newell, Bob Wilson, and Joe Bob Phillips. You tell a good story, and I hope I have done it justice.

Fill your glass with a shot of Weed...."To Fallen Comrades!"

C. R. Anderegg
Springfield, Virginia

IN MEMORIAM

Dedicated to the memory of
Brig. Gen. Larry R. Keith, USAF (Ret.),
who flew his final mission on June 21, 1999.
Husband, father, grandfather, mentor, leader, and the best damn
fighter pilot I ever saw.

About the Author

C. R. "Dick" Anderegg is a former U.S. Air Force fighter pilot who retired after thirty years of service. He flew over 4,000 hours in USAF fighters including the F–4C/D/E/G and the F–15A/C/E, flying 170 combat missions in the F–4D over North Vietnam and Laos. He was a Laredo fast forward air controller (FAC) for forty of those missions. He is a graduate of the F–4 Fighter Weapons School and served two tours of duty as an instructor pilot in the school. As an instructor, he taught specialized courses in precision-guided munitions, Maverick and laser-guided bombs. After a nonflying tour as a staff officer at the Pentagon, he commanded an F–15 squadron at Bitburg Air Base, Germany, and was the assistant director of operations at the F–15 training wing at Tyndall Air Force Base, Florida. In December 1988 he was reassigned to Seymour Johnson Air Force Base, North Carolina, as the director of operations, where he flew the new F–15E Strike Eagle on its first operational mission. In 1991 he assumed command of the 475th Weapons Evaluation Group at Tyndall, where he was responsible for conducting the weapons system evaluation program (WSEP).

He and his wife of thirty-two years, Jean, reside in Springfield, Virginia. They have two children. Son John is a police sergeant in Peachtree City, Georgia, and daughter Amy is a singer-performer in Marietta, Georgia. Both are married, and John and his wife, Michele, have a son, Ian.

PART I

THE VIETNAM SCHOOL
OF HARD KNOCKS

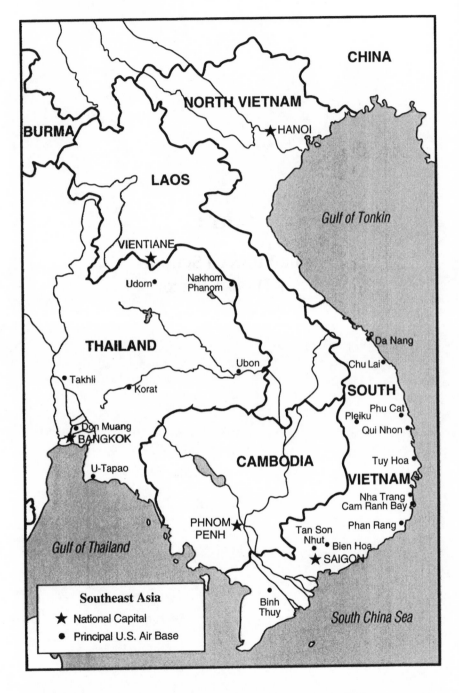

Figure 1.1 Southeast Asia during the Vietnam War, 1965–1975.

CHAPTER 1

✪

Fallen Comrades

Oh, there are no fighter pilots down in Hell.[*]

On November 2, 1969, an F–4D from the 555th Tactical Fighter Squadron (TFS) ripped along at high speed and low altitude above a dirt road through northern Laos. The big fighter *essed* back and forth across the track so the two-man crew could look for targets to strike—North Vietnamese supplies earmarked for use against U.S. forces and their allies. The jet's weaving flight path also made it more difficult for antiaircraft gunners to track the green, black, and tan camouflaged Phantom II. Suddenly, a single .50 caliber bullet smashed through the canopy quarter-panel and struck the back-seater in the chest. Only two years out of college, 1st Lt. Richard Lance Honey bled to death in the time it took his pilot to race at supersonic speed to the nearest air base.

Four decades have seen bitter debate among Americans about the morality of the war in Vietnam. Yet, to a fighter pilot, the answer to the question of why Rick Honey was in Southeast Asia was an easy one: his nation called. Others have written the story of why America asked him to be there, but this is a chronicle of fighter pilots, not politicians. The fighter pilot wonders why Honey was in such a vulnerable position where a golden BB could snuff out his life. "What were they doing right?" he might think, and "What were they doing wrong?"

Their call sign was Laredo 03, and their mission was to find targets along the stretch of dirt highway known as Route 7. The small, dusty road, not much more than a country lane, ran from the Laos–North Vietnam border westward to the Plain of Jars in central Laos. Laredo 03 was a fast forward air controller (FAC) mission. Once they found a target, typically a truck or two, or perhaps a poorly hidden supply cache, they would rendezvous with other fighters, guide them to the target, mark it with a white phosphorous smoke rocket, and then direct the other fighters' bombs onto the target. The scheme of fast FACs directing flights of other fighters onto small targets was the predominant interdiction tactic used in Laos along the Ho Chi Minh Trail, but it was very ineffective. Even the fast FAC familiar with his area had a difficult time finding targets, because he had to fly fast enough to survive AAA (antiaircraft artillery), and he had to fly high enough to stay out of the small arms fire such as that which killed Honey. Of course, the North Vietnamese were masters of camouflage who moved under

---

[*] First line of a fighter pilot drinking song.

Air Force F–4D
Phantom II in flight
over North Vietnam,
September 1972.
Official USAF photo.

cover of darkness and hid during the day. Even when the fast FACs did find a target, the fighters had a difficult time hitting it because their ordnance and delivery systems were ineffective.

Many bases in Vietnam and Thailand had their own fast FACs who flew with a call sign that designated their base of origin. Laredo flew out of Udorn, Thailand; Wolf flew out of Ubon, Thailand; Tiger flew out of Korat, Thailand. Each fast FAC had an assigned area of responsibility (AOR), and these AORs were typically in high-threat areas where slower spotter planes could not survive the intense AAA gunfire encountered there.

When Honey was killed in November 1969, it was "halftime" in the air war over North Vietnam, the time between Rolling Thunder, which lasted from 1965 until 1968, and Linebacker, which started in 1972. Attacks in North Vietnam were not allowed between the two major campaigns while negotiators attempted to end the war through diplomacy. Therefore, there were no large strike packages being ordered against important targets like railroad yards or industrial complexes in North Vietnam. The only targets were the difficult to find and harder to hit traffic along the Ho Chi Minh Trail. Waves of multimillion dollar jets sought, on a daily and nightly basis, to destroy trucks worth only a few thousand dollars each. The frustration level was very high among the fighter crews. So, again the question, "Why were Honey and his front-seater rooting around in the weeds looking for single trucks to attack with airplanes that could not hit them anyhow?" If they were so ineffective, what were they doing there? The answer was simple: with the equipment and training they had, it was the only way to try to get the job done.

The Phantom and Other Jets

The F–4D Phantom II, which Honey and his front-seater flew, was, like its older sisters, the F–100 and F–105, a child of the nuclear age. Such fighters were designed either to drop nuclear weapons or to defend against Soviet nuclear bombers attacking North America and Western Europe. Designers built the F–105 Thunderchief to go fast at low altitude and deliver a tactical nuclear weapon, and it did those things very well. Even today, the U.S. Air Force (USAF) has only one airplane, the F–111, that can go faster on the deck, and no others that can routinely exceed and maintain supersonic speeds at low altitude. For years a story circulated through fighter bars, told and retold countless times by beer-soaked revelers.

Following a strike on steel mills at Thai Nguyen in North Vietnam, an F–105 flight leader was heard to say on the radio, "Two, say your position."
His wingman responded in an excited voice, "South of the target!"
Flight leader: "Roger, what's your heading and altitude?"
Wingman: "I'm headed south and I'm on the deck!"
Flight leader: "I've got you in sight, two. What's your speed?"
Wingman (very excited): "A thousand miles an hour*!"
Flight leader: "Roger, let's push it up† and get out of here!"

Like the high-speed F–105, the F–4 was also a product of the nuclear age, but unlike the bomb-carrying "Thud," the F–4 was designed by the U. S. Navy (USN) to defend its fleets against Soviet nuclear bombers. In order to do that the F–4 had to be able to fly very fast at high altitudes to attack bombers before they could get to the fleet. It also needed a powerful radar to see the bombers at long range and a missile that it could shoot at bombers beyond visual range (BVR). A two-man crew divided the duties, so that the front-seater piloted the jet while the back-seater operated the radar. The USAF, in need of a fighter-bomber replacement for the aging F–100/F–105 fleet, adapted the Navy F–4 design to the Air Force mission. So the F–105, a nuclear fighter-bomber, and the F–4, a high-altitude interceptor, became the backbone of the fighter force in Southeast Asia. Thus, the USAF ended up fighting a tactical, conventional war over North Vietnam with aircraft designed for very different missions from those for which they were used in Southeast Asia.

Down the Chute

Of course, airplanes designed to drop nukes do not need to be especially accurate, since the large explosion compensates for aiming errors. However, in conventional warfare, with conventional bombs, bombing accuracy has to be very good. F–105 and F–4 pilots, never short on ego, thought they were pretty good at dropping bombs in combat. They were not. A 500-pound bomb must hit within 25 feet to destroy a truck, yet one study of fighter-bomber accuracy revealed that the circular error probable (CEP)‡ for all bombs dropped by the F–105 in combat was 323 feet.[1] The F–4 accuracy was about the same.

---

* A speed only the F–105 could attain, probably 20 percent faster than anything else could fly at low altitude.
† Accelerate.
‡ CEP is the radius of a circle within which half of all the weapons targeted for the center of that circle can be expected to land.

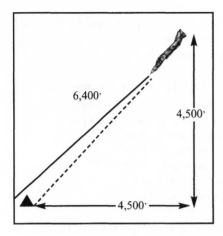

Figure 1.2 Bombing Geometry.

Dropping a bomb accurately without a computer, called manual bombing, is a very difficult task.* Typically, a fighter-bomber pilot drops bombs during gunnery training from a 45-degree dive at 4,500 feet, while flying at 450 knots indicated airspeed. Basic trigonometry (Fig. 1.2) shows that an attacker in a 45-degree dive who is 4,500 feet high is also 6,400 feet in slant range from the target. The task, then, is to position perfectly a fighter that is traveling at 450 knots and is more than a mile from the target. A fighter flying at 450 knots is moving toward the target at 760 feet per second. So in order to get the bomb within 25 feet of the target, the pilot must hit the pickle button† within 66 thousandths of a second of the proper moment.

Pilots employ a variety of techniques and procedures to arrive at the proper release point. The first task is to calculate the proper depression angle for the gunsight, a process relatively unchanged since the first gunsight was used. Ballistics testing of a bomb reveals the distance it will travel if dropped from a certain altitude at a certain speed. The results are then published in tables the pilot studies to select the release parameters he intends to use. The tables also show how much depression the pilot needs to set in his gunsight to indicate the proper release point. Note in Figure 1.2 that the nose of the aircraft (or zero sight line) points slightly beyond the target. The angle beneath the nose (dotted line) that is required to have the gunsight, or pipper, on the target at release is measured in degrees. Degrees are further divided into milliradians, and it is this "mil setting" that is dialed into the gunsight. The mil setting for an F-4 in a 45-degree dive, at 450 knots, releasing an MK-82 bomb, is 120 mils.

Before the pilot rolls in to attack the target, he sets 120 mils in his gunsight, so that the pipper is depressed that amount below the zero sight line. He flies his

---

* Both the F-4 and the F-105 had rudimentary computer bombing systems that were unreliable, so most pilots dropped bombs manually.

† Weapons release button on the control stick, usually red and operated by the right thumb.

jet with the target to one side, usually the left since fighter pilots prefer left turns, about two and a half miles away. This position is called a "base" position and is usually 5,500 feet higher than the planned release altitude and at a speed about 100 knots slower than the planned release airspeed.

As the pilot approaches a point where he will intersect the planned attack heading at 90 degrees, he rolls the wings left, to nearly inverted, then pulls the nose of the aircraft in a descending left turn to a point just beyond the target. He then rolls upright, wings level. If he has done everything correctly to this point, he will be wings level, in a 45-degree dive. Since he has rolled in well above the planned release altitude, the pipper will be short of the target, but "tracking" toward it along the ground. Airspeed will increase because the jet is in a dive. If the pilot has done everything perfectly, the pipper will touch the target when the aircraft passes through 4,500 feet at 450 knots. The pilot punches the pickle button with his right thumb, the bomb releases, and the pilot recovers from the dive. Just as the aircraft passes over the target, typically 1,500 feet above it, the bomb "shacks" the target—a perfect pass and a direct hit.

It is extremely unusual for any pass to be perfect, however, and pilots quickly learn that they must compensate for small errors in the pass that can produce large errors in the bomb's impact point on the ground. For example, if the pilot is one degree shallow in his dive angle, the pipper will reach the target a bit too soon. If the pilot does not notice the error and releases the weapon when the pipper hits the target, the bomb will hit 60 feet short of the target. Less airspeed at release also causes short hits. If the pilot is both shallow and slow, conditions that go hand-in-hand, since shallow means the aircraft accelerates more slowly than planned, then the errors are additive. A pilot who is only one degree shallow in his dive and is also 25 knots slow when he pickles will miss the target by over 100 feet.

One other issue will further define the difficulty of hitting a target with a manually released bomb. The pipper on the F–4 gunsight is a red dot that is 2 mils in diameter. A mil is a useful gunnery measurement because it subtends one foot at one thousand feet. So, the F–4 pipper covers two feet on the ground when it is 1,000 feet away from the target, or twelve feet at 6,000 feet, which is the slant range for release of a bomb under the parameters discussed above. If the pilot errs by as little as a pipper width during his pass, he will add 24 more feet of miss distance to other errors. These errors may seem small, but one must consider that a 500-pound, general purpose (GP) bomb must hit within twenty-five feet of a truck to effect a 50 percent probability of severe damage.

Combat greatly exacerbates the problem. Most bombing attacks in North Vietnam were made from higher altitudes so that the aircraft could recover from its dive before it flew low enough to be exposed to dense small arms fire, usually 4,500 feet. Therefore, pilots released their bombs at about 8,000 feet instead of the training/peacetime altitudes of 4,500 feet. The slant range for an 8,000-foot release is over two miles from the target, which accentuates the common delivery errors inherent in a manual dive bomb pass. Of course, getting shot at decreases accuracy as well. It is probably impossible to quantify how much. Peacetime weapons qualification required a pilot to put half of his bombs inside a 150-foot circle on the practice range from a controlled, 4,500-foot release altitude. However, combat CEPs from higher altitudes and under enemy fire were at least twice as large.

The easiest way to overcome aiming errors is to drop several bombs, and this the fighter bombers did. The F–4 typically carried six MK–82s* on a multiple ejector rack (MER) loaded to the center, belly station. Each inboard wing station carried a triple ejector rack (TER) that could carry three MK–82s. The outboard wing stations sported 370-gallon, jettisonable fuel tanks. The F–4 pilot therefore had the option of ripple releasing all twelve of his bombs on a single pass, a procedure that would produce a string of explosions about 250 feet long. Ripple releases from multiple attackers provided the greatest opportunity for success. However, killing a typical target was uncertain under the best of circumstances. One study of targets revealed that an attack of forty-eight fighter-bombers was required to give a 50 percent probability of knocking down a single span of a typical highway bridge. In other words, twelve flights of four F–4 or F–105s could roll in and drop 576 bombs. When the smoke cleared, there was one chance in two that the bridge would still stand. Such statistics were proved time and again during well-chronicled raids against the Doumer Bridge and other rail bridges that ran out of Hanoi.

Another way to improve accuracy was to increase tracking time, the time the pilot spent wings level down the chute, until pickle altitude. However, such a nice, steady pass also gave the enemy gunners a nice, steady target at which to shoot. Most pilots tried to limit tracking time to five seconds or less. Many joked that they got their flight pay for five seconds of tracking time, but they were not paid for one second more.

Delivery accuracy was not the only problem for the mud beaters in combat. The bombs were generally of two types, the MK–82 and the M–117, a 750-pound, general purpose bomb. Both were World War II vintage designs. Neither was good at penetrating hard targets because their cases were not thick enough to withstand the impact against something like a concrete bunker or a hard runway surface. When these bombs struck a hard target, the bomb case would usually fracture, thereby reducing the effect of the explosion dramatically. The fuzes were not much better. The MK–82 was fuzed by the M904 in the bomb nose and the M905 in the bomb body. The M904/5 fuze could be set to function instantaneously or to delay for up to 25 thousandths of a second. Even the instantaneous setting produced some penetration as the bomb, which impacted at several hundred feet per second, partially buried before the explosion happened. One popular solution was to add a fuze extender, a three-foot-long piece of hard pipe to the nose of the bomb with the fuze in the leading end of the pipe.

---

* 500-pound general purpose bomb.

F–4C Phantom taking off to attack targets in North Vietnam. *Official USAF photo.*

When the bomb hit the ground, the explosion would still occur with the bomb body above ground level (AGL). These "extenders" or "daisy cutters," as the air crews sometimes called them, were particularly effective against soft targets like troops, trucks, or unprotected supplies. They were useless against a target that had any strength to it.

Aerial Warfare

The F–4 Phantom was the primary air-to-air (A/A) combat machine for the USAF over North Vietnam. On paper it was a great design. It could carry four AIM–7 radar-guided missiles, the Sparrow, and four AIM–9 heat-seeking missiles, the Sidewinder. Sparrows were carried semisubmerged in depressions in the F–4* belly, two under each engine intake in the front, and two rear missiles on the aft belly stations. Each missile had an ejector foot that kicked the missile away from the aircraft at firing. When the Sparrow was about six feet clear of the jet its rocket motor ignited, and the missile started guiding. The radar-guided Sparrows were designed to be fired BVR. The GIB (guy-in-back)† locked the radar to the target and the pilot fired the missile. Against a large, bomber-type, high-altitude target, the Sparrow could be launched at more than ten miles from a head-on aspect. The radar had to stay locked to the target until the missile detonated by either a contact fuze or a proximity fuze, so the pilot had to always keep his jet pointed in the general direction of the target until the missile hit. Maintaining the lock-on to the target was crucial. If the radar stopped tracking the target, then the missile, no longer able to see reflected radar energy from the target, would go stupid. In its favor, the Sparrow was a large missile, nearly 500 pounds, and carried an excellent warhead. The warhead was an accordion

---

* The F–4 was the only aircraft that had a radar good enough to guide the Sparrow.

† Originally a pilot until the late 1960s, when navigators gradually transitioned into the cockpit. Navigators were sometimes called wizzos, a phonetic of WSO or weapons systems operator. Ultimately anyone who flew in the back seat was called a "pitter," since the back seat was often referred to as "the pit."

arrangement of steel rods around an explosive charge. When detonated, the rods expanded into a lethal circle of steel that ripped through the target with devastating effect.

The Sidewinder was a "launch and leave weapon," designed to be fired from behind the target at the infrared (IR) energy emitting from the target's jet exhaust. The Phantom could carry two Sidewinders under each wing on launch rails mounted to the weapons pylons. The Sidewinder, when the pilot selected it, produced a peculiar hissing noise in his headset. When the pilot pointed his F–4 directly at an IR source, such as the tail of a target, the Sidewinder produced a "growl" in the headset that indicated the missile had acquired the IR source. When the pilot heard the growl, he shot the missile by pulling the stick trigger with his right index finger. The Sidewinder launched straight ahead off its rail and flew toward the target in a peculiar corkscrewing flight path reminiscent of a sidewinder rattler scooting across the desert. Once the missile was shot, the pilot could turn away to seek other targets, since the Sidewinder was totally self-guiding after launch. It knew only that it had to home in on the IR source and detonate when it got there. Like the Sparrow, the Sidewinder was designed to be fired at large, nonmaneuvering targets such as Soviet nuclear bombers attacking the United States or its military forces.

When the F–4 was designed, many proclaimed that the day of the dogfight was over. They envisioned air warfare as a battle of high technology missiles arcing at opposing forces from many miles away. Certainly that was the Navy concept for defending the fleet against nuclear bombers, so the original Navy design did not have guns for close-in combat. The first two USAF versions of the F–4, the F–4C and the F–4D, did not have machine guns either. A 20-millimeter (mm) cannon—the same used in the F–104 and F–105—was put into a pod and carried on the centerline (belly) station of the early F–4s after the battles over North Vietnam indicated an aerial gun was needed. The F–4E, which came late to the war, was designed with an internal cannon located just under the radar package in the nose.

Sparrow and Sidewinder effectiveness over North Vietnam was horrible. Less than 10 percent of all Sparrow firings killed the target, and less than 25 percent of all Sidewinders fired brought down their targets.[2] Several factors contributed to these poor results, but they all fell into three general categories: missile design, aircraft design, and pilot proficiency.

Neither the Sparrow nor the Sidewinder was designed to be fired against the highly maneuverable, Soviet-built MiGs flown by the North Vietnamese, and the agile adversaries could easily outmaneuver the missiles. Furthermore, neither missile performed well at low altitude, especially when fired at a MiG that was below the F–4. At low altitude the maximum range of the Sidewinder was greatly reduced from that advertised, and the missile was easily confused by IR reflections from the ground and especially by sun glints off of clouds.

The Sparrow and its radar guidance scheme performed especially poorly at low altitude since the Sparrow guided on reflected radar energy from the target.

The shooter's radar had to track, or illuminate, the target throughout the missile's time of flight to the target. A Sparrow that was shot from two miles behind a MiG could take as long as twenty seconds to close the gap. As the Sparrow neared the target, it had to fly through an "altitude line" on the F–4 radar. This altitude line was the reflection of radar energy from the ground and was a band of "clutter" through which guidance was impossible. If the radar was tracking a target either beyond the altitude line or inside the altitude line, there was no problem, but if the missile transited the altitude line before impact, the radar had to employ a memory mode to predict where on the other side of the clutter/altitude line the target would reappear. The memory mode was no problem if the radar was tracking a nonmaneuvering bomber at 40,000 feet, but if the target was a hard-turning, small target at low altitude, the F–4 radar often could not track it through the clutter of the altitude line. Of course, if the radar broke lock, the missile went stupid and missed by a very wide margin. The radar had virtually no capability to find targets below its altitude. If the WSO pointed the radar antenna below the horizon, all he could see was ground clutter reflected back at the antenna dish.

Ultimately, the Sparrow/F–4 combination also pushed the Air Force's technological capability to the limits. The computer interface between the missile, the radar, and the launch system was difficult to maintain, especially in the high humidity of Southeast Asia. Many attempted Sparrow shots resulted in "hung" missiles, ones that never ejected from the missile bay. Many others kicked away, but the rocket motor did not light. Others that lit simply went stupid and never guided. Capt. Steve Ritchie* and others who enjoyed considerable success with the Sparrow personally selected the missiles that were loaded on their jets from ones that had undergone extensive analysis and "hand massaging."

More Problems

The nuclear war design of the F–4 extended to its cockpit layout and caused considerable problems for the pilots engaged in dogfights with small MiGs over North Vietnam. Visibility from both the front and rear cockpits was notoriously poor. To the rear, neither crew member could see much past the back of the wing line. Lookout to the front was restricted by a thick front windscreen that had a bulky structural frame around it. In an air force focused on nuclear weapons and defense against them, planners had determined that speed at high altitude was vital and that the days of visual combat were over. Apparently, somebody forgot to tell the North Vietnamese about modern warfare because they regularly engaged U.S. fighters at close quarters, well within visual range.

The layout of switches and controls in the cockpit was a nightmare. Perhaps most notorious were the Sparrow and Sidewinder controls. Four small switches

---

* Each of his five confirmed aerial victories used the Sparrow.

on a panel in front of the pilot's left knee controlled both missiles. The third switch from the left selected which missile fired when the pilot pulled the stick trigger. It was a three-position switch. The up position selected a radar missile, and the middle position selected the heat-seeking Sidewinder. Each depression to the down position stepped through the Sidewinders. In a swirling, twirling dogfight the pilot could tell the proper position of the switch by listening to his headset. If there was a Sidewinder hiss, he had the middle (heat) position selected. If there was no hiss, he had the up (radar Sparrow) position selected. Probably. Or he might be out of Sidewinders. Or he might have the tone volume too low to hear in the heat of combat. Or the Sidewinder he had selected might have a bad background tone. The only way to be sure was to look down into the cockpit, find the switch, and look at it. The pilot had to do all this while trying to keep track of a small maneuverable MiG.

Actually *changing* the switch was a trick in itself. Some pilots went to their crew chief and asked for a piece of the stiff plastic tubing the maintenance troops used to take oil samples from the engines. The pilot would then cut a two-inch length of the tubing and slip the end of it over the missile select switch, so that the end of the tubing stuck well out from the other switches. After takeoff, the pilot would then listen to each Sidewinder tone to determine which heat-seeker had the best tone, thus, hopefully, the best chance of success. He would then step through the missiles, so that the worst missile was selected, then move the piece of plastic tubing up to the radar position. With the switch thus positioned, the pilot went into the battle prepared to shoot a radar Sparrow. However, if he quickly needed a heater, he could swat the plastic tubing down with his left hand. This swat would carry the switch down to the bottom or step position, so that the system skipped to the next Sidewinder and put the worst missile last in the firing order. Several other cockpit switches were just as hard to manage.

The F–4 was a powerful brute of a machine with a higher thrust-to-weight ratio than any fighter of its era. However, it was not agile relative to the maneuverable Soviet-built MiGs. USAF pilots were accustomed to flying fighters less agile than their adversaries. The Zeroes and Messerschmitts of World War II and the MiG–15s of Korea could easily outturn the Americans' Lightnings, Thunderbolts, and Sabres. However, the Phantom also displayed a marked tendency to go out of control when maneuvered at high angles of attack (AOA), that is, low speed.* The main problem was a common characteristic of swept-wing aircraft called adverse yaw. During normal flight, the pilot controlled his turns by pushing the stick in the direction he wanted to turn. Most pilots like to turn left because it is easier to push the stick left than it is to pull it right.†

---

* High angles of attack, for purposes of this discussion, means slow speed, that is, below 300 knots. However, high angles of attack can occur at any speed, even though the pilot might pull the wings off the aircraft trying to attain high angles of attack at high speed.

† Try this yourself. While sitting in a chair, put your right forearm on your right thigh with

Suppose the Phantom pilot wants to turn left. He pushes the stick to the left. The aileron on the right wing goes down, proportional to the amount the pilot moved the stick, and a spoiler on the left wing proportionally goes up. The aileron on the right wing makes more lift on that wing because a section of the wing has more camber and length. The spoiler on the left wing lives up to its name and spoils lift on the topside of the left wing. The result is a roll to the left because the right wing is producing a lot more lift than the left. However, at low speeds, the situation changes considerably. When the pilot moves the stick to the left, the flight controls all move as discussed before. However, the aileron on the right wing produces more drag than it does lift. This drag causes the jet to yaw (skid) back to the right even though the pilot is commanding roll to the left, hence the name adverse yaw. Once the nose starts back to the right another very bad thing happens to our startled fighter pilot. As yaw increases to the right, the left wing effectively becomes straighter to the air flowing over it, and the right wing becomes effectively more swept. Therefore, the left wing very suddenly produces more lift than the right, and even though the pilot wants to turn left, the Phantom violently snaps into a right hand roll, and then into a spin. As Keith Jackson might say, "Whoaaa, Nellie!"

In order to control adverse yaw, F–4 pilots learned to use the rudder to control roll when maneuvering aggressively at low speeds. Buffet, a shaking of the aircraft, is a normal product of high angles of attack. Airflow across the wings is disturbed, and the turbulent air literally shakes the airplane. When the F–4 pilot starts to feel buffet, he knows he is approaching a moderate angle of attack. Also, he has a cockpit gauge to tell him the same thing. He knows that he can control his jet by using adverse yaw to his advantage. So, when he wants to turn left, he does not use the ailerons and spoilers by moving the stick to the left. Instead, he keeps the stick centered and pushes down the rudder pedal under his left boot, which moves the rudder on the F–4's vertical tail to the left. This causes the nose of the jet to skid to the left. The left skid causes an apparent decrease of sweep on the right wing and an apparent increase of sweep on the left wing. The result is more lift on the right wing than the left, and the airplane rolls to the left. Although it seems simple in discussion, the actual execution takes considerable practice and skill gained from many hours of flying the F–4. Many combat veterans claim that more than a few "combat" losses of the F–4 were actually losses to the adverse yaw demon.

The most vital part of any fighter system is the pilot, and in the F–4, the pilot and the WSO. With this point there is no disagreement. However, during the Vietnam War, the Air Force followed two policies that directly decreased pilot experience in

---

your fist between your knees as though you were holding a fighter stick. Now hold your right fist firmly in your left hand and push with your right fist to the left against the resistance of your left hand, then reverse it and pull with your right fist to the right. It takes less muscle to push than to pull. That's why, if at all possible, landing patterns, instrument patterns, and gunnery practice patterns are set up around left turns.

the combat theater. The first of these policies was the "universally assignable" pilot. The Air Force considered every graduate of pilot training capable of flying any aircraft in the inventory. Nothing could have been further from the truth. After the intense competition of fifty-three weeks of pilot training, the classes were ranked from top to bottom based on flying and academic skills. Fighters were often the first choice of the top graduates, and the top grads quickly skimmed off the few fighter assignments available. The bottom of the class was left to choose less desirable assignments to bombers and air refueling tankers. Thus, the best students got the hardest jets to fly, and the slower students got the slower aircraft. Nonetheless, the institutional arrogance of the Air Force insisted that any pilot could fly any aircraft in any mission. Exacerbating the "universally assignable" pilot policy was another policy, implemented by then-Chief of Staff Gen. Joseph P. McConnell, that no pilot would be required to do two tours of duty in Vietnam until every pilot had done one. Of course, since it was the policy that any pilot could fly any mission, a regular rotation of pilots through the combat theater seemed reasonable. It was a noble and well-intentioned policy, but its effect was devastating to the combat capability of the tactical forces. When the U.S. bombing of North Vietnam started in 1965, the average fighter pilot had over 500 hours of flying experience in his aircraft. However, as these experienced fighter pilots finished their tours of duty, inexperienced pilots replaced them. By 1968 the experience level was less than 250 hours. In 1966 pilots were lost to enemy action at the rate of 0.25 aircraft per month, yet by 1968 they were lost at 4.5 per month. On the other hand, the Navy, which had no such policies, rotated their experienced pilots continuously through the combat zone and maintained a steady loss rate.[3] One combat pilot, who later became an Air Force lieutenant general, recalled that "the universally assignable pilot concept really hurt a lot of guys."[4]

Close Air Support

Chasing MiGs across North Vietnam and bombing targets "Downtown"* was only a part of the Air Force mission in Southeast Asia. Although the bases in Thailand focused their efforts in the North, air bases throughout South Vietnam were dedicated to supporting allied ground forces. The close air support (CAS) mission during the long war was carried by a variety of aircraft, but the bulk of bombing support for ground forces was conducted by the F–100 and the jack-of-all-trades F–4.

Slow-mover FACs who lived and worked with their Army counterparts controlled CAS missions. Flying light, slow, and maneuverable spotter airplanes like the O–1 and O–2, the FACs found targets and called for an allocation of fighters to be sent to them. When the fighters arrived, the FAC marked the target with a smoke rocket and then controlled the fighters as they delivered their

---

* Nickname for area around Hanoi.

ordnance, usually high-drag MK–82s and napalm. F–100s, with their built-in guns, also strafed targets if requested by the FAC. Most CAS missions were conducted at low altitude since there were very few, if any, enemy flak guns in the South. Of course, small arms fire could and sometimes did bring down a jet, but CAS missions required the pilot to get close to his work because there were usually friendly forces in the area. Low-altitude bomb deliveries were much more accurate than the steep, diving kind used to stay above enemy flak. The low-altitude deliveries were more accurate because the bombs were dropped from a much closer slant range; therefore, the errors inherent in a bombing pass were diminished greatly.

An innovation that reduced the slant range for delivery even more was the Snakeye, or high-drag bomb. The high-drag was a standard 500-pound, MK–82 bomb body with a clamshell contraption on the rear. When the fighter released its bomb, the clamshell opened instantly into four large panels that rapidly slowed the bomb. As it fell to the earth, it looked somewhat like an opened umbrella. The drag device made the bomb slow down so fast that the bomb hit well behind the airplane, so the bomber was well clear of bomb fragments, or frag, after the explosion. The ultimate result was that the pilots could get very close to the target with better accuracy.

However, there were many flaws with the fast-moving F–4s and F–100s in the CAS role. First, they were too fast to stay near the target and often had problems keeping the small, CAS targets in sight. Second, they had poor loiter time. Their big engines gulped fuel at low altitude, so the fighters could not hang around and wait until the right tactical moment for the FAC to put them onto the target. Third, they could not talk to the Army units they supported. The fighters were designed with radios to talk among themselves, but their radios had different frequencies than those used by the Army. Fourth, the airplanes and the pilots were vulnerable to small arms fire, which sometimes was very heavy.

As in the interdiction mission over North Vietnam, the CAS mission found itself shortchanged by the fighters of the nuclear era. The flawed vision of military planners had incorrectly predicted the circumstances under which Rick Honey and his comrades would lay down their lives. The fighter crews of Vietnam did the best they could with what they had, but they were woefully equipped and badly trained.

---

1. "USAF Conventional Weapons Delivery Capability," Air University Library, M-U 30905–4, no. 28, p. 23.

2. Craig C. Hannah, "Counterflow: the Demise and Rebirth of the USAF Tactical Air Command in the Vietnam Era," Air University Library, M-U 43567–777, 1995, p. 66.

3. James W. Alder, "It Never Troubles a Wolf," Air University Library, M-U 32893 A 3613I, p. 26.

4. James R. Brown, telephone interview with author, April 20, 1999.

CHAPTER 2

✪

The Schoolhouse

It wasn't much fun.[1]

No one who attended a replacement training unit (RTU) during the Vietnam War would deny that the mission of those squadrons was to mass-produce fighter pilots to fill wartime cockpits. Squadrons at bases in Arizona, California, and Florida cranked out F–4 crews as fast as possible to accommodate the USAF policy of no pilot doing two combat tours until every pilot had done one.

Classes were a mix of "universally assignable" pilots and navigators who came from every nook and cranny in the Air Force. Some pilots came to the F–4 cockpit from the Strategic Air Command (SAC) bombers and tankers, and others came directly from pilot training. Some had thousands of hours of flying time and were field grade rank.* No matter what their rank, though, they shared a common denominator—no experience in the F–4. Everything they needed to know to survive combat and become an efficient killing machine had to be learned in the RTU. These schoolhouses for fighter crews were the only chance for learning before the crucible of combat. Nonetheless, most who attended them remember the schoolhouse as a poor learning experience that did not adequately prepare them for the rigors of war.

The Students

Often the problem was the student himself. Students who came from bombers and transports often did not fare well in the fast, dynamic fighter world, so the Air Force tried to improve their skills by sending them first through a transition course in the AT–33. The venerable "T-Bird" of Korean War vintage was an old friend to many pilots who had learned to fly when it was the primary jet trainer in the pilot training program

So the Air Force formed AT–33 units to refresh pilots' basic skills before they went to fly the faster, more complex F–4. One student, who transitioned† from the C–7 Caribou, a small tactical transport, to the F–4, remembers the course as very rudimentary and of little value. Instructors in the transition course were

---

* Major, lieutenant colonel, and colonel.

† Transition training is Air Force jargon for learning how to fly a different aircraft. For example, an F–100 pilot "transitions" to the F–4.

less than motivated because the AT–33 duty was viewed as a "second team" operation.[2] Nonetheless, pilots who finished the AT–33 program pressed on to the F–4 schoolhouse.

Takeoff and Landing

The first few sorties of the F–4 syllabus were devoted to transition training, the basic skills a pilot needed to fly the jet: takeoffs, landings, basic aerobatics, and basic instrument flight. If there was one thing Phantom pilots enjoyed it was the beast's incredible power. The jet's twin J79 engines produced nearly 36,000 pounds of thrust with the throttles in full afterburner. A clean jet* weighed 45,500 pounds, so the acceleration down the runway during takeoff was both impressive and exhilarating. The takeoff procedure called for the pilot to stop on the runway and run both throttles to 85 percent of full military power† while holding the brakes. Once engine instruments were checked in the green, the pilot released the brakes and smoothly advanced both throttles to 100 percent power, rechecked the engines, then moved both throttles outboard and forward into the full afterburner position. The roar outside the airplane was thunderous to those near the runway as the afterburners shot cobalt blue plumes behind the jet. Inside, the crew could barely hear the roar, but the acceleration was unmistakable as the airspeed indicator quickly came alive at its minimum operating speed of 80 knots.

During the initial takeoff roll, the pilot steered the fighter by using nose gear steering, controlled by the rudder pedals, to steer down the runway. At 70 knots, there was enough airflow over the aircraft to make the rudder effective for steering. During the takeoff, the pilot kept the control stick all the way back in his lap, so that as the big jet reached flying speed the nose would slowly lift off the runway. When the nose got to about 10 degrees of pitch up, the pilot relaxed the back-stick pressure to maintain the takeoff attitude as the Phantom thundered toward its takeoff speed of about 170 knots. Immediately after liftoff, the pilot used his left hand to raise the landing gear handle to command the main landing gear to fold inward and the nose gear to retract aft. As soon as the gear was retracting, the pilot raised the flaps with a small airfoil-shaped switch located just behind the throttles. Although the takeoff roll was very quick, perhaps twenty seconds from brake release to airborne, the powerful jet accelerated even faster once airborne. As the speed approached 300 knots, usually when the jet reached the end of the runway, the pilot pulled the throttles out of afterburner (max) to military power and let the jet accelerate to climb speed, 350 knots, in military (mil).[3]

As breathtaking as the takeoff was to every F–4 crew that flew the powerful jet, it was one of the easier tasks they had to perform. Landing was a different

---

* One with no external stores such as fuel tanks, missiles, or bombs.
† Full engine thrust without the afterburner.

matter altogether. Pilots in the RTU learned the same basic landing pattern used at training bases and fighter bases everywhere in the United States Air Force. Some jets were not difficult to land and some were harder. The F–4 was, by most accounts, somewhere in the middle. It was not difficult to land safely, but was hard to land with any points earned for style and grace.

In a typical landing pattern, called the overhead, the Phantom pilot lined up with the runway from about five miles and 1,500 feet above ground level. He flew toward the runway, on the same heading as the runway, at 300 knots. As he flew over the near end of the runway, the pilot "pitched out" by making a hard level turn—to the left if he had a choice—to reverse his heading. During this turn, the book said to use 60 degrees of bank and pull 2 g to maintain altitude. At the end of the turn, the pilot would then be abeam his intended landing point, at 1,500 AGL and offset from the runway about a mile. Because he had reduced his power a little in the turn, the airspeed was below 250 knots, so the pilot then lowered his landing gear and immediately lowered his flaps to full down.* The extra drag of the gear and flaps further slowed the jet until the pilot reached a point one mile away from the end of the runway, still at 1,500 feet, at 180 knots and configured for landing. There, the pilot started a descending 180-degree turn back toward the runway.

His goal was to arrive one mile from the end of the runway, at final approach speed of about 150 knots at about 300 feet AGL. From this point the pilot flew a constant angle of attack to touchdown, and that was the part of landing the Phantom that many pilots found difficult. Most were used to flying aircraft that were "flared" at touchdown. This flare procedure entailed a significant power reduction on short final approach to further slow the aircraft. Then, as the airplane got close to the runway, the pilot gradually raised the nose as the aircraft slowed in order to gently settle onto the runway. The F–4, though, had been designed for "controlled crashes" onto aircraft carrier decks, and the technique was entirely different. Many pilots, especially those who had come from slower, older aircraft, found it hard to adjust.

An important aspect of the landing pattern learned by new fighter pilots in the RTU was an attitude the instructors instilled in the impressionable students. Instructors made it clear, through their example, if not their words, that only wimps flew the overhead pattern in the manner described above. The common fighter pilot logic of the day was "if a little is good, more is better, and a lot more is a lot better." This logic of extreme applied to the traffic pattern. If the book said to use 60 degrees of bank in the pitch out, then 70 was better, and 85 was *sierra hotel*.†

---

* For purposes of this discussion, a "hard-wing" F–4 is described. The "soft-wing" F–4 and the changes it enjoyed are discussed later.

† Sierra hotel, the phonetic letters for s and h, was a common derivation of the vulgarity "shit hot," meaning "the absolute best."

Fledgling Phantom pilots soon learned that the tighter, or closer to the runway, they could keep their landing patterns the better. Although the practice was dangerous, the RTU instructors encouraged it and in many instances demanded it. Although they never actually taught the students how to fly very tight patterns, their attitude toward teaching was the same as their teachers had shown them. The students were expected to learn by watching and copying the actions of their teachers. There was little true verbal instruction by the flying instructors. Granted, they briefed each pilot before the mission on what was expected, but these briefings typically emphasized procedural items and not techniques. There was an attitude among the instructors that "I learned the hard way, and you must learn that way as well."

Basic Fighter Maneuvers

It would be a gross understatement to say that F–4 crews left the RTU unprepared for the air-to-air combat some would experience over North Vietnam. Throughout the war years, air-to-air training was on-again, off-again. Mostly it was off. The primary rationale for curtailing training was the belief of Tactical Air Command (TAC) that dogfight training was too risky. Many F–4s, and other types as well, were lost to the adverse yaw demon that plagued that generation of swept-wing fighters, particularly the Phantom. Of course, TAC* was not fighting the war since its responsibility ended at the West Coast. Therefore, the fighter command could afford the luxury of placing a higher priority on safety than it put on combat capability.[4] At the RTU bases, the students received little, if any, actual training in the handling characteristics of their aluminum steeds. For many RTU classes, particularly those unlucky enough to be attending the course immediately after an accident, the entire aerial combat portion of the syllabus was simply not flown, and the graduates were sent to war without it.

For those who did fly the limited sorties dedicated to aerial combat, they remember the training as confusing at best. The primary formations and tactics used were the same as those employed in Korea nearly twenty years earlier, in a war where the only AAA armament was the gun.

In fact, many RTU instructors used *No Guts, No Glory* as the primary tactics manual from which they instructed even though it was written about fighter aviation in the Korean War before the advent of A/A missiles.[5] The primary fighting unit was the four-ship employing the Fluid Four formation. In Fluid Four, the four-ship operates as two elements of two planes each. The leaders of the elements are Number 1 and Number 3. Number 2 and Number 4 fly as their respective wingmen. The element leaders fly about one to three miles apart, and

---

* Tactical Air Command, responsible for all fighter operations in the United States, carried the burden of training fighter crews for combat in Southeast Asia.

the wingmen fly off the element leaders. The wingmen fly 1,500–2,500 feet behind their element leaders, in a maneuvering cone of 45–60 degrees behind. When the flight leader wants to turn while on patrol, he simply turns gently and constantly to a heading. The element leader can then maneuver by diving for air-speed to catch up or by climbing to trade airspeed for altitude. These maneuvers are called fluid maneuvering, thus the Fluid Four appellation.

One very important aspect of Fluid Four is the responsibilities of each flight member. The flight leader, Number 1, makes all decisions for the flight, including when to engage the enemy and when to disengage. He also directs defensive reactions to an enemy attack on the flight. The flight leader is the primary shooter. Although the element leader, Number 3, is given the responsibility of being a back-up shooter, in practice, Number 1 does the lion's share of the killing. The job of the wingmen, simply stated, is to protect the element leaders. As the element leader maneuvers for a kill, the wingman continually watches the area behind his leader's jet, the "six o'clock" vulnerable area hidden from the leader's vision. They may leave their maneuvering cones only as a last ditch measure to save themselves from enemy attack. The wingman's position was called "fighting wing," although some called it "welded wing" because the wingman was there to stay, no matter what happened.

Fighting wing is a difficult formation to fly when the element leader begins to maneuver aggressively. The wingman, unless he is very experienced, must concentrate totally on maintaining the formation position, making it impossible to watch for attacks from behind. Of course, new pilots always flew in the wingman position. Many pilots, including one who ultimately won the Risner Award as the best fighter pilot in the Air Force, later recalled that they never saw anything of the "fight" because they were just trying to "hang on and not get spit out [from the maneuvering cone]."[6]

At the same time as RTU and combat wingmen were earning their spurs by thrashing around the skies in fighting wing, the Fluid Four formation and tactics were coming under considerable fire from those who questioned their usefulness in a modern air battle that featured air-to-air missiles. Later chapters will discuss those concerns.

Pod Formation

Fighting wing was not the only difficult formation the RTU crew had to learn. Hours were spent practicing pod formation. Simply called "pod," the formation was designed to counter the surface-to-air missiles (SAM) threat over North Vietnam. When SAMs first entered the air battle, the fighter pilot's only option was to evade the missile by outflying it. The SA–2 SAM used by the North Vietnamese was fast but not agile. If the F–4 or F–105 pilot saw the missile coming, he could evade it easily by first diving to pick up some airspeed. Then, once the missile committed down toward him, the pilot would pull back up into the

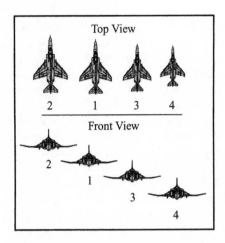

Figure 2.1 Pod Formation.

SAM and cause it to overshoot and miss. Aircraft hit by SAMs were almost always jets whose pilots never saw the missile.

Self-protection devices, called pods, were developed to electronically spoof, or jam, the SAM guidance radar. These pods were small, about six feet long, and could be carried on one of the fighter's weapon stations. When the pods were tested against radars similar to the SA–2 radar, it was quickly determined that several pods jamming at the same time were more effective than a single pod. However, the aircraft had to be close enough together and in the proper relative positions to present one large jamming blob in order to confuse the SA–2's radar operators. Thus, pod formation was born. All aircraft flew line abreast, and each was 1,500 feet laterally and vertically displaced from the ones next to it to optimize the jamming pattern. (Fig. 2.1)

Pod was extremely difficult to fly. The higher aircraft were looking down, just over their canopy rails, to see their formation mate below. If they drifted a bit too close, they had to correct out immediately, or the airplane below them would disappear from view. If they got too wide, the effect of the jamming was lost. If the formation was difficult to fly, it was impossible to turn without pre-positioning everyone either forward or behind the leader's wing line. It was not unusual for an RTU pod formation to scatter to the four winds because someone flinched and broke away from a potential midair collision. During weapons delivery, students learned how to roll in on dive bomb passes from pod, drop the bombs, and then reform quickly into pod to egress the target area. The orchestration of this dance of twenty-ton sugar plum fairies left all with the same impression—there had to be a better way.

Weapons Qualification

Rockets, dive, skip, and strafe. Those four events comprised virtually every gunnery range mission in the schoolhouse during the Vietnam era. The F–4 in the air-to-ground (A/G) gunnery configuration had two 370-gallon fuel tanks, one on each outboard wing station; a LAU–3 pod with three 2.75-inch rockets on one inboard wing station; and a SUU–21 practice bomb dispenser on the other inboard station. F–4C/D carried a SUU–16 or SUU–23 20-mm cannon gun pod on the centerline or belly station. Thus armed, the fledglings headed for Cutty Back, Avon Park, or Gila Bend, gunnery ranges in California, Florida, and Arizona, to learn the finer arts of gunnery.

On the way they might practice the dreaded pod formation or perhaps fly a low-level navigation route. If timed perfectly, the external fuel tanks would be dry just before the flight entered the range for the spacing pass. On the spacing pass, the flight would fly in an echelon formation over the range center. Then the flight leader would pull, or "break," up and away from the flight, followed by Number 2 ten seconds later, then Number 3 after ten more seconds, then Number 4.

The first event was rockets fired from a 30-degree dive. Each pilot would make three firing passes in turn. Following each pass, the range safety officer, who sat in a small tower on the range, would call out the score as the shooter was climbing back to altitude for a subsequent pass. Since the rockets were powered and had a relatively short time of flight, they essentially fired like a bullet and were therefore quite accurate. A score inside 30 feet was expected, and a "shack," or bull's-eye, was not unusual.

Dive bombing came next. The flight leader would climb to a higher altitude and roll in for the 45-degree dive bomb pass. The difficulty of dive bombing accurately has already been discussed. At the RTU, since dive bombing was difficult, it was the manly man's event. Everyone wanted to be good at all aspects of gunnery, but the ones who were good at dive bombing got extra respect. A good bomb landed inside 100 feet, an excellent one inside 50. Shacks were rare for the students and almost as rare for the instructors.

After each airplane had made its four dive bomb passes, the flight dropped to lower altitude for skip bombing. The skip bombing target was a box 100 feet long by 50 feet wide with a canvas panel at the far end. The objective was for the fighter to drop a simulated high-drag bomb* into the box from a low-altitude, nearly level pass. If the bomb hit in the box, it was adjudged a "skip hit;" if it hit the canvas panel, it was a "hit on the fly." Either counted as a qualifying bomb delivery. The minimum altitude for skip bombing was 100 feet. Because the bombs were dropped so low, it was unusual for a pilot to miss the target.

The last event was strafe. The target was a canvas panel, or "rag," strung between two telephone poles. The fighters swooped around into a low-altitude,

---

* The orange MK–106 practice bomb had a blunt nose and was sometimes called a "beer can." The other practice bomb used for dive bombing was the BDU–33, which was a miniature bomb that weighed twenty-five pounds and was painted blue. Both types of practice bombs carried a small white smoke charge to mark their impact point.

low-angle pass, and fired the 20-mm cannon at the target. Each pilot usually made two or three hot passes, and his total ammunition was limited to 100 bullets by a governor set in the electrically-driven Gatling gun. In order to qualify, the pilot had to put 25 percent of his bullets through the target. Pilots were not allowed to shoot closer than 1,500 feet from the target.* The danger of the event was getting too close to the target and picking up ricochets as the jet roared low over the panel after firing.

After the last shooter was winchester,† the flight rejoined and returned to the base. In the flight debriefing not as much was said about weapons delivery techniques as about the wager. Each pilot bet 25 cents on every pass. Whoever had the best score for a pass won the quarters. Since a four-ship gunnery mission made nearly 50 passes, it took much discussion and, if the mission was the last of the day, several beers to identify the winners and losers. Instructors were notoriously closemouthed about their gunnery techniques. Again, students were often expected to learn the hard way, by watching and losing a lot of quarters.

Perhaps one of the most interesting aspects of the gunnery range missions flown in the RTU was the targets used for weapons deliveries. For rockets and dive bombs, the target was almost always a pylon, a large post made of steel planking, surrounded by concentric circles of tires at 50-foot intervals out from the target. The pylon and tires were painted white, so the effect from the attacker's cockpit was that he was attacking a bull's-eye drawn on the ground. The circles helped new pilots learn the techniques of dive bombing more quickly. For example, a wind drift correction could be made more easily since the pilot could clearly see how far a 25-foot correction was from the target by judging half the distance between two circles. In combat, though, the enemy seldom drew white circles around his targets. So most gunnery ranges featured a set of tactical targets—old trucks or heavy equipment—to attack during tactics missions. There was usually no scoring on these tactical targets. Another flight member had to judge from the air, or "air score," the bomb miss distances. RTU students flew only one or two of their gunnery missions on the tactical ranges; the majority of their gunnery was done on the bull's-eye targets.

In order to qualify as a mission-ready pilot, the F–4 pilot had to drop 50 percent of his ordnance within qualifying criteria. Most pilots qualified in every event during the six to eight range rides of the RTU syllabus. Some never qualified. They were graduated and sent to combat anyhow. The war was on, and the bodies were needed to fill the cockpits. Even though a steep dive bomb pass was the desired way to deliver bombs in combat, there was a ban on 45-degree bomb

---

* Some "old heads" recall the days when the minimum range was 1,200 feet, while new pilots shot from 1,800 feet. In typical bureaucratic fashion, the Air Force moved the line 300 feet further away, following a series of mishaps during which fighters were struck by ricochets from their own bullets.

† Code word meaning all ordnance was expended.

training during the heart of the war. Too many mishaps had happened during the steep passes, so TAC restricted the RTUs to teaching only 30-degree dive bombing.[7] For many graduates the first bomb pass they saw in combat was from a 45-degree pass at twice the release altitude they had seen in training.

Armed Reconnaissance

At the end of the RTU syllabus, students were required to fly tactics missions that would introduce them to the tactics being used in Vietnam. One such tactic was armed reconnaissance or "road recce," as it was called, with recce being pronounced "wrecky." The idea was to employ a four-ship formation along a major transportation artery. The flight leader and his WSO visually searched the highway or railroad. As they searched, the rest of his flight flew a modified Fluid Four above and behind them. When the leader spied a lucrative target, he radioed its position to the rest of his flight, and the entire flight would attack this target in a preplanned manner. Road recce in the RTU was fun. Everyone got to fly fast and maneuver hard. Plus, it was inspiring to be practicing what the students thought would be an actual combat skill. As much as the training crews enjoyed the mission, it was useless. Crews in Vietnam seldom, if ever, flew armed recce. The flight leaders could not find vehicles and supplies the enemy cleverly camouflaged, and the flight zooming around the jungle at low altitude was an easy target for any soldier with a rifle and a juicy target for antiaircraft gunners.

Close Air Support

One training area that proved valuable for combat were the tactics missions devoted to learning how to work with a forward air controller. FACs flew light observation planes like the O-1 and O-2 in support of Army and Marine ground units. The FACs lived with the grunts they protected and knew the battle areas intimately. FACs marked targets with white smoke rockets, and fighters delivered ordnance where the FAC directed.

In the RTU, new pilots learned the rules of the road for working with a FAC. The hardest part was finding the small aircraft as it circled over the target area. The fast-moving fighters used directional finding/steering equipment to get close enough to the slow, low FAC until someone in the flight could get an eyeball on him—a tally-ho. Once the FAC was in sight, he would give the fighters a target briefing—type of target, elevation, attack heading, location of friendlies, enemy defensive fire, best egress heading if hit by enemy fire, and other pertinent data. Usually the fighters would set up a circle, called a wheel or wagon wheel, over the FAC, and wait for him to mark the target. Once the target was marked, the flight leader would attack first. The absolutely inviolable cardinal rule was that each pilot had to have the FAC in sight, and say so on the radio, before he attacked the target. More than one small spotter plane had been run over by a big, fast fighter in the heat of battle. Most RTUs were able to get FAC aircraft to their bases to help train the new fighter crews, many of whom remember the close air support tactics rides as the best training they had in the RTU.

Enthusiasm

The schoolhouse had many shortfalls, not the least of which were the students themselves. Many of the bomber and transport "retreads" did their best to learn fighter ways, and some transitioned well into the fighter community. However, many did not. Adequate pilots or not, these men, because they were older and senior in rank, were thrust into leadership positions in the war for which they were woefully unprepared.

As for the young, inexperienced pilots who went through the RTU as their first flying assignment, most of them just hung on and tried not to get spit out of the fight. They went to war poorly prepared for aerial combat and nearly as badly prepared for "beating dirt."*

This is not to say that they found their combat tour unrewarding. One pilot, who was part of an experimental program to put second lieutenants directly into the front seat of the F–4†, recalled, "It was the time of my life. I took off every day with snake and nape‡ and put it on the enemy. It never occurred to me that I had been poorly trained."[8] Others found mentors in the combat arena who taught them what they should have learned at RTU. One young F–100 pilot took several hits from enemy gunners early in his tour. Fortunately, they were small caliber hits that missed vital spots on his aircraft. One day, a captain in his squadron, Ron Fogleman, approached him and said, "Buzz, haven't you ever heard of a curvilinear approach? I'm going to show you how."[9] A curvilinear approach is a constantly turning bomb pass until just before the instant of release. The constant turn makes it much harder for an enemy gunner to track and hit the attacker. Fogleman, who would later become Air Force chief of staff, taught the trick to the new pilot who successfully completed his combat tour.[10]

All of these pilots were inculcated early with the fighter pilot desire to excel no matter the odds. They flew their patterns very tight.

---

* "Beating dirt" is a slang phrase for air-to-ground attack.

† Prior to this new pilots went to the back seat first. The test was a success, and navigators started to be assigned to the back seat, with all new pilots going directly to the front seat.

‡ High-drag bombs were called Snake Eyes. Nape refers to napalm.

1. Lt. Gen. Donald L. Peterson, interview with author, Bolling Air Force Base (AFB), Washington, D.C., January 15, 1999.

2. Gen. John P. Jumper, interview with author, Ramstein Air Base (AB), Germany, February 27, 1999.

3. T.O. 1F–4E–1, February 1, 1979, C–2 September 15, 1979, published by authority of the Secretary of the Air Force, 1979, pp. 2, 22–23.

4. James W. Alder, "It Never Troubles a Wolf," Air University Library, M-U 32893 A 3613I, p. 27.

5. John Madden, interview with author, Springfield, Virginia, July 9, 1999.

6. Maj. Gen. Timothy A. Kinnan, interview with author, Springfield, Virginia, February 19, 1999.

7. Russ Everts, briefing given at 50th Anniversary Celebration of USAF Weapons School, Flamingo Hilton Hotel, Las Vegas, Nevada, June 19, 1999.

8. Maj. Gen. Ronald E. Keys, interview with author, Stuttgart, Germany, February 23, 1999.

9. Charles L. Buzze, interview with author, Springfield, Virginia, July 11, 1999.

10. Peterson interview.

CHAPTER 3

✪

Glimmers of Hope

*The bomb just obliterated the exact
point they were trying to hit.*[1]

By halftime, the period between Rolling Thunder and Linebacker, several efforts were underway to improve combat capability within the fighter forces. The shortcomings of the F–4 and its weapons delivery system were well known. The Air Force was beginning efforts to improve the Phantom and the training of its crews. A few combat squadrons had the new version of the Phantom, the F–4E, with an internal gun, and an even newer version with a modified wing and improved cockpit switches was in the process of development. More importantly, though, a cadre of handpicked aircrews participated in a focused aerial combat training program at Nellis Air Force Base, Nevada, that was intended to improve their ability to kill MiGs. Furthermore, a technological leap in bombing accuracy was just getting off the ground in the forms of rudimentary laser-guided bombs (LGBs) and television (TV)-guided bombs.

Papa Whiskey Charlie

On a January morning in 1970, Capt. John P. Jumper, Laredo 04, entered the mission planning room at Udorn Royal Thai Air Base to plan his upcoming fast FAC mission with his back-seater, Lt. Dick Anderegg. Anderegg had been breaking out the frag* to determine what fighters had been allocated to them for the mission and what ordnance the fighters would carry.

Anderegg, pointing to the frag, asked Jumper, "Do you know what a Papa Whiskey Charlie is?"
Jumper shook his head no, and asked, "Who's got it?"
"A flight of four from Ubon," Anderegg answered. "I've looked in the code book, but there's no reference to PWC under the ordnance column."
Jumper shrugged his shoulders and said, "Guess we'll find out when we get there."

A couple of hours later, Laredo 04 had finished searching for targets just west of the Fish's Mouth on Route 7, the same stretch of dirt road where Rick Honey

---

* The fragmentary order was the part of the war order for the day that pertained to their unit.

had been killed a few weeks earlier. As Jumper pulled the F–4D from the Triple Nickel (555th Tactical Fighter Squadron) into a rocketing climb out of the dangerous low-altitude arena, Anderegg changed the radio to the rendezvous frequency designated on the frag for their mission with Ubon's F–4s.

> The Ubon flight leader transmitted, "Good morning, Laredo, this is Buick flight of four, at 18,000, ready to work."
> Jumper responded, "Okay, Buick, we have a suspected storage area that looks pretty good just on the north side of the road."
> The fighter leader answered, "Ah, well, that's not a good target for our ordnance. We need a small, pinpoint target for what we have."
> "Well, we haven't seen any trucks yet," said Jumper, "but we have a single 37-mm gun that's been shooting at us pretty good. How's that?"
> Buick leader responded instantly, "That's perfect. Where is it?"

The next few minutes were taken by the two missions finding each other, and then Laredo led the Ubon jets to the gun's location. Jumper rolled in and fired a white-smoke marking rocket at the gun. Immediately a clip of seven red golf balls from the gunners zoomed past the Phantom as Jumper jinked* the big jet off the pass.

Between the white rocket landing nearby and the dust kicked up from the firing AAA piece, the Buick leader immediately announced that he had the gun in sight. He also transmitted, "Laredo, I want you to stay high; we'll take it from here."

Jumper took his plane to 16,000 feet, orbited away from the gun and watched as the Buick flight leader started a left-hand orbit right over the gun but well above the gun's effective range. They heard the Buick leader clear his wingman to drop down, and both were amazed to see the wingman rolling in from well above the normal altitude. Anderegg commented, "Jeez, what's he doing up there? He'll never hit anything from there," and Jumper agreed.

Almost immediately, with virtually no tracking time, the Buick wingman pulled off his pass and called, "Bomb gone," on the radio. The Laredo crew was very confused. Neither had ever seen anyone drop a bomb from such a high altitude. They watched the gun position. The gunners were not firing anymore. Suddenly a huge explosion blew a 2,000-pound bomb hole right where the gun had been. It was vaporized. A direct hit. The Laredo crew had just seen their first personal demonstration of the future of fighter aviation.

> The Buick leader calmly transmitted, "Ya got another target for us, Laredo?"
> Jumper replied, "No. But we'll find one. Don't go away!"[2]

By the time Linebacker started, the boys from Ubon's Wolfpack had perfected their laser-guided bomb delivery techniques, and had graduated from

---

* Moved the airplane in an erratic, violent manner to spoil the enemy gunners' aim.

Capt. John Jumper (left) and the author beside their F–4D from the 555th Tactical Fighter Squadron after a combat mission. *Courtesy of Jean Anderegg.*

the old Zot system to the Pave Knife designator. The Zot* system used an aiming device out of the left side of the airplane. The pilot had to keep the airplane in a left turn, so the WSO could aim the laser at the target and keep it there during the time a wingman dropped his bomb. Zot had some clear disadvantages. The designator could not drop a bomb and guide it himself. It took two airplanes to get one bomb to the target, and the coordination this required sometimes resulted in miscommunication. If at any time the laser moved off the target or stopped transmitting, the chance of a hit was very low. In addition, the Zot put the designator in a dangerous position, since he had to hold a steady left-hand orbit around the target while the bomb fell, a dangerous tactic over North Vietnam where the flak and SAMs were thick.

A newer designator, Pave Knife, arrived at Ubon just in time for Linebacker. Pave Knife was a large pod with a bulbous nose that was carried under the wing of the F–4. The bulbous nose housed a gimbaled designator that could rotate fully 360 degrees under the aircraft. Therefore, the pilot could roll in and point his nose at the target, thereby letting the WSO see the target on his radar/TV screen. The WSO then tracked the target with the laser designator, and the pilot dropped his LGB. As the pilot recovered from the dive and started his egress, the WSO could continue to lase the target until bomb impact. The success of Pave Knife and LGBs was dramatically illustrated when Capt. D. L. Smith led a mission

---

* Zot, surprisingly, is not an acronym. It comes from the "B.C." comic strip, wherein an anteater frequently fires his long tongue out of his mouth to snatch an ant. The "sound" his tongue makes is represented by the word "zot" in the cartoon panel. The laser, therefore, was likened to the lightning fast anteater's tongue, a blindingly fast, straight line to the target.

against the Thanh Hoa bridge during Linebacker. In one attack Smith's eight F–4s with LGBs destroyed the bridge, a feat the old-fashioned dive bombers had been unable to do in hundreds of missions. Those missions started an Air Force love affair with laser-guided bombs and laser designators that still burns brightly today. The era of smart bombs had dawned.

The Soft-wing Phantom

Although it is easy to criticize TAC for clamping down on dogfight training for the RTU crews, credit must also be given to the fighter command for leading the way in the development of the soft-wing F–4E. The modification was a totally new wing for the spin-prone beast that featured hydraulically operated slats on the leading edge of the wing controlled automatically by the jet's angle of attack sensing system. When the angle of attack reached a preset value, the slats popped out and forward to add lift and energy to the wing. The result was two-fold. First, the pilot no longer had to worry about controlling roll with rudder at high angles of attack. If he wanted the airplane to roll left, all he had to do was push the stick to the left, and it would roll that way even at a high AOA. Second, the airplane became virtually spin proof, and accidents from spins dropped dramatically. In fact, many pilots thought the soft-wing F–4E flew much like the T–38 in which they learned to fly during pilot training. Of course, there were some penalties to pay. The slats increased drag slightly, so acceleration and top speed were reduced somewhat, but these were adjudged small prices to pay for controllability and confidence at low speeds while dogfighting.

Visual Identification (VID)

During most combat periods over North Vietnam, rules of engagement (ROE) required Phantom crews to visually identify MiGs before shooting. With such restrictive ROE, the beyond visual range capability of the F–4 and the AIM–7, radar-guided Sparrow, were nearly useless. The problem was in the head-on or nose-to-nose aspect. The F–4 could fire its Sparrow at over ten miles from a MiG if the two aircraft were approaching head-on. However, the MiG was so small that the F–4 pilot could not identify the MiG as an enemy in time to shoot. Closure speeds in a head-on pass are very high. Two fighters flying at 500 knots are closing at the rate of a mile every three seconds. The minimum range for a Sparrow in the front aspect was nearly three miles. (The performance envelope in Fig. 3.1 shows a representative Sparrow envelope.) It was impossible to see the MiG far enough away to get a missile shot before the MiG was inside minimum range.

The F–4 (on the left) can shoot his Sparrow at the MiG (on the right) anyplace within the shaded area. If he shoots outside the shaded area, the missile does not have enough flight time to hit the target. If he shoots inside the small white area, the missile cannot turn fast enough to hit the MiG.

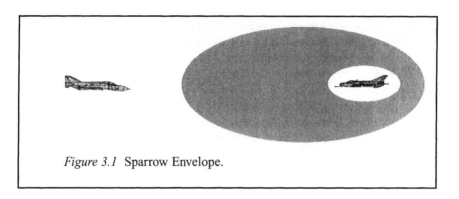

Figure 3.1 Sparrow Envelope.

An ingenious attempt to solve the VID problem was the target identification system electro-optical (TISEO). The TISEO was an electronic telescope mounted in the left wing of the F–4E. It had 4-power and 10-power magnifications. When the WSO locked onto a target with the radar, the TISEO could be moved to look exactly where the radar looked. The WSO could then select the TV mode of his radar/TV scope and look in the black-and-white TISEO picture for the target. If he saw the target, the WSO could then command the TISEO to optically track the target while he selected 10-power magnification. Tests of the TISEO indicated that it provided the aircrew a positive VID of a MiG-sized target well outside minimum Sparrow launch range. The technological advances that permitted the crew to see a TV picture inside the cockpit were nearly beyond the comprehension of the F–4 pilots and pitters. Suddenly it seemed that flying fighters was getting very close to science fiction. The best, for them, was yet to come.

The Pinkie Switch

Not all improvements to the F–4 were such gee-whiz advancements, though. Some were nothing more than commonsense modifications to a horribly designed cockpit. Many MiG kills were lost because the pilot did not or could not set his switches properly. As discussed earlier, pilots went into combat in three-million-dollar fighters with a piece of plastic tubing jammed over switches to make them easier to find in the heat of combat. In response to this horrible design, the Air Force fielded a modification to the F–4E that was numbered 556. Pilots called it the five-five-six mod, which significantly redesigned parts of the F–4E cockpit.

The 556 mod added a switch on the outside of the pilot's left throttle. The multipositional switch selected which air-to-air ordnance the pilot desired. In its forward setting, the radar, or Sparrow, missile was selected; in its middle position, the heat, or Sidewinder, missile was selected; and in its aft position, the gun was selected. The switch was designed to be operated by the pilot's left little finger, so it quickly became known as the pinkie switch. No longer did the pilot have to look down into the cockpit or feel around the instrument panel for the proper switch. Since the pilot seldom moved his left hand from the throttles, the pinkie switch was immediately available.

Another switch, added to the front of the left throttle, allowed the pilot to change all his systems from bombing to dogfighting with a single push. If he depressed the switch, his radar, his gunsight, and other systems transferred immediately into the dogfight mode. Hugh Moreland, then a captain, transitioned from the F–104 to the F–4E with the 556 mod. He recalls, "I didn't need a lot of hours in the jet to know that a single switch that would put everything instantly into air-to-air was a good thing."[3]

The mod also dramatically changed the F–4E's capability to drop bombs. Several selections were added that allowed the crew to salvo bombs (drop bombs simultaneously from each station) rather than ripple them in a long string. More intervals were also available so that more firepower could be concentrated on the target. Finally, because the switches were all consolidated on one panel, the pilot did not have to search around the cockpit for the Rube Goldberg kluge of switches seen before the 556 mod. Soft wings and new switches clearly moved the F–4 out of the nuclear war role and into the conventional arena.

Rivet Haste

The program that tied aircraft modifications and air crew training into one package was nicknamed Rivet Haste, and was a clear sign that the Air Force realized how poorly it had equipped and trained its fighter forces. The Rivet Haste program spawned the slat, TISEO, and 556 mods for the F–4E, but more than that it emphasized pilot experience and training. TAC, under the Rivet Haste aegis, handpicked highly experienced crews, all combat veterans, to form an elite force of MiG killers. In the late summer and fall of 1972, the crews went through an extensive training program at Nellis Air Force Base, Nevada, in brand-new slatted F–4Es. As part of their training they each flew three missions against MiG–17 and MiG–21 fighters, which had been obtained by the Air Force and flown by pilots under the top-secret programs nicknamed Have Donut and Have Drill.[4] Without question, those flights against the actual aircraft they might encounter in combat were the best training missions the pilots had ever experienced.[5] Even though the Rivet Haste crews were seasoned combat veterans, they had never experienced aerial combat training against the real thing in a controlled environment.

During the Nellis "top off," the Rivet Haste crews went through training in three groups of six pilots and six WSOs, with each group a month behind the previous one. By the time the second group started, some of the pilots, ones who had experience in an aerial attack system of tactics called Double Attack, proposed that the Rivet Haste squadron adopt Double Attack as an alternative to Fluid Four.[6]

Double Attack had been around for years and was even taught briefly in the F–100 Fighter Weapons School (FWS) in the mid-1960s. The basic fighting unit of Double Attack was the two-ship. During a dogfight, or engagement, both aircraft were equal partners in prosecuting the attack. The premise was that fighters that were not as agile as the adversary should not attempt to turn with the adversary. Of course, U.S. pilots had never had aircraft that could outturn their adversaries in any previous war, and Vietnam was no exception. In Double Attack, Fighter A would threaten the adversary by pointing at him, which would force the adversary to focus his attention on Fighter A. Meanwhile, Fighter B would position for a shot from outside the adversary's line of sight. Under no circumstances would Fighter A slow down to try to match turns with the adversary. If Fighter A could not get a shot, he would accelerate away from the adversary, and then turn the engagement over to B. The system was designed to take advantage of speed and coordinated firepower.

When Rivet Haste pilots tried to convince the Nellis Fighter Weapons School instructors of the value of Double Attack, they were rebuffed. The Nellis position was that Double Attack required very experienced pilots to make it work, and the experience level of the RTU pilots going to Vietnam was so low they were not capable of doing anything except hanging on in the welded wing position of Fluid Four. Undaunted, some Rivet Haste pilots saw Double Attack as the attack system that would work over Vietnam. Indeed, Navy F–4 and F–8 pilots flying over North Vietnam were getting good results with their version of Double Attack called Loose Deuce.

Rivet Haste seemed to be doing all the right things based on lessons learned from the Vietnam experience. All the pilots and WSOs were experienced and were kept together in the same squadron. They had the best aerial combat training of any crews to go to war. Their aircraft were modified to improve shortcomings in handling qualities, weapons employment, and target identification. Unfortunately, the Rivet Haste concept arrived too late to have any impact on the war. Although the crews flew a handful of combat missions, they never shot down any MiGs, and another bombing halt, the final one before the end of the war, came less than two weeks after the Rivet Haste forces arrived.[7]

---

1. Gen. John P. Jumper interview with author, Ramstein AB, Germany, February 27, 1999.
2. *Ibid.*
3. Col. Hugh Moreland, USAF (Ret.), telephone interview with author, March 4, 1999.
4. Marshall L. Michel III, *Clashes: Air Combat over North Vietnam, 1965–1972* (Annapolis, Maryland: Naval Institute Press, 1997), pp. 76–77.
5. Moreland interview.
6. *Ibid.*
7. *Ibid.*

PART II

CHANGING OF THE GUARD

CHAPTER 4

✪

The New Officer Corps

During the Vietnam War years, the United States Air Force officer corps underwent some profound changes that were reflected in the makeup of the fighter force. Several factors were simultaneously at play, and the two most significant results were that fighter pilots were younger and better educated.

Exodus of the Graybeards

By the mid-1960s, the huge block of World War II veteran officers on active duty began retiring. The number that left the Air Force, and the experience they took with them, was staggering. In 1965 alone, 35,000 officers became eligible for retirement as compared to 2,500 a decade earlier. More importantly, though, the 35,000 who became retirement eligible in 1965 included nearly half of the total number of officers who wore silver wings.[1] During the twenty years after World War II, from 1946 to 1966, the average age of a pilot had increased from twenty-four to over forty. As that generation left active duty for bass fishing in Florida and golf in Arizona, the average pilot age, and of course the flying experience that went with it, plummeted.

Another factor that affected pilot age in the fighter force was the demand of pipeline training for Vietnam combat. The pipeline was the entire training flow needed to qualify a pilot for combat, and usually progressed through several bases over many months. A universally assignable C–7 pilot selected for a combat tour in the F–4 entered the pipeline when he got his orders. He then went to water survival school at Homestead Air Force Base, Florida, followed by land survival and escape and evasion training at Fairchild Air Force Base, Washington. After these basic survival courses, he next went to the AT–33 program, then to the F–4 RTU, and then on to jungle survival school at Clark Air Base, Republic of the Philippines, just before reporting to duty at his base in South Vietnam or Thailand. The entire pipeline took nearly a year.

The catch to the pipeline, though, was that there were actually two pilots in training for every slot in Vietnam—the C–7 pilot in this example who was going to fly the F–4 in Vietnam, and the pilot who had to replace him in the C–7. The result was a staggering training load. TAC's manning was under 80 percent, and a six-day workweek was standard policy throughout the command. One instructor pilot at the Homestead RTU recalls that everyone was exhausted, morale was very low, and each new class that piled on top of the one before made life miserable.[2] Air Training Command instructor pilots routinely worked over 70 hours a week.[3] At any given time there were over 4,500 pilots in the pipeline.

One way of reducing the training load was to increase the number of recent undergraduate pilot training (UPT) graduates in the pipeline. Since these new aviators were not coming from a flying job, there was no need to train a replacement for them. By 1969, over 75 percent of all new UPT graduates were being assigned to the pipeline, headed for combat in Southeast Asia.[4] Of course, such large numbers of new pilots entering the fighter force dramatically reduced its age and experience level. At the start of the Vietnam War, the average flying time for a fighter pilot in combat was over 1,000 hours; by the end of the war, it was less than 250. From 1965 to 1968, the percentage of fighter pilots in combat that came directly from UPT rose from 12.5 percent to 21.1 percent.[5]

Another decision that lowered the average age in fighter squadrons was the move to replace F–4 back seat pilots with WSOs or navigators. Originally, the Air Force manned both cockpits of the F–4 with pilots, maintaining that it took two pilots to employ the aircraft properly.* That position quickly became unpopular with both the front- and back-seaters. Many aircraft commanders (ACs) came from single-seat fighters, and so they were not used to flying with anyone, let alone another pilot. They did not know how to use the young pilots in the back seat properly, and in some cases did not want to learn. The young pilots, called the guy-in-back, were dissatisfied that their primary duties did not include flying the airplane, at least not as much as they thought they deserved. Their frustration was understandable, since they had just competed in what was arguably the Air Force's most intense program, UPT, against the cream of the new officers and had succeeded in securing a coveted fighter assignment, only to find that they would get little "stick time." In many cases, squadron supervisors elected to crew a strong GIB with a weak AC, a practice that only exacerbated the frustration many GIBs felt.

In 1968, under pressure from the Department of Defense, the Air Force initiated a test program that put UPT graduates directly into the front seat of the F–4 and navigators in the back. It was declared a success, and the transition continued for four years. In 1972 the last of the pilot GIBs was checked out in the front seat. Interestingly, the decision to take pilots out of the back seat was forced onto the service by Secretary of Defense Robert McNamara, who did not believe the Air Force had a pilot shortage as it claimed. One solution McNamara saw to the shortage was to take the pilot out of the back seat of the F–4, judging that the Air Force was wrong in its claims that it took two pilots to fly the big fighter. Tired of being stonewalled, McNamara directed the change in policy even before the test results were known.[6]

---

* The Navy never put pilots in the back seat.

The impact of McNamara's decision on the age and experience level in fighter squadrons can be seen in the experience of the 78th Tactical Fighter Squadron, stationed at Royal Air Force (RAF) Base, Woodbridge, England. During an eighteen-month period from the summer of 1971 to the winter of 1972, no new pilots came to the 78th TFS. As the front-seaters finished their three-year* overseas tours and rotated back to the states, they were replaced by pilot GIBs, who upgraded to the front seat. The WSOs in turn replaced the GIBs. The effect on age during this period was remarkable. Before the conversion, the top seven leadership positions in the squadron (commander down through the flight commanders) were held by three lieutenant colonels and four majors. After the conversion, those same positions were held by two majors and five captains. In fact, one of the majors progressed through the squadron's command structure, one step at a time, all the way from flight commander to squadron commander.

Hitting the Books

No less remarkable than the drop in age was the increase in the educational level of officers. As the 1960s dawned, about 45 percent of the officer corps had college degrees. Two programs, Aviation Cadets and Officer Candidate School (OCS), were popular with high school graduates because they provided a road to commissioning and silver wings for those without college diplomas. However, the Air Force gradually closed both of those programs and dramatically increased officer accessions from AFROTC† (Air Force Reserve Officer Training Corps) and Officer Training School (OTS),‡ both of which required college graduation. By 1965, the Air Force was no longer commissioning officers without a college diploma. The larger impact on the percentage of officers with degrees, though, was the World War II retirement hump. During the 1960s, nearly 55,000 officers

---

*There were two kinds of tours—long and short. A long tour was three years, and the service member could take his family, car, and household goods. Most overseas tours were long tours in countries like Germany, England, and Japan. A short tour was one year, usually at remote bases or combat bases. Family members were not permitted to accompany the service member on short tours.

† Air Force Reserve Officer Training Corps, a two- or four-year program offered on college campuses. Students take one military training course per semester, one drill period per week, and attend one four-week military training session in the summer. Upon graduation, they are commissioned as second lieutenants in the Air Force Reserve and enter extended active duty almost immediately. During the late 1960s, about 10 percent of the cadets were given scholarships if they took courses of study particularly valuable to the Air Force like engineering, mathematics, and physics.

‡ OTS is a three-month, concentrated military training program for college graduates. After completion, candidates are commissioned as second lieutenants in the Air Force Reserve and go directly to active duty. Although sometimes referred to as "ninety-day wonders," their service and promotion records are comparable to USAF Academy and ROTC graduates.

retired, and another 40,000 younger officers completed their service obligation and left the service. Out of this population of almost 100,000 were over 40,000 with no college degree. After they were gone, the percentage of officers with college degrees jumped to 85 percent by 1974.[7]

Supplementing AFROTC and OTS college graduate officers were graduates from the newly opened U.S. Air Force Academy (USAFA) in Colorado Springs, Colorado. The first class graduated in 1959, and although the number of "Zoomies" was small, their impact was significant. AFROTC and OTS commissioned about 8,000 a year, whereas the academy produced about 500 per year.[8] Even though USAFA graduates comprised less than 10 percent of the officer corps, they formed an intelligent, highly educated cadre that was academically oriented. Some cadets had carried academic loads as much as 75 percent higher than their contemporaries in civilian colleges, and many took pride in their academic accomplishments. One engineering graduate recalled that he took more English courses than an English major at a liberal arts college.[9]

The emphasis on academics at the academy was not without some sacrifices. Academics took 77 percent of the curriculum, whereas military training took 15 percent and athletics 8 percent. Class standing added to the pressure to achieve academically, for class standing almost exclusively dictated choice of assignment after graduation. Graduates were displeased with the military environment, and more than one fact-finding congressional commission observed that military training was weak. Ultimately, the pressures to succeed in the classroom overcame discipline, and a huge cheating scandal erupted in 1965. Over a hundred cadets resigned. Even though graduates and observers called into question the academy's military training, the academic excellence of its students was rock solid.[10]

Finally, by 1966, every officer coming into the Air Force was a college graduate. Candidates and cadets from the USAFA, AFROTC, and OTS stood in front of an American flag, took the oath of office, and had their mothers or girlfriends pin the gold "butter" bars of a second lieutenant on their shoulders. When they reported to their first assignments, they were not any smarter than the warriors who wore the same rank in two world wars and two Asian conflicts before them, but they had an academic approach to problem solving. For those who became fighter pilots and WSOs, that approach would serve them well in the forthcoming technology explosion.

1. Vance O. Mitchell, *Air Force Officers: Personnel Policy Development, 1944–1974* (Washington, D.C.: Air Force History and Museums Program, 1996), p. 201.

2. Lt. Gen. Donald L. Peterson, interview with author, Bolling Air Force Base (AFB), Washington, D.C., January 15, 1999.

3. Mitchell, p. 248.

4. *Ibid.,* p. 249.

5. Marshall L. Michel III, *Clashes: Air Combat over North Vietnam, 1965–1972* (Annapolis, Maryland: Naval Institute Press, 1997), p. 167.

6. Mitchell, p. 256.

7. *Ibid.,* p. 201.

8. *Ibid.,* p. 224.

9. Maj. Gen. Timothy A. Kinnan, interview with author, Springfield, Virginia, February 19, 1999.

10. Mitchell, p. 228.

CHAPTER 5

✪

Changes in Attitudes

The fighter pilot culture that emerged from the smoke, dust, and blood of Vietnam was multifaceted. The three things that mattered most in fighter squadrons were flying skills, flight discipline, and unit cohesion.

Good Hands

A fighter pilot who was adept at maneuvering and controlling his jet was said to be a "good stick" or to have "good hands." Those who were less adept were referred to as "ham fists" or "hamburgers." Every fighter pilot aspired to be the best in his squadron. The highest compliment was to say a pilot was a good stick. Even though that was an understatement, there was no such thing as best stick. Even those who won squadron gunnery competitions were never referred to as "top guns." Ones with good hands usually presented an air of humility, but beneath the humble exterior roiled competitive souls who viewed any losing effort as abject failure.

Tom Wolfe described well this competitive drive of the fighter pilot in *The Right Stuff.* But if Wolfe thought the pre-Vietnam astronauts were competitive, he would have been more impressed with the group of fighter pilots who came into the Air Force in the 1960s and 1970s.

The competition began before a fledgling aviator ever stepped onto a training base. USAFA cadets came from the very top of their high school classes in academics, leadership, and sports and had endured four intense years in a highly technical college curriculum. AFROTC cadets competed for four years for coveted pilot training and navigator training slots. Many worked outside jobs to pay for college. Those few who had ROTC scholarships had to maintain 3.0 grade point averages in scientific and technical major fields of study. A third route to commissioning was through OTS, which was the officer accession "shock absorber." Since its course was only three months long, it could increase or decrease officer production very quickly. During the Vietnam War years, it expanded dramatically, but even during those years it was difficult to gain admission to OTS, and it was not unusual for the number of applicants to exceed the number of appointments by 300 percent. The reason was simple. Many thought it better to go into the Air Force as an officer than to be drafted into the Army.[1]

No matter which of the commissioning sources put a young man in pilot training, the selection process was very competitive. The candidate first had to pass physical requirements that less than 10 percent of the general population could meet. He then had to compete against other applicants nationwide based on college grades, class standings, test scores, and recommendations. Once selected for aircrew training, the candidate was thrown into a pressure cooker at pilot training or navigator school. Pilot candidates' days were divided into halves. In the morning half the class flew while the other half had academics. In the afternoon they switched places. Every day was a flight, and every flight required extensive preparation. Examination flights, or check rides, were frequent, as were written tests at the end of each academic phase. It was a grueling course, but when one considers the goal was to take a man who may have never flown an airplane and make him into a universally assignable jet pilot, fully instrument rated, proficient in formation flying and aerobatics in only fifty-three weeks, the intensity is understandable.

Nearly one in five could not pass the course, a number that is somewhat misleading.[2] Most washouts occurred in the first few months of training, so the pressure early in training was enormous, as candidates watched classmates drop like Southern belles in a heat wave. OTS graduates suffered most with a washout rate of 36 percent, as compared to 17 percent for AFROTC graduates and 12 percent for USAFA graduates. OTS failure rates were higher for two reasons. First, some candidates were only trying to stay out of combat in the United States Army. Therefore, they resigned from aircrew training as soon as they arrived, knowing that they would likely never see Vietnam as a ground officer, and if they did, it would be in a safer location than as an Army lieutenant in the field. Second, OTS provided no flight screening programs as did AFROTC and USAFA, so initial washouts were very high for those graduates.[3]

For many years, class standing at the undergraduate pilot training and undergraduate navigator training (UNT) programs was the sole factor in determining what aircraft the new graduate would be assigned. Such was the case up to nearly the end of the Vietnam War. Class standing was determined by averaging academic averages and check flight averages. About a month before graduation, a block of assignments was given to each class at the several training bases nationwide. The block was different for every class, but it was common for each to have a few fighters. Typically, most of the fighter slots were snatched up by the top graduates. Of course, those were pipeline assignments to the war.

By the time a new pilot or navigator reported to his F–4 RTU class, he had been through an extensive filtration process. It was a process that demanded he compete, compete, and compete again under pressure that was nearly palpable. These newly minted aviators brought an attitude to RTU. That attitude was, "I'm good, and I know it. I can learn anything quickly and well. There is no challenge too great, and no task I cannot master. I prefer that you teach me, but if you will not or cannot teach me, then I will teach myself. I seek only one reward: someday someone will say of me, 'good hands'."

Life after Combat

Life in a fighter squadron outside the combat zone during and immediately after Vietnam was a venue where the crews flew hard and, some might say, played even harder. By the end of the Vietnam War, every F–4 squadron was loaded with combat veterans, and nearly all the pilots had two combat tours. Despite the official policy of no pilot having to serve a second nonvoluntary tour in Southeast Asia, a carrot was held in front of the dissatisfied pilot GIBs that made consecutive combat assignments more common. If they would volunteer for a second combat tour, they would do it in the front seat. Every F–4 squadron had several pilots who snatched the carrot and chomped it up. They graduated RTU as GIBs, did a combat tour, went directly to the RTU to repeat it in the front seat, and then immediately returned to the combat zone for a second tour. Most of these two-tour pilots had nearly 400 combat missions, where they provided the tactical leadership within the combat squadrons. With few exceptions, the rest of the postwar squadron pilots and WSOs had one combat tour of 150 to 200 missions. All of them had survived the final distillation of the competitive process. They were the best the Air Force had.

In the early 1970s, when the conversion to navigator back-seaters was nearing completion, the upgrade of the pilots out of the back into the front seats got ahead of the training of navigators, and some navigators came directly from nonfighter aircraft assignments to the back seat of the F–4 without even going through the RTU. One such navigator, Capt. J. W. Smith, arrived at his F–4 squadron having never flown in anything faster than the propeller-driven C–130 in which he had navigated for several years. After a few weeks of flying with the combat veterans on the gunnery range, and partying with them afterwards, Smith, a Lousianian, went home on leave to visit his mother. The first evening he was there, his mother asked him, as they sat in porch rockers looking across the bayou, "Tell me, J. W., what's it like being in one of them thar fighter squadrons?" J. W. rocked for a moment, then smiled and said to her, "Well, momma, it's like bein' paid $30,000 a year to be a Hell's Angel."[4]

Some observers of peacetime fighter squadrons after Vietnam would have echoed Smith's characterization that these units were wild and undisciplined. Many crews were nonconformist and frequently disregarded regulations about uniforms, flying, and social behavior. They left the Vietnam conflict distrustful of not only their national leadership, but Air Force leadership as well. The supreme lesson from combat was that the only people one could trust were the other members of the flight and squadron peers. No matter how bad things got in a battle, the wingman never abandoned his leader, and the leader always took care of the wingman. Those who were dependable survived. Those who were undependable usually survived the enemy's bullets, but they never survived the scorn of their peers. Therefore, although flying skills remained the most admired attribute, discipline ran a close second.

Lt. Tim Kinnan, one of the first pilots without combat experience to arrive at his postwar squadron, recalls his first taste of flight discipline in an operational

Capt. Tim Kinnan's right hand zooms to a position of advantage as he teaches aerial tactics at Clark Air Base, the Philippines. *Courtesy of Sue Kinnan.*

squadron. Kinnan was the wingman in a flight of two F–4s scheduled to fly a low-level training route. When the flight arrived at the point where they had to descend to the low-level starting point, the weather was not as good as they expected. Kinnan's flight leader told him to drop back into a trail position two miles behind. Kinnan did so and was surprised when the flight leader promptly dropped down through a very small hole in the clouds, a move Kinnan viewed as both illegal and dangerous. He did not follow. When the flight returned to the base, the flight leader told Kinnan, "If you had done that in combat, you would have been sent to the staff in Saigon and never flown another mission." Kinnan recalls that he was very angry with the flight leader for chewing him out, but he vowed, "I'd never leave his damn wing again. No matter what!"[5]

In contrast though, discipline in the air did not extend outside of the flight or squadron. A wingman might hang doggedly to his flight leader, the epitome of discipline, but the same wingman flying alone might "shine his ass" at the drop of a hat. Every fighter pilot of the early 1970s, and earlier generations, recalls a pet target that the squadron would dust off whenever the opportunity presented itself. One familiar request from radar controllers was a "bubble check." The radars that monitored and controlled fighters were enclosed in enormous white bubbles that were usually located on a hilltop in some remote area. After a mission, if the radar controller requested a bubble check, it was really a request for the fighters to fly as low and fast over the radar dome as they could get away with. Just before the fighters arrived, the controllers would all run outside and enjoy the free air show.

Another practice that was equally as dangerous and illegal, and thus just as appealing, was the "doors check" on the gunnery range. One version of the practice bomb dispenser carried by most fighters had sliding doors that opened and closed. The doors were opened while on the range but closed while flying to and from the range to ensure no practice bombs fell out inadvertently. Normally, as flights departed the range, they would check each other to make sure all the dispenser doors were closed. Occasionally, though, a single fighter would use the dispenser on the range, and the range safety officer, who sat in a 50-foot tower to the side of range, was required to check that the doors were closed. The standard procedure for this process directed the pilot to fly past the tower at a safe airspeed and altitude. To most pilots, though, a good door check was flown if the jet was so low that the pilot had to rock the wing up so that the range officer could see the bottom of the dispenser.

John Jumper, a captain with two combat tours in Vietnam, serving at RAF Bentwaters in the early 1970s, remembers there was little or no effort on the part of the combat veterans to follow the rules. Each squadron had its own code of right and wrong. One example he recalls were the constant mock attacks that RAF and USAF fighters made on each other. What little A/A training the Phantoms did was against each other. However, their low proficiency did not stop them from jumping RAF Lightnings, Hunters, and F–4s* at every opportunity. Even though strictly forbidden by USAFE (United States Air Forces in Europe) rules, swirling, twirling dogfights over the North Sea with national pride at stake were commonplace. Jumper recalls, "We had no idea what we were doing. It was just a free-for-all. Sometimes it was so dangerous it wasn't even fun. It was plain stupid."[6]

In short, a contradiction existed in the fighter force. Within the fighter culture there was unquestioning loyalty to one's mates that demanded total discipline in the air. But there was also a common disregard, even disrespect, for authority above the squadron level.

If the F–4 pilots and WSOs flew their Phantoms hard, they played even harder. The mainstay of social life was the officers' club, and alcohol use was the linchpin of camaraderie after duty hours. Fighter pilots have always loved games and competition, especially drinking games, and the officers' club environment provided the perfect venue for both. All clubs had a stag bar where women were forbidden to enter, and the penalty for even a telephone call from a wife was a free round of drinks paid for by the chagrined husband. "Happy Hours" on Wednesday and Friday afternoons offered drinks at half price, or less, through most of the evening. Dice games, "Horses," "4–5–6," and "21 Aces," were continuous as one pilot or WSO after another lost, then bought rounds of drinks to the point where it was common for a man to be behind, with several lined up in front of his place at the bar.

As the evenings wore on, dice games, darts, and "dollar bill" games soon progressed into more physical events, some carried along as part of the fighter culture from previous wars. Whole squadrons linked arms and conducted "MiG sweeps" of the bar area as they steamrolled over tables, chairs, and people in their path. Another game was for a small group of men to attempt to throw a buddy over the bar. Of course, it was the victim's job to resist with all his might by holding onto whatever or whomever was available. Ultimately, he would lose

---

* The RAF had its own version of the F–4, powered by Rolls Royce engines, of course.

and be launched into the glassware and bottles behind the bar, often dragging a thrower or two along with him. The more dangerous the game, the better, and Sockey, a hybrid of soccer and hockey, was the most hazardous of all. A crushed steel beer can served as a puck that teams of players attempted to kick through the opposing goal. Adding spice to the game was the practice of sloshing beer on the hard linoleum floor. Players always had to carry a beer in one hand. There were no other rules. Injuries were sometimes serious. Many commanders attempted to ban Sockey, not because it was stupid, but because injuries caused disruption in the flying schedule if an injured player had to be replaced the next morning. Flying hard and drinking hard were expected among the peers of the fighter squadrons. Those who did not do both were suspect, and those who did were expected to be perfect the next day on the mission, following a fighter pilot's breakfast—a Coke, a candy bar, and a cigarette.

Despite social behavior incomprehensible to outside observers, some fighter crews came out of their combat experience with positive goals. One was a burning desire to teach the next generation a better way to learn the fighter business. Some had their opportunity to teach in the RTU, and a handful had the chance to teach at the highest level—The USAF Fighter Weapons School (FWS) at Nellis Air Force Base, Nevada.

Learning to Teach

In 1974 there was a large sign on the front of the 414th Fighter Weapons Squadron (FWSq) at Nellis. The centerpiece of the sign was the famous bull's-eye patch that identified the building and the squadron as the F–4 Fighter Weapons School, or simply "weapons school," as it was usually called. Under the large patch, an imposing statement proclaimed, "Home of the World's Greatest Fighter Pilots."

Nellis had been the cradle of fighter weapons and tactics since the Air Force established a fighter training and gunnery training school there in 1949 in an effort to capture the lessons and experiences fighter pilots had learned in World War II. Later the school became the Fighter Weapons School, and each successive fighter model, like the F–86, F–100, and F–105, had its own squadron within the weapons school. The mission of the weapons school was to provide a "doctorate in flying fighters." Although there were three weapons schools in the mid-1970s, one each for the F–4, A–7, and F–111, the F–4 weapons school was the largest and most influential because nearly every fighter base worldwide was equipped with the Phantom. Typically, three classes of fifteen pilots and ten WSOs each, selected from the best of the best, attended the weapons school every year. Competition at every base was intense for the one or two slots per year earmarked for each F–4 wing. It would be no exaggeration to say that aviators selected for the weapons school ranked in the top 5 percent of their contemporaries.

The syllabus consisted of both classroom and flight instruction on every weapon and every weapon system used on the F–4. "Academics," as the classroom work was called, met every day for a half day and were very detailed and fast paced. At the end of the block of instruction on the Sparrow, a student who worked hard nearly believed he could build one from scratch. A written examination concluded each course. Each written test contributed to the students' class rankings—more competition.

The flying missions introduced every mission area of which the F–4 was capable: intercepts, dogfights, nuclear weapons delivery, precision-guided weapons, conventional weapons delivery, and tactical considerations for every phase of flight. Standards were incredibly high, and students often observed that every ride seemed like a check ride. Students who graduated from the four-month course were expert in every aspect of operating the Phantom. When they went back to their home units, they became squadron weapons officers, the person all aviators turned to for expert advice on everything from how to make a hard turn to how to compute the length of a string of bombs dropped from a certain altitude and speed. The instructors at the weapons school were handpicked by the squadron commander and operations officer, and they chose only those who had done well as students themselves. The claim of being the home of the world's greatest fighter pilots seemed obnoxious and boastful to some, but it was not an empty claim.

Certainly the weapons school carried a reputation throughout the tactical forces. A favorable aspect of its reputation was that its aviators were deeply experienced and "good sticks." An unfavorable aspect was that the school was rigidly dogmatic, and its instructors overbearing and egocentric. One student recalled, "they were just so damn intimidating" with their cocky attitude and seeming indifference to standard grooming practices.[7]

In July 1974 attitudes started to change at the F–4 Fighter Weapons School with the arrival of a new operations officer,* Maj. Larry R. Keith. Surprisingly, Keith was not a graduate of the FWS, but he was picked for the job because of his reputation as a strict disciplinarian and stern task master. His credentials were impeccable—a career fighter pilot who was credited with the kill of a MiG–17 over North Vietnam. When Keith arrived at the squadron, the commander, Lt. Col. Paul N. Chase, told Keith that he would go through the next weapons school class, which started in September, because it was important that Keith be a graduate of the same school everyone else in the squadron had attended. While Keith was a student, Chase continued, Keith's two deputies would run squadron operations so he could devote his full attention to the rigors of the course.

It did not take Keith long to determine that the squadron had more than its share of prima donnas, and when he started taking the school academics and flights, he became very concerned over "their whole attitude." It was clear that the instructors were more concerned with proving that they were better than the

---

* Number two ranking squadron officer who is responsible for the flying program.

students than they were in teaching them how to be weapons officers. It did not take long for Keith's displeasure with what he was seeing to come to a head. One evening he was standing at the duty desk accounting for flights and flight hours while talking with one of his subordinates, a flight commander.* An FWS student approached the flight commander and asked for information concerning his mission the next day. The flight commander "exploded in anger" and told the student he should already know that information. After observing the flight commander's actions, Keith took him into his office and fired him on the spot. The next day Keith told Chase the arrangement was not working. He would continue as a student but take over the operations authority immediately, or he would leave the squadron altogether. Chase agreed, and that afternoon Keith called a meeting of all the instructors of every rank and position. He told them what he thought of their attitude and their reluctance to teach the students. He was not satisfied with the squadron's de facto policy of making the weapons school nothing more than a rite of passage wherein the students were harassed and hazed rather than instructed. The meeting lasted until midnight. One instructor openly resisted Keith's new policies. He was fired as well.[8]

Keith was not the only flier to arrive at the FWS that summer who had not been through the weapons school. Eight others came who were not "target-arms."† These eight new officers, who comprised over a third of the squadron, also got their marching orders from Keith one evening when he called them all into a briefing room and closed the door. "We're going to change things around here," Keith told them.[9]

Within the next year, the "Home of the World's Greatest Fighter Pilots" sign came down so the squadron building could undergo routine painting. The sign never went back up.

1. Vance O. Mitchell, *Air Force Officers: Personnel Policy Development, 1944–1974* (Washington, D.C.: Air Force History and Museums Program, 1996), p. 260.

2. *Ibid.*, p. 235.

3. *Ibid.*, p. 262.

4. Capt. James W. Smith, conversation with author, RAF Woodbridge, England, 78th TFS, circa 1972.

5. Maj. Gen. Timothy A. Kinnan, interview with author, Springfield, Virginia, February 19, 1999.

6. Gen. John P. Jumper, interview with author, Ramstein AB, Germany, February 27, 1999.

7. Kinnan interview.

8. Brig. Gen. Larry R. Keith, USAF (Ret.), telephone interview with author, March 31, 1999.

9. Jumper interview.

* Typically a flying squadron has four flights, each of which is subordinate to the operations officer.

† Reference to the bull's-eye patch graduates wore on their flight suits.

CHAPTER 6

✪

Making It Happen

The most difficult problem to overcome in a safe and effective low-altitude training program is finding people with experience to teach the techniques required.[1]

The cultural change that evolved during the next four years, during which Larry Keith* served as operations officer and then commander of the F–4 Fighter Weapons School, can be clearly traced through the *Fighter Weapons Review (FWR)*, a quarterly magazine published at Nellis Air Force Base. The *FWR* published articles of interest to fighter crews on tactics, bombs, missiles, fuzes, and ancillary equipment. Most fighter pilots eagerly anticipated each issue because it was a great source for the newest and most innovative ideas to come out of Nellis[†] as well as from other fighter bases worldwide that were experimenting with weapons and tactics. Many of the articles were written by aviators from bases other than Nellis. In fact, the editors were always seeking articles from the field, outside the Nellis influence.

The Watershed Articles

In early 1976 Tactical Air Command was falling behind in its training programs at the RTU bases because budget cuts in aircraft spares and maintenance were reducing flying hours. In an effort to catch up, TAC ordered the F–4 Fighter Weapons School to conduct RTU training at Nellis instead of FWS training. Furthermore, it canceled the last two weapons school classes of 1976. Suddenly, the 414th Fighter Weapons Squadron, always throttles to the wall, went into the coaster mode as they assumed the duties of teaching new pilots the basics of flying the F–4. After listening to his instructor pilots and WSOs complain about extra time on their hands, Keith challenged them to take the initiative by documenting the training methods that were evolving within the squadron.

---

* Keith was operations officer from July 1974 to February 1976 and commander from February 1976 to February 1978.

[†] Nellis had been the cradle of fighter weapons and tactics since the late 1940s. Initially, fighter pilots had gone through fighter and gunnery training at Nellis in a school established in 1949. Later that school became the Fighter Weapons School, and each fighter model, such as the F–86, F–100, F–105, and F–4, had its own squadron within the weapons school. The *FWR* put onto paper the latest buzz at Nellis.

He ordered them to produce a series of articles for the *FWR* that would document their efforts as well as show the fighter world a way to "make it happen." He put Capt. John P. Jumper, one of his more articulate and prolific instructors, in charge of the effort.[2] After months of work, Jumper and a host of weapons school instructors produced two complete volumes of articles for the *FWR*, all of which were printed in consecutive issues.

The "Winter '76" and "Spring '77" issues were a watershed for fighter training in the USAF. Those two issues, authored entirely by instructors from the F–4 weapons school, laid the foundation for training techniques that would spread throughout the tactical air forces (TAF) over the next decade. Prior to those seminal issues, *FWR* articles were technically oriented descriptions of how a particular bomb operated with a particular fuze to produce a desired effect. Sometimes the articles discussed tactics, especially air-to-air tactics, a subject near and dear to the heart of every fighter pilot. A/A tactics are notorious for being contentious, and discussions of them in the *FWR* were nothing short of that. However, prior to the Keith era, the FWS responses to some articles were nothing short of arrogant. The attitude seemed to be, "We're Nellis and you're not. We know more than you do, so just shut up and do it our way."

The change in content and attitude in the "Winter '76" and "Spring '77" issues was remarkable and represented a turning point in the fighter community. Essentially, the two issues outlined a training method and continuum for teaching fighter crews everything from basic aircraft handling to the most complex tactics. The heart of the training system was the "building block approach" (BBA). The BBA was nothing more than a description of the FWS F–4 syllabus, a program that had evolved significantly over the previous two years under Keith's leadership. The BBA began with the idea that the final objective must drive every aspect of the training program. If, for example, the goal of the FWS syllabus was to produce an F–4 crew that could lead a composite force* successfully against a numerically superior enemy force, then every mission in the syllabus had to have specific training goals that led directly to the end objective. Each of these missions was a building block upon which the more difficult objectives rested. Without one of the blocks, the structure was unstable. By the time a student arrived at a complex level, he would have individually experienced each facet of the complexity.

Of course, the basic idea of using training objectives was nothing new to experienced educators, but it was to the FWS. Jumper, who wrote the BBA article, also tied the training objectives to specific, *measurable* criteria in a new way that appealed to everyone. For example, during a bombing attack, the specific objective was not only the score, but also the tracking time the pilot used before he released

---

* Air Force jargon for an attack force composed of several different aircraft types and mission areas, i.e., bombers, fighters, electronic countermeasures (ECM), search and rescue, and so on.

the bomb. If the pilot could not drop an accurate bomb using only five seconds of tracking time, then he could not progress to the next level. Another good example was in the A/A phase. Specific parameters were designed for every attack on every mission. The students knew exactly what they would see before they became airborne. Therefore, they had to produce the desired result for those parameters. If the student was the attacker at a 6,000-foot range from the defender, then the student was expected to achieve a valid Sidewinder shot, as measured exactly from the gun film and tape recorder every pilot carried. If he was unable to attain the parameters, then he continued flying the engagement until he could. If he could not do so within a limited number of flights, usually four, then he was given a "bus ticket to Amarillo," slang for elimination from the course. It was not long before the phrase, "building block approach," was in use throughout the tactical air forces as the model for fighter training.

The impetus for these changes to training practices came from two frustrations felt by most fighter pilots, and certainly those instructors at the weapons school. The first difficulty was the hangover from the Korean War veterans' way of doing business through brute force. Before the Vietnam War, it was not unusual for a fighter pilot to fly thirty to forty hours a month,[3] which equated to a flight every working day, sometimes two a day. If a pilot was having trouble qualifying in gunnery, he simply flew twice a day, every day, until he got it right. However, after Vietnam, defense budgets continued to fall, and pilots were flying less than half that time. Flying hours were precious, and every drop of fuel counted.* There were no extra sorties to throw at a weak pilot. The other frustration was the rite of passage attitude within the fighter force. Many "old heads" had learned their lessons the hard way, through the school of hard knocks. They figured that if it was good enough for them, it was good enough for the next generation. However, the next generation was better educated and more scientifically oriented. Those pilots were seeking logical, controlled solutions to problems. To this new generation it was not good enough to be told that they were unsuccessful because the old head said so. They wanted evidence and explanation. Further, they wanted to learn the techniques that were not always forthcoming from the instructors.

Exacerbating these frustrations was the overall decline in flying experience in the tactical air force. One of the strange, but predictable, results of combat is that after every war, the combat experience of the military declines rapidly. The TAF in the 1970s was no exception. During that time, the FWS watched in amazement as the requirements to attend FWS dropped from 1,000 hours of fighter time, and 250 hours of instructor time, to 500 hours of fighter time. New qualifications required candidates to have merely qualified as an instructor. Keith was

---

* These were also the years of the Organization of Petroleum Exporting Countries' (OPEC) oil embargo. The impact was great enough on the Air Force for it to change the Thunderbirds, its famous acrobatic demonstration team, to the fuel efficient T–38. It was the first time the team did not fly a frontline combat aircraft.

stunned to see some students arrive "with the ink still wet on their instructor check rides."[4] Put another way, the flying experience of the FWS students plummeted to lows never before seen. Keith and other leaders in the squadron, like flight commanders Dick Myers and Dixie Alford and operations officer Hugh Moreland, knew there had to be a better way to train these students, and the building block approach was the method upon which they settled.[5] The days of self-taught skills learned by many hours as a wingman observing experienced leaders were over, as were the days of impatient leaders demanding better performance without personal involvement and attention.[6]

The long months of work on the watershed articles were not without humor. Jumper, in need of graphics support for the issues, approached Blake Morrison for help. Morrison, a former fighter pilot and a renowned aviation artist in his own right, was in charge of graphics for the *FWR*. As they planned illustrations for the articles, they also planned a surprise for Larry Keith. Jumper, an inveterate practical joker who once poured a pool of oil under the engine of a friend's new, very expensive sports car, plotted with Morrison to produce a fake cover for the first issue. Then they enlisted the wing commander, Keith's boss, to help them pull off the prank. The day before the first issue was supposed to be released, the wing commander walked unannounced into Keith's office, slammed down the magazine and boomed, "Keith, tomorrow 3,000 of these are going to hit the street. So, you hit the street, too. You're fired!" As the wing commander turned on his heel and strode out of the office, the stunned Keith looked down at the magazine cover. In the middle was a Soviet pilot, red star on his helmet, hanging in a parachute, agony on his face as he was ripped apart by bullets from an F–4 behind him strafing him in his parachute. Bold letters across the page proclaimed that this issue was produced by "Larry Keith and the rest of the world's greatest fighter pilots!" Keith yelled at the top of his lungs, "Jummmm-ppper!" and came roaring out of his office only to find his entire squadron rolling in laughter in the hallway.[7]

The Building Blocks at Work

The first building block was aircraft handling. Each pilot flew two sorties during which he learned to fly the soft-wing F–4E to its limits. The briefing guides for those rides were four pages long and meticulously detailed the maneuvers the pilot would fly. Every maneuver had a specific purpose that related to an event that would come later in the syllabus. For example, a slicing turn was performed under two different parameters: the first was as hard as the pilot could pull, and the second was at an optimum turn angle of attack. The student quickly learned from this demonstration that the optimum turn took only a few seconds longer but ended up at a much faster airspeed, maintaining future maneuvering potential. Steve Hanes, then a young captain assigned to the weapons school, remembers thinking, "I thought I knew how to maximum perform the jet until I went through the weapons school. I didn't have a clue!"[8]

After the advanced handling flights, the crews flew three basic fighter maneuver (BFM) rides—one as attacker, one as defender, and one where neither had the advantage. Each of these was against another F–4 flown by an instructor under rigid parameters. After the BFM phase came the air combat maneuver (ACM) phase. All ACM flights were flown against a dissimilar type of fighter, usually against the Nellis Aggressors, about whom more will be said in Part III. The last A/A phase was air combat tactics (ACT) that had four missions. In the ACT phase, two F–4s fought against two dissimilar adversaries. It was the last building block of the A/A phase and was an important preparation for the graduation missions that took place at the end of the school.[9]

The air-to-ground missions followed the A/A missions and started with single-ship navigation and single-ship, low-altitude maneuvering missions. The missions then built to two-ships during the terminal guidance (TG) weapons phase where the students learned how to employ the AGM–65 Maverick and the Pave Spike laser-guided bomb designator. At the end of the A/G phase, the flights expanded to four-ships, and the students practiced every kind of A/G weapons delivery of which the F–4 was capable, and there were dozens. Six A/G missions were flown, but throughout the phase the lessons of the A/A phase were reinforced with "enemy" dissimilar aircraft continually attacking the dirt beaters enroute to and from the gunnery ranges at ever-lower altitudes.

The final course of study was the ground attack tactics (GAT) phase. The first GAT mission was a close air support sortie with a FAC. The F–4s dropped live bombs on the mission under the control of a slow mover FAC reminiscent of the Vietnam era, except that the scenario called for sophisticated defenses, including enemy fighters.

The World's Most Demanding Peacetime Mission

The last two flights of the F–4 weapons school were called GAT 5 and 6. Graduates consistently recall those missions as the most challenging they ever flew outside of actual combat. GAT 5 and 6 were always flown together and comprised the final examination before graduation. GAT 5 was a flight of four F–4s. Number 1 and Number 3 carried Pave Spike laser designator pods, and all four aircraft carried two GBU–10 laser-guided, inert* bombs. GAT 6 was a flight of four F–4s configured for air superiority. Both missions were led by student crews in the number one, three, and four positions with an instructor crew as number two. GAT 5/6 missions flew into the teeth of the multiple defenses on the Nellis ranges against targets defended by SAM and AAA simulators. The eight F–4s always encountered "enemy" fighters in greater numbers than the F–4s.

---

* A standard 2,000-pound bomb body filled with sand instead of explosive.

The students received one point for every target on the ground they destroyed with an LGB and one point for every enemy fighter they "shot down" in the air. For every F–4 that was "lost," the team lost two points. The pass/fail criterion was simple: the students had to finish with a positive score. Every A/A shot was scored by gun camera, and every bomb impact was scored by special video recorders onboard the Pave Spike aircraft. Scoring was strict. If a friendly or enemy camera malfunctioned, nothing that airplane did was counted. If the package failed to score positive points, the whole package failed the ride and had to try again. Keith's instructors were not content to throw the students into the fray without seeing that the very difficult objective could be attained. So the first GAT 5/6 for each class was flown with all instructors. Usually the instructors passed on the first attempt, but not always. If they failed, they, like the students, flew it again.

The F–4 pilots were not the only ones to put everything they had into the GAT 5/6 missions. Enemy fighters, usually represented by Nellis Aggressor squadrons of F–5s, challenged by the realism and competitiveness of the mission, tried their best to defeat the students. Often the students elected to fight their way into the targets at low altitude, whizzing across the desert floor where one mistake meant disaster. Earl Henderson, who was so respected by his subordinates that they nicknamed him "Obi-wan," recalled, "Some of my guys came in from their first GAT 5/6 with ashen faces and wide eyes."[10]

Ron Keys, whose great intellect contributed to the A/A portions of the BBA, recalled a GAT 5 and 6 where the score ended at zero with one roll of F–4 gun film yet to review. Eight pilots, eight WSOs, and a few interested bystanders crowded into a small flight debriefing room. The student had claimed a kill with an AIM–7 Sparrow on an enemy fighter. The film rolled, and one by one the parameters were checked. A good fire signal meant the pilot had actually pulled the trigger, and there was a blue sky background that was required for targets below 10,000 feet altitude. The range bar on the gunsight showed 9,000 feet from the enemy F–5 at missile launch. As the film rolled, it was apparent the F–5 saw the F–4 because the wily Aggressor pilot started a hard turn into the F–4 and popped his only bit of chaff out of the speedbrakes to make the F–4 radar break lock. Would it? The radar had to stay locked to the target only until 3,000 feet range under the mission rules. Sixteen pairs of eyes were glued to the range bar on the gunsight of the flickering film as the red stripe slowly decreased. Five thousand feet. Four thousand feet. Three thousand feet. It had held lock! A mighty explosion of cheers and *sierra hotels* burst out of the room. They had passed. By one point, but they had passed on the first try. The film was still running onto the floor as the assemblage burst out of the room headed for the officers' club stag bar to celebrate.[11]

GAT 5/6 was the culmination of the building block approach. Each block had measurable objectives, but the final objective was measured as well. Such obsession with combat capability was not prevalent in most fighter units, but the

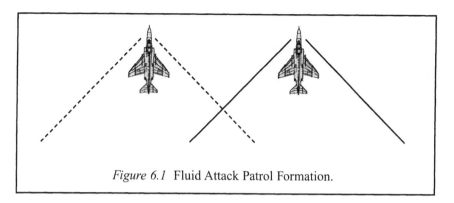

Figure 6.1 Fluid Attack Patrol Formation.

students of the weapons school saw how important it was, and they took what they learned back to their home units. There, they pressed their commanders for more realism in training and stricter accounting of success and failure, so that their home units could improve despite continuing reductions in flying hours and decreasing combat experience.

The Death of Fighting Wing

Another system the students took home with them was the Fluid Attack system. After much conflict and struggle within the fighter community in general and the weapons school in particular, Fluid Four, the primary A/A formation and tactic since Korea, had died a timely death at the hands of those who saw a better way.

The Fluid Attack system had its genesis in the Double Attack system that was invented in the jet age by an F–100 pilot named Everest Riccioni. Essentially, the Fluid Attack patrol formation is two aircraft flying line abreast about a mile apart. The objective is to give both aircraft unrestricted visual coverage of the rear, or six o'clock, of the flight mate. (Fig. 6.1)

These large areas of lookout are especially effective in an arena where the enemy has A/A missiles that can be fired from as far away as two miles in the stern. Plus, when the fluid pair adds an altitude stack into their formation, it complicates an enemy's problem to see both of them at the same time. When the fluid pair is on the attack, one attacks and becomes the "engaged" fighter, while the other maneuvers for a subsequent attack and becomes the "free" fighter. Each has specific duties, but the job of *both* is to kill the enemy. Of the many advantages Fluid Attack enjoys over Fluid Four, the essential doubling of firepower is the most significant. Instead of one fighter shooting, there are two, or if two Fluid Attack elements are flown together as a four-ship, there are four shooters.

The Fluid Attack pair turns in increments of 90 degrees while they are patrolling. If the flight leader wants to turn into his wingman, he does so and rolls out after 90 degrees of turn. The wingman delays his turn until the leader is

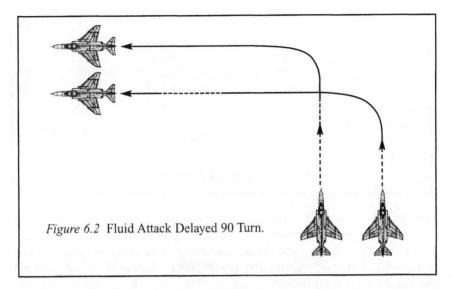

Figure 6.2 Fluid Attack Delayed 90 Turn.

halfway through his turn; then the wingman turns 90 degrees and rolls out line abreast again. (Fig.6.2)

If the leader wants to go 90 degrees the other way, he calls on the radio for the wingman to turn 90 degrees, the leader delays his turn, then turns and rolls out line abreast. These types of turns came to be known as "delayed 90s." The pair can also turn 180 degrees simply by both turning at the same time. They can also turn in increments less than 90 degrees. If the flight leader wants to go 45 degrees to the right, he turns that way and rolls out. The wingman simply crosses over the leader, then turns 45 degrees and rolls out line abreast again. All of these turns are done without radio calls. The leader flashes his wing at the wingman to indicate direction. So, if the leader wants to turn 90 degrees away from his wingman, he rolls up to the left, giving the wingman the wing flash signal. The wingman then turns 90 degrees, and away they go.

When You Have to Go Low

The primary consideration for any tactician is the threat. What are the enemy's capabilities? After the Vietnam War, the primary threat the Air Force had to face came from the Warsaw Pact that opposed NATO (North Atlantic Treaty Organization). Unlike the situation the United States faced in Vietnam, NATO forces were greatly outnumbered and faced a force that was the most modern possible. During the fifteen years between the end of the Vietnam War and the fall of the Berlin Wall, every analysis of the Soviet and Warsaw Pact forces showed them to be formidable. While some claimed that the Air Force had painted Ivan to be ten feet tall when he was really shorter, to the fighter pilots who had to fly into the teeth of his defenses he was tall enough to be taken very seriously.

The Soviet integrated air defense system (IADS) combined MiGs, which by most counts outnumbered NATO fighters by two to one, and overlapping SAM systems that went from very low altitude to high altitude. Complementing the SAMs and MiGs were some wicked AAA systems. One major weakness of the system, though, was its centralized command and control (CCC), and it was this weakness Air Force pilots hoped to exploit. The Soviets depended heavily on their ground based radars to give their enemy's location to the MiGs and SAMs. If NATO forces could operate at very low altitudes, then they could fly under the radar coverage and thus deny acquisition to the SAMs and MiGs. Just as important as the Soviet threat was the European weather, where the ceiling was below 3,000 feet and the visibility less than three miles more than 50 percent of the year. Fighter pilots had to see the targets in order to hit them, and in Europe, that meant going in under the weather.

Not everyone, though, was in favor of training fighter forces for low-altitude combat and low-altitude flying, and tactics threw many red flags in front of the establishment bulls. Low-altitude flying had been tried by the F–105s in Vietnam, and AAA had forced them to higher altitudes. True, argued the low-altitude advocates, but the Soviet SAMs at medium altitude are much worse than the AAA. Low-altitude training is dangerous, claimed the establishment, plus it is too difficult to find the targets from low altitude. The advocates responded, yes, it is dangerous because we do not know how to do it. We can learn. The targets will be there. Unlike Vietnam it will be a target rich environment. "Yeah. Target rich is what Custer had," skeptics replied.

Another charter of the weapons school was to develop and evaluate tactics. The instructors, led by low-altitude advocates like Tommy Dyches, Joe Bob Phillips, R. G. Evans, and others, proposed a low-altitude tactics test to validate the tactics they had been working on for nearly two years.

The tactics assumed that some basic things would be needed to survive and operate at low altitude. One was that the formations would have to spread out and fly line abreast to provide visual acquisition of not only MiGs but also SAM launches. Another assumption was that communications would be jammed by the many Soviet radio jammers that traveled with their troops. A third assumption was that the Air Force fighter pilots should strive to kill more than one target per pass.

One hotbed of low-altitude tactics was the instructors in the terminal guidance flight of the weapons school, who taught Maverick and laser-guided weapons to the students. During the mid-1970s, Maj. Dixie Alford commanded the flight, and his flight members, most notably Capt. John Jumper, Capt. Tosh McIntosh, and Capt. Jack Sornberger, came to the conclusion that the best way to employ the TV-guided, rocket-powered Maverick missile was to fly at low altitude the same way they flew when they were flying A/A at higher altitudes. They would fly line abreast for good visual lookout. They would maneuver in delayed 90 turns, so that only one jet was turning at a time while the other was searching for threats. And they would have one fighter engaged while the other was free during attacks on targets. Essentially, their vision was to move the techniques of A/A into the A/G realm. One system all the time. No confusion. Maximum proficiency and efficiency.

Jumper and the others were particularly interested in maneuvering the formation and executing attacks at low altitude without using the radio. After months of experimentation through the end of 1975 and into 1976, they finally struck upon a solution—a thing they called the low-altitude contract. It was simple: the wingman would always strive to be line abreast, and the leader would always strive to let him be line abreast. As long as both pilots went into the mission with the contract in mind, the logic of comm-out maneuvering (as it came to be called) was easily understood. Turns into the wingman were easy: the leader just turned 90 degrees into him; the wingman delayed and then turned as well. Turns away were nearly as easy. The flight leader did a check turn of 30 degrees in the direction he wanted to turn. When the wingman saw the check turn, it was a signal to turn 90 degrees into the leader. When the wingman passed behind the leader, the leader finished the turn. Ultimately, the two airplanes were able to maneuver completely without the radios and attack targets. The system worked so well that it soon spread to higher altitudes, and within a year the entire weapons school squadron was flying its missions at any altitude totally silently, without depending on the vulnerable radios to direct the flights. A few years later, radios, called Have Quick, were delivered to the fighter force. Have Quick radios take a time signal generated by a common atomic clock. Once all the radios in a mission are "hacked" to this superaccurate clock, they are set to hop from frequency to frequency tens of times per second. Thus, it is impossible for a jammer to find the frequency they are on and jam it. Have Quick is a great invention, but fighter pilots still make all their patrol formation turns silently, thus freeing the radios for more important matters.

---

1. John P. Jumper, "When You Have To Go Low," *USAF Fighter Weapons Review,* Spring '77, p. 55.

2. Brig. Gen. Larry R. Keith, USAF (Ret.), telephone interview with author, March 31, 1999.

3. *Ibid.*

4. *Ibid.*

5. Jumper interview; Keith interview; Maj. Gen. Ronald E. Keys, interview with author, Stuttgart, Germany, February 23, 1999.

6. John P. Jumper, "Tactics, Training and Evaluation: Toward Combat Capability," unpublished monograph, Air Command and Staff College, 1978, Maxwell AFB, Alabama, p. 28.

7. Keith interview.

8. Steve Hanes, interview with author, Peachtree City, Georgia, December 27, 1998.

9. Syllabus, F–4 Weapons School, Nellis AFB, Nevada, 1977.

10. Earl J. Henderson, interview with author, Las Vegas, Nevada, September 12, 1998.

11. Keys interview.

CHAPTER 7

❂

Let's Get Serious about Dive Toss

Like a golfer looking for the right putter or a Casanova searching for the appropriate words, fighter pilots are always looking for that magic technique that will transform them into the Top Gun.[1]

Fighter pilots and WSOs were always looking for a better way to deliver unguided bombs and cluster bomb units (CBUs).* By the early 1970s there had been several schemes installed in fighter and attack aircraft that used computerized delivery systems. The venerable F–105 employed a "baro-toss" mode that was more accurate than the old manual system described in earlier chapters. The A–7 used a computer system that was very accurate, but the Air Force bought so few A–7s that its impact was small. By 1974 the fighter force was a force of Phantoms. Every overseas base in Europe and the Pacific was equipped with them, as were most of the stateside bases. The USAF's first Phantoms, the F–4C, or Chucks as they were called by some, had no computer delivery systems, but the F–4Ds and F–4Es that followed were equipped with a weapons release computer system (WRCS) that provided the crew with several computer weapons delivery options. The most useful of these was the dive toss mode.

Dive toss was designed to be used in a diving delivery similar to the normal dive bomb pass. The pilot rolled in the same way, but pointed his gunsight directly at the target. Then the WSO locked on to the ground with the radar. Once the radar was tracking the ground, the WRCS computer knew slant range to the target. Aircraft altitude and dive angle went to the computer from the aircraft navigation systems. The WSO told the computer what kind of weapon was to be released by dialing a drag coefficient into the black box. Once the radar was solidly tracking the ground, the pilot hit his pickle button and held it down while he recovered from the dive. When the computer arrived at a proper solution, it automatically released the bomb. When everything worked perfectly, dive toss could drop a bomb better than the average pilot could during a manual pass.

Of course, the problem was that it often did not work perfectly or even close to perfectly. WSOs quickly discovered that each airplane/WRCS had its own personality. WSOs in weapons offices around the world tracked every aircraft

---

* A canister that opened after release and dispensed smaller bomblets over the target.

and its quirks. Often, small errors that were consistent could be corrected by fudging the drag coefficient or other computer settings to make the WRCS think a different type of weapon was aboard. In the worst cases, the bomb would release as soon as the pilot hit the pickle button, or very late during the pull-off from the pass. Such monumentally short or long bombs were a continual source of embarrassment to the F–4 crews and sometimes a danger to troops on the ground. Many crews learned the hard way to distrust their dive toss system.

Dive toss faced another obstacle, but it was not a hurdle of wires and chips; it was a cultural hurdle. Dive bombing in the direct mode, where the bomb dropped when the pilot commanded it, was the manly man's way to attack a target. Fighter pilots learned to depend foremost on themselves early in their flying careers. Instructors insisted that fledglings become self-reliant immediately. The fighter pilot culture through Vietnam demanded hard-core individualism. In many squadrons, although the official policy might be to use dive toss as much as possible, using the system sometimes brought scorn and derisive hoots of laughter from old heads.

Not all units ridiculed dive toss, though, and the new generation of pilots was predisposed to seek technical solutions to technical problems. The F–4Es stationed at Korat, Thailand, during the late 1960s and early 1970s used dive toss almost exclusively in combat over Laos and Vietnam and achieved excellent results. However, many units did not trust the system and did not use it. Of course, a system that is not exercised atrophies quickly. Therefore, dive toss in most F–4 units was suspect, and the more suspect it became the less it was used, and the downward spiral continued. Despite the fact that the F–4 had dive toss as part of its standard equipment, starting with the production of the F–4D in 1966, fighter pilots were still figuring out ways to be better manual, or direct, dive bombers well into the 1970s. More than one article on how to be a better manual bomber graced the pages of the *Fighter Weapons Review*. Capt. Alex Harwick, an instructor in the USAFE Tactical Employment School at Zaragoza Air Base, Spain, produced a series of detailed articles on the mathematics and techniques of dropping manual bombs. Harwick's articles became the bible for every fighter pilot on how to win quarters on the gunnery range. Even though dive toss had the potential to drop more accurate bombs in the heat of battle, Harwick's and other articles did not acknowledge the computer system's abilities. They made no effort to give any credit to computerized deliveries.

Not everyone in fighters was consumed with the science and art of dropping manual dive bombs. Since the advent of navigator WSOs filling the back seats of F–4s, many WSOs started putting the systems to work that the disgruntled pilot GIBs had ignored. Many articles started appearing that advocated scientific application of the WRCS and the powerful F–4 radar. The first of these with great impact was "Let's Get Serious About Dive Toss," written in 1970 by Capt. Bob Baxter. Baxter's point was that if the crews would only use dive toss to its maximum capabilities, the computer would give them more combat capability.

The culture was slow to change, however. Five years later articles still appeared discussing the finer points of winning quarters on the range without the computer.

When Capt. John Jumper was a student pilot in the fighter weapons instructor course in the fall of 1974, he recalls being ridiculed by some instructors for devising a way to use dive toss from long ranges on a tactics mission. Jumper's idea was to use dive toss to literally toss a bomb a few miles so that the fighters would not have to fly over the target. If he could do that, he could stay away from the simulated enemy defenses that surrounded the target. In fighter parlance, it was an effort to "stand off." He consulted with the civilian company that built the WRCS and determined that the system was capable of delivering bombs from much longer slant ranges than most pilots realized. Jumper, an electrical engineering graduate of Virginia Military Institute, planned to fly at low altitude to the target, pop up to a few thousand feet, and then point at the target from five miles away. Once the WSO locked onto the ground return, Jumper would hold down the pickle button, pull his nose up through an extended line toward the target, and literally toss the bombs at the target from three or four miles away, letting the WRCS computer decide the proper release moment.

Jumper's idea brought immediate scoffs from the hard-core instructors who pointed out that the accuracy of the computer from such long ranges would not get a bomb within a few hundred feet of the target. Jumper was not thinking of just one bomb, though. His plan would use a new delivery mode in the 556-modified jets to salvo twelve bombs in four groups of three. Jumper was fully aware of the problems inherent in the dive toss system, but rather than turn away from it, he studied the problem in depth and looked for a technical solution, instinctively shunning the offhand dismissal of computer deliveries he saw within the F–4 force.

He got to taste his pudding on a tactics mission that was planned by students who then flew as leaders on the mission. Jumper took his flight of four F–4s into the tactics range low and fast behind a broad, conical mountain that stood between them and the airfield parking apron that was their target. At six-and-a-half miles from the target they popped up to 3,000 feet one by one and pointed at the airfield target that had been bladed into the desert floor to look like a Warsaw Pact runway. The WSOs locked onto the ground, and the pilots tossed four bombs each at the target from nearly five miles away. Immediately after the small practice bombs released from the jets, the pilots sliced hard away from the target and back down to low altitude heading away from the target. The attack was so quick that none of the crews even saw their bombs hit the ground as they screamed away.[2]

The results were spectacular. Three of the four strings of bombs walked through the target; one string was well short. Although none of the individual crews would have won a quarter for accuracy for a single bomb, the aggregate effect of the salvo release directed by the dive toss computer shacked the target. Ultimately the attack became known as long-range dive toss. Although it never saw combat use, the change in the fighter pilot culture it signaled was important.

Capt. Ron Keys.
Courtesy of Ron Keys.

Throughout the F–4 fleet, pilots, and WSOs took notice. There was always a better way to get the job done, and an in-depth knowledge of available technology was the path to success.

The Other Side of the Coin

There was another meaning to the phrase "let's get serious about dive toss" that had nothing to do with dive toss. It also meant to look at something realistically and honestly. Fighter pilots live in a personal world of pragmatism. They must in order to survive. If the left fire warning light is flashing, and the left side of the airplane is engulfed in flames, it's a pretty good bet that the airplane is on fire, and the fighter pilot accepts that for what it is—nothing less and nothing more. He sees no sense in worrying about things he cannot control, so he presses on to the next step, which in this case is a bailout. Although such an attitude is perfect for flying fast jets into dangerous places, it is not an attitude or outlook that serves well in the political arena where nothing is black or white.

At the end of the Vietnam War, a considerable strain of skepticism ran through the fighter force that was aimed at national and Air Force leadership. Most pilots, like Rick Honey, saw a job to be done and simply did their best to do it. Yet, these well-educated officers, smart and capable, privately asked themselves how their leaders could have screwed up the Vietnam effort so horribly. Unfortunately, some of them concluded that their leadership did not care about them. In the peacetime years after Vietnam, as budgets fell, pilots' flying hours declined, and their benefits eroded, pilots watched in dismay as the Air Force assumed what was, in their view, an attitude of "make everything look better than it really is." Often, when one of these young men heard of some cheery face painted on a disaster, he might say, "Ah, come on. Let's get serious about dive toss!"

Less than five years after the war ended, an exodus of pilots, displeased with the Air Force, voted with their feet and went to commercial airline jobs. The most eloquent expression of their feelings was written by Ron Keys, then a captain at Nellis, in a paper that has since become famous as the "Dear Boss" letter. As Keys tells the story, he was given the task of writing down concerns young officers had about the Air Force. These concerns would then be gathered into a package to be sent to the TAC commander, Gen. Bill Creech. Keys, who was about to leave on a trip to Alaska, was already swamped with work, but he took the time at home late that night to write down his thoughts. He decided to do it in a letter that would speak for his buddies who had left the service.

Keys had absolutely no intention of "putting in his papers." He saw lots wrong with the Air Force, but like others in the hard core, he planned to work for change and not give up. The next morning, before he departed for Alaska, he left the draft letter with the squadron secretary to type up for the commander. However, the letter was never compiled with other inputs, and the scathing indictment, of even General Creech himself, made it directly to the general's desk. By the time Keys returned from his trip, copies of the Dear Boss letter were everywhere, and Creech wanted to see him immediately.

Keys hardly had time to change his clothes before he was on another airplane, heading for Langley Air Force Base in Virginia and an appointment with the four-star general. During his meeting with the TAC commander, he found that the general was very interested in the details of Keys' observations. Furthermore, Creech was interested in ways to fix the problems. He thanked Keys for his honest feedback and sent him on his way.[3] (The Dear Boss letter is in Appendix 2.) The letter eloquently expressed many of the frustrations the fighter force felt at the time, and some of the reasons pilots were leaving by the droves for commercial airline flying, frustrated that their leaders never seemed to "get serious about dive toss."

---

1. Dewan Madden, "Dive Deliveries and the Iron Sight," *USAF Fighter Weapons Review*, Spring 1972, p. 10.

2. Gen. John P. Jumper, interview with author, Ramstein AB, Germany, February 27, 1999.

3. Maj. Gen. Ronald E. Keys, interview with author, Stuttgart, Germany, February 23, 1999.

PART III

THE TRAINING REVOLUTION

Nellis Air Force Base, Nevada, home of the Fighter Weapons School. *Official USAF photo.*

CHAPTER 8

✪

The Aggressors

> *You don't wish a MiG to death; it takes training to kill him, and that's what air combat tactics are all about— training the way we plan to fight.*[1]

If one statistic from the air war over North Vietnam is most stunning, it is this: 58 percent of the USAF aircraft shot down by enemy MiGs "were totally unaware of the pending attack." Further, another 25 percent "received such short-term warnings that they were required to take immediate defensive reactions" to avoid being shot down.[2]

Many factors contributed to such findings, and by the end of Rolling Thunder, the first major air campaign over North Vietnam from 1965 to 1968, USAF and USN fighter pilots understood those factors well, and the most important one was training. Air-to-air, or dogfight, training, though, was poor to nonexistent. Few USAF pilots had ever trained against a dissimilar adversary, a fighter of different performance, size, and armament flown by a pilot with different tactics and temperament.

In the skies over North Vietnam, U.S. fighter pilots with little to no air-to-air training faced off against dissimilar adversaries in aerial combat. While the MiG–17 and MiG–21 jets flown by the North Vietnamese air force (NVAF) were much more agile than the F–105 and F–4 and could outturn the heavier fighters with ease, perhaps the MiGs' biggest advantages were their small size and smokeless engines. The wingspan of the MiG–21 was only 25 feet as compared to the 38 feet of the F–4. Not only was the F–4 a very big fighter for its day, but its J79 engines were notorious "smokers." The twin engines poured a long black smoke trail easily seen from many miles. Although no extensive debriefings of NVAF pilots have been published, it was clear to U.S. Air Force pilots that their adversary frequently had, by a considerable margin, the first tally-ho;* thus, a significant advantage. U.S. pilots and aircrews did, however, have an advantage in terms of armament. The F–4 carried radar-guided and heat-seeking missiles, while NVAF armament on the MiGs consisted of only a gun, with the exception of the MiG–21 which also featured the Atoll, a heat-seeking missile that was a carbon copy of the USAF Sidewinder.

---

* Visual sighting.

View of a Soviet MiG–21 Fishbed fighter aircraft. *Official U.S. Navy photo.*

NVAF tactics varied dramatically and evolved over the course of the war. Sometimes the MiGs attacked singly, other times in pairs close together or in pairs with a "trailer" two miles behind his leader. Throughout the war, though, the NVAF relied on ground control intercept (GCI) radars to vector them into positions of advantage as they had been trained and equipped to do by their Soviet advisors. Relying on GCI and using the small size of their fighters, the NVAF used hit-and-run attacks to successfully shoot down U.S. fighters. When F–4s were tasked solely in an A/A role, they did well against the MiGs, achieving kill ratios similar to those enjoyed by U.S. fighter pilots in Korea and World War II. However, when the F–4 was used in the A/G role, the bomb-laden Phantoms, like the lumbering F–105 "Thuds," fared poorly, often struggling to maintain an even exchange ratio.

The showing of the USAF in aerial combat concerned many veterans when they returned to peacetime assignments. In Vietnam the USAF heavily outnumbered the NVAF. However, many believed the next war would be fought in Europe, where the Soviet-sponsored Warsaw Pact forces outnumbered the NATO air forces by more than two to one. Fighter pilots, especially F–4 crews, who would fly a considerable percentage of their missions loaded with bombs, wondered how they would succeed against a numerically superior force, given the mediocre results they had achieved against the smaller NVAF.

Learning Ivan's True Height

One way to improve the combat performance of the U.S. Air Force fighter community was through a better understanding of their adversary beyond the Iron Curtain. Capt. Roger Wells had graduated as the outstanding overall student from his weapons school class and shortly afterwards transferred to Nellis as an instructor. Wells believed that he had learned everything there was to know about the F–4 and its weapons, but felt that the weapons school did not teach enough about the Soviet fighter pilot, his aircraft, or his weapons. When he arrived at Nellis, one of his first tasks was to approach the operations officer and say that he wanted to create an academic course that would teach their students about the enemy. His proposal was quickly approved by the weapons school squadron, but when Wells approached the commander of the intelligence squadron, he was stunned to hear that he did not have a "need to know"* the kind of information he sought. He persevered, though, and found an ally and mentor in Lt. Col. Lloyd Bootheby, an officer assigned to Nellis' commanding general's staff. Bootheby took Wells to another Air Force base, and an organization that gathered foreign military equipment for analysis. This intelligence organization proved less fanatical about the rules, and Bootheby, known for his persuasive tongue, talked their way past the front door.

Finally, Wells was admitted to a vault where he found the mother lode. The vault contained thousands of photos of Soviet equipment, training manuals, and aircraft and weapons technical data. Wells requested copies of everything he could get his hands on and arranged for it to be shipped back to Nellis. When the shipment arrived, it filled twelve four-drawer safes. Wells studied the documents carefully and crafted an academic course on the Soviet fighter pilot, the man and his machine. In January 1971 he presented it for the first time to the F–4 weapons school students, who gave it rave reviews. It was the first time any of them had heard how their potential adversary lived, worked, and flew. The briefing quickly gained renown, and Wells traveled the world telling U.S. fighter pilots what they might face in a showdown with the Soviets.[3]

Victory in some future conflict would require more than knowledge about the enemy. Veterans of the air war were also convinced that air-to-air combat training had to be improved. During the Vietnam War, the performance of U.S. Navy pilots against the NVAF convinced Navy leadership of the need to improve the capability of their fighters against the MiGs by providing dissimilar air combat training (DACT) in their now-famous Top Gun school at Miramar Naval Air Station, California. The USAF was slower to respond. Initially, some F–4 pilots bound for Vietnam flew dissimilar training against the Air Defense Command (ADC) F–106 interceptor. Earl Henderson, then a captain, participated in some of this dissimilar training as an F–106 pilot who previously had flown a combat tour in the F–105. He remembers the F–106 as being an excellent dogfighter with nearly the agility of the MiG–21 and maintains that the engagements provided excellent training. In fact, later analysis demonstrated that the F–4 pilots who had training against the F–106 fared better in combat than those who did not.[4]

At Nellis, fighter weapons school instructors were keenly aware of the benefits of dissimilar air combat training from their experiences in flying their F–4s against other aircraft types on a regular basis as part of tactics validation and testing programs. The idea of a special unit to fly DACT with the weapons school had been around for years, and some weapons school graduates recall the idea

---

* Even though one has a security clearance, one may not necessarily have access to all classified information. The individual has to have a specific purpose, approved by supervisors, for the information.

bouncing around in the mid-1960s.[5] There was no lack of ideas around the 414th FWSq in the early 1970s about how to set up such a special unit. Maj. Moody Suter, the 414th air-to-air flight commander, wanted to create an adversary flight in the 414th with all the Nellis old hands to share their accumulated experience with the students. Gary Skaret, who worked for Suter, advocated using the Navy Top Gun squadron as a joint unit that would service Nellis and the Navy. Based on his knowledge gained from studying Soviet tactics, Roger Wells wanted to build an exact duplicate of a Soviet squadron at Indian Springs* that could operate within the Nellis complex and beyond, as capability would permit.[6]

The idea of a specialized dogfight adversary got a major boost from the 414th assistant operations officer, Maj. Randy O'Neill, who often flew with the new commanding general of the Nellis Tactical Fighter Weapons Center (TFWC), Maj. Gen. William Chairsell. The general was an engaging personality who loved to fly, and O'Neill accompanied him whenever he flew, a common practice since Air Force generals of the day often did not fly frequently enough to maintain currency. It was O'Neill's job to keep the general out of trouble when he flew. In a phrase of the time, he was the general's "seeing-eye instructor pilot." In a conversation one day, while returning from a business trip, O'Neill was bemoaning the poor training Tactical Air Command was giving its fighter pilots. Chairsell put him on the spot and asked what he would do to improve it. O'Neill answered that they needed a DACT adversary that they could use on a regular basis. The idea was not new to Chairsell because he had heard Wells's briefing, so he directed O'Neill to prepare a new briefing on such a project. When it was complete, Chairsell and O'Neill took the briefing to TAC headquarters, where it received a cold reception from the TAC assistant director of operations, who thought it a radical and dangerous idea. In fact, the general would not let the briefing be given to the TAC commander, Gen. William W. Momyer. The team returned to Nellis discouraged and defeated for the time being.

Yet the Nellis group was not the only one working on the idea. Col. William Kirk, a Vietnam MiG killer, was working in the basement of the Pentagon as the chief of the tactical division under the Air Force director of operations. In early 1972 he attended a meeting with Air Force Chief of Staff Gen. John D. Ryan to discuss the poor air combat results of pilots in Vietnam. Ryan was not happy about an account of a MiG that had escaped death because the F–4 pilot attacking the MiG had fumbled his switches. Ryan, clearly irate, turned to the general in charge of flight operations and asked a question. What, he said, would be the result if every fighter pilot took a written examination on his aircraft and weapons? How many would pass? The operations general responded 10 percent. Ryan was incredulous. Did he really think their knowledge was that poor?

---

* A nearby auxiliary base that had a runway, taxiway, and parking apron maintained by a skeleton crew.

He might have believed 60 percent, but 10? Ryan directed the operations general to do just that—take a test to the TAC aircrews as a survey to determine their knowledge or lack thereof. Further, he told them to not tell the TAC commander, Momyer, that they were doing the survey.[7]

The operations general picked Kirk to head the survey team. Kirk knew there was no way to travel throughout TAC without Momyer finding out, so he asked two TAC colonels to accompany the team and keep their headquarters informed about the progress of the survey. Kirk, in turn, asked a young major, John Corder, to write and administer the test as they traveled across the command. Corder, a weapons school graduate and combat veteran, wrote a test that he thought was fair and combat oriented. He gave the test at every TAC fighter base in the United States to over 200 pilots and WSOs. Corder, confident he was giving a valid test, made the following offer at every test session—if you see a question that you think does not apply to combat, line through it, and it will not be counted against your score. In all of the testing sessions, only one pilot lined out one question. Despite the fairness of the exam, after Corder tabulated the scores, the results were as bad as feared. The average score was about 40 percent, and only about 10 percent of the crews had passed the test.[8] Corder recalls being stunned that virtually none of the TAC instructor pilots were able to determine the range of a MiG by comparing its wingspan to the pilot's gunsight.* Further, he was amazed when he discovered that several, in an attempt to draw the proper relationship, drew the MiG to look like an F–4 with bent-up wingtips—further testimony that the crews had no idea how to fight against a different adversary.

Kirk and his team prepared a briefing that summarized the results of their survey and provided recommended solutions. Then they went to the lion's den at TAC to present their findings before returning to the Pentagon to brief the Air Force chief of staff. The team members knew that their reputations, if not their careers, were on the line. If Momyer decided to shoot the messengers, they would be finished in the Air Force. But to a man they also felt it was their duty to tell the truth as they saw it. In his original briefing, Kirk had written that the results were poor. Corder convinced him to rephrase the conclusion and say that the results were "understandably poor." When Kirk briefed Momyer, he related that TAC was swamped by training crews for Vietnam and was emphasizing A/G training for the Phantoms; thus, the crews had little opportunity to dogfight. Moreover, there was no opportunity for DACT because all the units were equipped with F–4s. An exacerbating factor was poor maintenance, especially because experienced flight line supervisors were siphoned off to man combat units in Vietnam. When the aircraft systems did not work properly, the crews did

---

* The process is called reticle matching. Remembering that a mil is a foot at 1,000 feet, a MiG–21 with a 25-foot wingspan will be 25 mils wide (the inner circle on the F–4 sight) when the F–4 is 1,000 feet from the MiG.

not use them, which made the systems even worse due to neglect. After the briefing, Momyer spoke to the team and his staff philosophically for over an hour, an unusual thing for him to do. He said there are some guys who are eager to engage MiGs, and some who say they are but find a way to avoid the fight when the chips are down. When you find a guy who really wants it, he continued, you should give him the "golden supper." One of the team's recommendations was to form an adversary training squadron at Nellis to provide DACT for TAC crews. Kirk's effort to make the bad news palatable did not go unnoticed. As Momyer rose to leave the conference room, he paused and wryly said to Kirk, "You've been as *understandably* objective as you could be, colonel."[9]

The team's timing could not have been better because, unknown to them, Momyer had just heard the aggressor concept briefing during a visit to Nellis. Chairsell, the commanding general at the base, had played golf with Momyer and suggested to the TAC commander that he hear the briefing. Of course, Momyer did not have all his staff with him on this visit to Nellis, so there was no bureaucratic stonewall for Chairsell to overcome.[10]

At the time there was considerable resistance within TAC to begin a program that was viewed as risky. The reigning philosophy was that safety was the ultimate goal. If there was an accident resulting from a 45-degree dive bomb pass then the fix was easy—stop doing 45-degree dive bombing. Twice during the second half of the Vietnam War, TAC discontinued air-to-air training for nearly a year because of midair collisions. Of course, the problems were not all of TAC's making. The one pilot-one tour policy instituted by the Air Force meant that TAC had become a training command. Every TAC fighter base, save two, was devoted to RTU duties. Almost the entire focus of the command was on cranking out the cannon fodder to fill the cockpits in the war. It was not an environment conducive to realistic training. TAC was under pressure from the chief of staff to improve training, and the press was having a field day with what it perceived as a failure of U.S. forces to deal adequately with the tiny NVAF. The next day Momyer sent a message to the Pentagon saying he was forming an aggressor squadron at Nellis. When the action officer, Maj. John Corder, brought the package to General Ryan a few days later for Ryan's concurrence, Ryan asked, "Does this package start an aggressor squadron?" When he was told it did, Ryan flipped the package open, and without reading it, put a "big, black R" in the approval block. The Aggressors were born.[11]

Iron on the Ramp

The concept for the Aggressors envisioned them flying the F–5, a fighter version of the T–38. However, the Air Force did not have any F–5s. The aircraft manufacturer, Northrop, had been unable to sell the F–5 to the USAF, but by selling the little fighter to foreign nations who had an interest in an inexpensive fighter with limited capability, the company had managed to keep the aircraft in production.

T–38 Talon jet trainer near Edwards Air Force Base, California.
Official USAF photo.

The Nellis fighter pilots favored the F–5 because of its similarity to the MiG–21. Drawing on the work of John R. Boyd, a former fighter pilot, to compare aircraft performance, they found that the F–5 matched the MiG–21 in nearly every parameter. Boyd was such a proficient pilot that he often challenged less experienced pilots to a contest in which Boyd would put the pilot directly behind him in a perfectly advantageous position and tell the pilot to try to shoot him. The bet was that Boyd could turn the tables by spitting the attacker out in front of Boyd's airplane where Boyd could "shoot" him, with the entire fight lasting less than 40 seconds.[12] Boyd, or "40-Second-Boyd" as he came to be known, had developed a system that plotted aircraft performance on graphs measuring energy levels at various speeds and weights. Using what he called energy maneuverability (EM) data, an F–4 pilot, for example, could see at a glance that the F–4's quickest, tightest turn (corner velocity) was at 420 knots, whereas the MiG–21's corner velocity was nearly 100 knots slower. Therefore, the wise F–4 pilot would try to avoid a slow speed fight against the MiG–21.

In addition to the EM comparisons, there were other similarities as well, most notably in size, cockpit visibility, and smokeless engines. The F–5 and the MiG–21 were both small fighters with virtually smokeless engines that did not give away their position. The cockpit visibility from the MiG–21 was very poor, especially in the rear quarter, and not much better from the F–5. In sum, the two little fighters were remarkably similar, but in 1972 there were no F–5s available for dissimilar air combat training. A close substitute for the F–5 was the T–38, also made by Northrop. The T–38 did not have as much power as the F–5 and its cockpit visibility was somewhat better, but in other respects it was very similar. Best of all, the T–38 was an Air Force aircraft and available in large numbers.

As soon as the fighter pilots started the effort to get their hands on the T–38, they ran into stiff resistance, mainly at the Pentagon. Everyone agreed that the concept was a good one. However, Pentagon officers are, by definition, advocates for their specific programs. Those who controlled T–38 assets were very reluctant, in fact refused, to reprogram any of the trainers from Air Training Command despite the fact that the jets would be in less demand as the war in Vietnam wound down. The fighter pilots viewed the situation in stark terms, with officers interested in improving combat capability pitted against those who were interested in improving their careers. A disgruntled senior officer who thought his rice bowl* was under attack could badly damage a young officer's career in the blink of an eye. Ultimately, the fighter pilots steamrollered the careerists by showing the package with the big, black R on it. Showing the same determination and heroism they had in the skies of Vietnam, the young fighter pilots pressed on, dismissing the risks to their careers to build a better Air Force.

The Golden Supper

In late 1972 the 64th Aggressor Squadron finally started operations at Nellis Air Force Base with a squadron of T–38s and a handpicked group of fighter pilots. The commander was Lt. Col. Lloyd "Boots" Bootheby, the officer who had helped Roger Wells break through the intelligence iron curtain, and the operations officer was Maj. Randy O'Neill. As soon as he knew he had the job, O'Neill flew to TAC headquarters, where he worked with the chief of officer assignments, Maj. Jack Petry, to choose the pilots. Many of the Nellis pilots wanted the squadron manned by highly experienced combat veterans, "old heads." O'Neill did not. He wanted younger guys who, after their tour as an Aggressor was over, would go back to operational units and provide expertise in regular squadrons. O'Neill feared that if he selected all old heads, they would go on to staff jobs, and their knowledge would be lost to the line jocks.[13]

The concept behind the Aggressors was straightforward. Pilots would deploy with a small number of jets to a TAC base. While there, they would fly their T–38s against a unit's fighters at whatever skill level the local commander wanted. The most basic mission was one on one, but the Aggressors, who had undergone an extremely rigorous, forty-mission training program, were prepared to fly in larger scenarios such as four on four. During the missions, the Aggressors flew enemy tactics they knew the Soviets used. They even "tried to think like Ivan."[14] When they were not flying, they taught academic courses, similar to the one Roger Wells invented, on Soviet weapons, training, and tactics. One course of great interest to all USAF fighter pilots was one that described the daily life of a Soviet fighter pilot, from how much he flew (little) to how much

---

* Resources.

vodka he drank (a lot). Along with the Aggressor pilots, two other officers completed the training package. One was a GCI controller, who trained alongside the Aggressor pilots and controlled Aggressor aircraft in the same way the Soviets relied on their GCI to get them into the fight. Another member of the team was an instructor from the fighter weapons school of the type of aircraft hosting the visit. Of course, in the early 1970s, this meant an F–4 instructor pilot and often a WSO, who would instruct the host pilots in both flying and academic matters in flying the Phantom against the T–38s.

No Joy

Perhaps the most difficult task for a fighter pilot engaged in aerial combat was seeing his adversary. With the advent of the jet age, this problem became more difficult as closing velocities jumped dramatically; with second generation fighters such as the F–4 and the MiG–21 flying head-on at 500 knots, closing velocities became staggering. They would come together at one mile every three seconds. At two miles, the frontal area of a small fighter like the MiG–21 is smaller than the end of a pencil eraser; yet that distance would be closed in six seconds.

The difficulty in seeing an adversary of this size gave the MiG pilot a significant advantage. In practical terms, only after a fighter pilot saw his enemy could he orient himself in the battle scheme, quickly determine the best course of action, and then begin maneuvering. John Boyd, innovator of the energy maneuverability concept, described the steps as observe-orient-decide-act, the so-called OODA loop. Boyd believed that a pilot who could cycle through his OODA loop faster than his adversary would create confusion in his opponent that would ultimately render the adversary defenseless. His treatise, which took more than twelve hours to brief in the long version, was an articulate expression of what military men have always known, and its tenets were points of common discussion among tactical thinkers in the 1970s.[15]

Boyd started developing his OODA loop concept during the Korean War when closing speeds were slightly less, and fighters had to close within 2,000 feet in range to use their guns. With the advent of higher speeds and long-range missiles in Vietnam, the OODA loop was compressed significantly. When the Aggressors took to the road in their MiG-sized T–38s, the post-Vietnam fighter pilot found it difficult to get his OODA loop even started because his Aggressor opponent invariably saw his big, ugly, smoking F–4 first.

The first Aggressor road show, as they came to be known, traveled to Homestead Air Force Base, Florida, an F–4 base. Earl Henderson, one of the original Aggressor pilots, went on the trip. Henderson had been an Air Defense Command F–106 pilot as his first flying assignment, then went to Thailand, where he flew a combat tour over North Vietnam in the F–105. Like many veterans, Henderson returned to the United States disappointed in the training he had received before his combat tour, and in the general ineptitude of the tactics and pilot skills he saw during the war. Henderson returned to the interceptor world of the F–106 after his combat tour, but as soon as he heard about the Aggressor squadron forming at Nellis, he volunteered for the job. He remembers being the only non-TAC pilot in the unit, and one of the few who had flown more than a handful of dissimilar air combat training missions before arriving in the squadron.[16]

The first obstacle the new squadron faced was finding a unit that wanted them to come. One Aggressor said, "We were all ready to give a war, but nobody wanted to come."[17] The aircraft accidents during air combat training over the previous few years had spawned a culture of extreme conservatism within TAC. A squadron commander or wing commander who lost a jet in training was immediately under the gun, and air combat training posed the greatest risk, mostly because of the F–4's proclivity to go out of control when not handled with kid gloves. Few commanders were willing to stick their necks out as the test site for the shiny, new program, no matter what long-term benefits it promised.

Contributing to the commanders' reluctance was the TAC operational readiness inspection (ORI) grading system. Every unit underwent an ORI each year or two. It was easy for the inspectors from TAC to measure bombing accuracy, since the bomb scores on the range were easily quantified. Assessing aerial combat proficiency was a different matter. Since there was no puff of smoke from a practice bomb on the ground to measure, evaluators flew with the crews on air combat missions and subjectively assessed their performance. No F–4 unit ever failed an ORI because they were poor at air-to-air, so the local commanders understandably put little emphasis on it.[18]

Despite the roadblocks, the Aggressors headed to Homestead, and Henderson recalled that they took so much equipment in an effort to respond to any contingency the road show was "overkill." Randy O'Neill, who had been in on the program from day one, was the Aggressor operations officer and went to Homestead as the on-scene commander for the two-week deployment. They took extra pilots, airplanes, spare parts, and every conceivable item to insure that the trip was a success.

The first missions were very basic—mostly one on one. During the preflight briefing, the Aggressor pilot would describe the performance characteristics of the T–38 and how it simulated the MiG–21. He stressed the small size of the airplane and how difficult it was to see. The F–4 would take off first, followed 20 seconds later by the Aggressor. As they flew out to the training area, the T–38 did ranging exercises on the F–4. The T–38 flew 45 degrees back from the F–4, about 9,000 feet away, and parallel to the F–4 course. In this position, it was relatively easy for the F–4 crew to see the T–38 since they were looking at the length of its fuselage. After cruising that way for a few moments, the Aggressor would then turn slightly toward the F–4 and accelerate towards it. F–4 crews, accustomed to seeing larger aircraft, immediately noticed the difference. As they described it, as the Aggressor presented the much smaller nose aspect, he "hit his disappear switch." In other words, they lost their tally-ho, or tally, on him. The point was

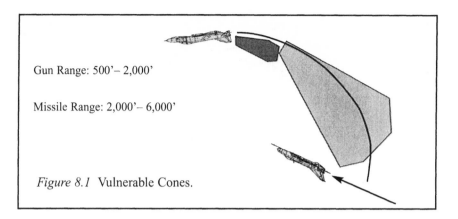

Gun Range: 500'– 2,000'

Missile Range: 2,000'– 6,000'

Figure 8.1 Vulnerable Cones.

well taken—at this range, the Aggressor was within Soviet missile capability. It was impossible to cycle through the OODA loop when the crew could not accomplish the first step—observe. An old fighter pilot axiom is "lose sight, lose fight," a point driven home the first time a fighter pilot and his WSO saw the T–38 hit his disappear switch.

Once the jets arrived in the training area, a series of engagements, or dog-fights, were flown from perch setups whereby one pilot would position his jet behind the other, offset slightly so the front aircraft could see the one behind. The Aggressor would set up just outside the defender's vulnerable cone, the area behind the defender where the attacker can fire a missile or shoot his gun. A typical one is shown in Fig. 8.1.

When the front jet, the defender, called on the radio that he was ready, the rear jet, the attacker, would call, "fight's on," and begin the attack . When the attacker was the Aggressor pilot, the defenders quickly learned that keeping the small jet in sight in a hard turn was even more difficult than it had been during the earlier ranging exercises. The proper maneuver in such a setup was a break turn, a maximum performance turn into the attacker that would move the vulnerable cone away from the attacker, immediately taking him out of missile parameters. (Fig. 8.2)

Such a break turn requires the most g available.* Typically, the F–4 break turn was done at around 6 g. When the pilot is subjected to high g, blood pools in the lower extremities. In an extreme case, a pilot might lose consciousness from the lack of blood flow to the brain. The anti-g leg and belly garment worn by fighter pilots squeezes the lower extremities to maintain blood pressure in the brain and continue to supply oxygen. Even for a pilot accustomed to pulling g, it is not

---

* A g is one force of gravity and is the centrifugal force on an aircraft in a turn. If one holds a bucket of water at arm's length and starts spinning around, the bucket will extend the arm parallel to the ground. The faster the turn, the more the bucket weighs. The measurement of this weight is g or g-load.

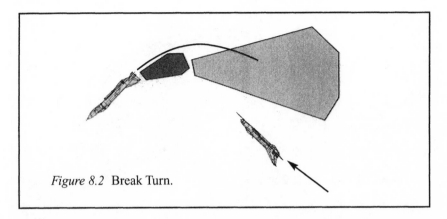

Figure 8.2 Break Turn.

unusual for the decreased blood pressure to reduce visual acuity. Not surprisingly, when the F–4 pilot did a break turn against the T–38, the little jet sometimes "disappeared" again, and the radio call "No Joy"* resounded on the radio. Since the rules of engagement required both adversaries to have sight, the Aggressor would have to discontinue his attack and tell the F–4 crew where to look to see him.

Henderson recalled that "being little was a big deal." The small, MiG–sized T–38 often could maneuver against the F–4 totally unobserved, just as the real MiGs had done over the skies of North Vietnam.

By the time it was the F–4 crew's turn to be on the attack, frustration and embarrassment often were at a high level, and their fangs were out so far they were poking holes in the tops of their boots. Then they learned some more lessons. As they started their attack on the more maneuverable T–38, it was certain failure to slow down in an attempt to stay inside the Aggressor's break turn. Accustomed to fighting against another F–4 with identical performance, the inexperienced pilots learned quickly that Boyd's energy maneuverability charts were perfect. A fighter that attacked in an area where he had no advantage was in trouble, and the hunter quickly became the hunted.

The crews at Homestead were no slouches. They were experienced fighter pilots with hundreds of hours in the Phantom and all instructors, but few of them had flown DACT missions prior to the Aggressor road show. One F–4 weapons school instructor's experience was typical. He arrived at Nellis with well over 1,000 hours in the F–4, including 365 combat hours in Vietnam, but he had never flown an air combat tactics mission against an aircraft other than F–4s from his own squadron.

During the first deployment to Homestead, the Aggressors flew only the most basic sorties against the F–4s, who were "a little overwhelmed by the newness of it."[19] Nevertheless, the F–4 crews proclaimed the training the best they had ever had, and all agreed that the deployment was a smashing success. Soon, other units were clamoring for road shows as the word spread around TAC. Lessons learned were many, and sometimes they were surprising. Earl Henderson remembers that communications improved dramatically at each unit they visited. The two-man F–4 crew had a unique problem not encountered by the single-seat fighter pilots. Not only did the crew have to hear, interpret, and respond to radio calls, they also had to fit intracockpit chatter into the fight. While on the attack, the WSO operated the attack radar and when he was locked to a target, he had to be able to steer the pilot toward the bogey using voice commands. The pilots quickly learned that looking inside the cockpit at their own radar scope was a recipe for humiliation, since no one was looking outside to see the little Aggressor sneaking up behind them. A brevity code, short phrases and words that conveyed a lot of meaning, quickly evolved. The system became more refined as TAC fighter crews became more proficient in dogfighting.

Defensive maneuvering produced some interesting results. Before exposure to the Aggressors, pilots flew their own defense as they watched their attacker over their shoulder and maneuvered the jet accordingly. They did this in part because they were fighting against other F–4s that were big and easy to keep in sight, and partly because their WSOs had not been trained to direct an adequate defense. They quickly learned that fighting against the Aggressors was a different story. The WSO had better rearward visibility and could see the small attackers more clearly. Soon, pilots were training their WSOs to direct the defense using a brief, succinct code of intercom calls. WSOs learned to call for a "break left" or an "extend" or a "guns break."

The Aggressors forced the F–4 crews to work together to win the fights, and the fighting unit of pilot and WSO bonded more closely than ever.

Check Left and Extend!

There is no better example of the "train the way you're going to fight" axiom than the effect the Aggressors had on the development of fighter tactics in the decade after Vietnam. After the advent of the Aggressors, Fluid Four with its welded wing position died a quick and timely death. As one Aggressor put it, "Fluid Four sucked," and the point was driven home with riveting clarity every time one or two of the small, agile jets attacked a flight of big, lumbering, smoking F–4s. With the wingman only 2,500 feet from his leader and trailing him, there were now two big smoking fighters in the sky for the Aggressor to see long before the Phantoms knew the T–38 was there.[20]

The Fighter Weapons School started to loosen up its formations in a fashion that emulated the Navy's Loose Deuce, the Double Attack of the small Air Force F–104 community, and the Six Pack with which the F–106 pilots of ADC had experimented. These schemes were very similar because they used the two-ship as the basic formation and flew line abreast about a mile apart with an altitude

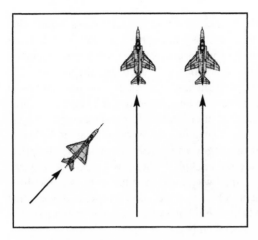

Figure 8.3
Line Abreast Patrol Formation.

"stack," or differential, of a couple of thousand feet. When attacking, the pair had only one fighter, the "engaged" fighter, press the bandit, while the other, the "free" fighter, maneuvered away from the fight to pick an opportune entry. The system had the advantage of spreading out the big fighters so that it was not so easy to see both of them. In addition, the less agile F–4 would stay engaged until his airspeed started to deplete. Then he would use superior thrust to separate away from the bandit so that the free fighter, who had been conserving his energy advantage, could engage the bandit. Thus, the two continuously switched roles so they did not have to slow down into the more agile bandit's area of advantage.

When defending, the spread formation gave each airplane an unobstructed view of his flight mate's vulnerable rear hemisphere, or "six o'clock." Each WSO could see nearly two miles behind the other's jet with relative ease. Further, if the left fighter was under attack, the right WSO had a side view, or even a belly view, of the attacker, thereby increasing his tally range. (Fig 8.3)

When the crews initially experimented with the formation, their fighting wing upbringing made them reluctant to let the fighters get too far apart. After all, they were trained to believe that the wingman was inexperienced. Therefore, he had to be closely supervised and told exactly what to do and when. This mind-set immediately got them into trouble when they started devising "initial moves" to counter an attack from their "six." The first scheme was a move called "check and extend." If the bandit attacked the left aircraft, whoever saw the attacker first would call for the aircraft under attack to check left and extend. The defender would then turn hard for thirty degrees away from his flight mate and then roll out to accelerate away from the attack. The hard turn was intended to move the defender's vulnerable cone away from the attacker and put the attacker out of the F–4's blind cone, so either the WSO or pilot could get a tally. (Fig. 8.4)

Against another F–4, the move had promise. The check turn denied a missile shot, and the defending F–4 usually picked up the big F–4 attacking them.

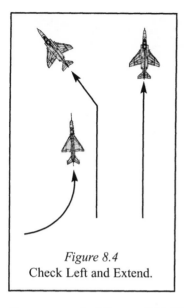

Figure 8.4
Check Left and Extend.

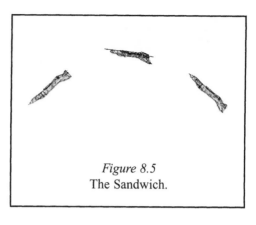

Figure 8.5
The Sandwich.

However, against the small T–38, which was also more maneuverable than the F–4, the move was often a disaster. The Aggressor pilot simply attacked at very high speed, so as the F–4 rolled out of his check turn, the Aggressor was already inside 6,000 feet and had very little angle on the F–4 in his sight for a missile shot. If the F–4 did another break turn, the wily attacker then pulled his power back, slowed down, and turned inside the F–4 for a gun shot. Of course, the small T–38 was very difficult for the defending crew to pick up, and often they did not.

After getting their brains gunned out too many times, F–4 tacticians developed a simpler plan for their clumsy jets against more agile attackers. When the attack commenced, the defending fighter would go into a hard, break turn and hold it, thus denying a missile shot until one of the crew got a tally; from that point on, they would fly the best one on one defense they could, with their only objective being to survive. The other fighter would start a hard turn into the bandit, too. If the bandit stayed on his initial attack, the outside fighter would effect a "sandwich," and either shoot the bandit down or force him to disengage. If the bandit switched to the outside fighter, then he was already in a good defensive turn that would allow him to defend himself. (Fig. 8.5)

During the decade after Vietnam, Aggressors and the fighter weapons schools continued to devise tactics. Often the progression seemed like the old *Mad* magazine feature of "Spy vs. Spy," wherein the white-cloaked spy countered the black-cloaked spy, who in turn countered the counter and so on. Although tactics continued to evolve and a better idea always seemed to pop up, one thing was constant: the tactical evolution was based on an aircraft that simulated as closely as possible the real threat the pilots might face during a war.

F–5Es of the 57th Fighter Weapons Wing, painted in the Aggressor colors, fly over the Nellis ranges. *Official USAF photo.*

Furballs over Dogbone Lake

Perhaps the most exciting peacetime dogfights many pilots of that era experienced occurred as part of exercises sponsored by the Aggressors. These exercises usually took place on Saturday at Nellis. The Aggressors invited Navy Top Gun pilots to bring as many of their fighters as they could muster to Nellis on Friday. During the afternoon, the USN, Aggressors, and Nellis Fighter Weapons School crews met to brief each other on tactics, weapons, and training developments in their respective services. They would also brief the scenario for an air-to-air war the following day. A large square of airspace, forty miles on a side, was designated as the battle area. Red forces, composed of the Aggressors and anyone else they could get to fight on their side, had to enter the battle from the west, and the Blue forces, F–4s assigned to the Fighter Weapons School and the 422d Test Squadron, had to enter from the east. The battle started with four Red and four Blue aircraft launching from Nellis and heading to the exercise area. Two minutes later, two more Reds took off, followed two minutes later by two Blues. Frequently there were nearly 100 aircraft involved, so the launches out of Nellis lasted close to an hour.

Dogfights swirled and twirled throughout the exercise area as the continuous launches of new players "fed the fight." Pilots had to be vigilant every moment because the conditions of battle could totally change in a second. A Phantom pilot intent on pouncing on an unsuspecting Aggressor probably was being stalked simultaneously by a Navy jock in an A–4 looking for an easy shot. Everyone learned quickly to avoid a furball—a close-in, roiling dogfight that depleted maneuvering energy and anchored the adversaries' position over a fixed point on the ground.

Of course, those overly concerned with the safety aspects of such large fights need not have been concerned. The fights seldom, if ever, developed into a situation where all the fighters were in the same small piece of air. Fighters tried to avoid maneuvering as much as possible, and focused their energies on slashing attacks that made them less vulnerable to unseen bogies. Several of these fights involving 80 to 100 aircraft took place at Nellis and the Navy Top Gun school at Miramar without incident.

Frequently the exercises were conducted "comm-out." No one was allowed to talk on the main frequency except to call shots and kills. Not all the fights were intense at all times. The dogfights ebbed and flowed as pilots jockeyed for the best position they could find. On one occasion, the commander of an Navy A–4 squadron brought several of his airplanes to one such exercise. The commander, whose call sign was "Skipper," made the following radio call during a long lull in the battle. "Hey, this is the skipper. I'm over Dogbone Lake at 15,000 feet. Doesn't anybody want to fight!??" Clearly, someone had been stalking the unsuspecting skipper for a long time, because less than 30 seconds later the voice of a Phantom pilot came over the fight frequency, "Fox 2,"* kill, on the skipper in a left-hand turn, 15,000 over Dogbone!"

New Jets

Although the original Aggressor concept envisioned the F–5 as the aircraft of choice for the mission, at that time there were no F–5s in the USAF inventory, but the T–38 was an acceptable substitute. However, the Aggressors soon discovered that the T–38 could not stand up to the continuous pounding dogfighting put on the airframes. For instance, the doors that covered the landing gear after it retracted would, under certain conditions, pop open and get ripped off by the slipstream. In the worst cases, the door would gash the underbelly and damage flight controls or hydraulic lines, resulting in a major mishap or crash.[21]

A serendipitous series of events at the end of the Vietnam war brought the Aggressors the airplanes they needed to do the job better and more safely. The U.S. government had been buying new F–5s to supply the South Vietnamese air force. However, when it became apparent that the Saigon government would fall, the United States withheld the F–5s. The fighter pilots pounced on the opportunity with all guns blazing, and three squadrons of F–5s went to the Aggressors. A second squadron, the 65th Aggressor Squadron activated at Nellis, and both Aggressor squadrons got the new F–5. A third Aggressor squadron was formed in Europe with the remaining F–5s. PACAF (Pacific Air Forces) jumped on the bandwagon as well, taking more new F–5s to upgrade their Aggressor squadron at Clark Air Base, the Philippines.

---

* Fox 2 denoted a Sidewinder missile shot. Fox 1 was a Sparrow shot. Gun attempts were called "guns."

The Legacy

Less than five years after the end of the Vietnam War, fighter pilots through-out the Air Force were fighting regularly against the Aggressors. Only a few years earlier, not only had there been no dissimilar training, but there had been very little air combat training of any kind. The fighter pilot culture changed so dramatically that new regulations actually encouraged dissimilar training. Navy and Air Force units around the world could pick up the telephone and schedule a dissimilar mission between different fighters. Aggressive, productive air combat training became a way of life for the generation of pilots who came after Vietnam. The war wrote its lessons in blood, but it was not for naught.

1. Ronald A. Keys, "ACT—The Run for the Roses," *USAF Fighter Weapons Review*, Spring '76, p. 45.

2. Report, Project Red Baron III, USAF Tactical Fighter Weapons Center, Volume 1: Overview Report, January 1973, p. 18.

3. Roger Wells, telephone interview with author, April 28, 1999.

4. Ronald L. Rusing, "Prepare the Fighter Force—Red Flag/Composite Force," thesis presented to the US Army Command and General Staff College, June 11, 1980, p. 11.

5. John A. Corder, telephone interview with author, April 29, 1999.

6. Dawson R. (Randy) O'Neill, e-mail to author, April 28, 1999.

7. William L. Kirk, telephone interview with author, April 29, 1999.

8. Corder interview.

9. Kirk interview; Corder interview.

10. O'Neill interview; Wells interview.

11. Corder interview.

12. Bob Herculson, briefing at 50th Anniversary Celebration of the Fighter Weapons School, Flamingo Hilton Hotel, Las Vegas, Nevada, June 19, 1999.

13. O'Neill interview.

14. Earl J. Henderson, interview with author, Las Vegas, Nevada, April 12, 1999.

15. Alexander Cockburn, "The Radical Colonel," *The Nation*, April 7, 1997, Vol. 264, No. 13, p. 9(2).

16. Henderson interview.

17. Ronald W. Iverson, interview with author, Burke, Virginia, March 5, 1999.

18. Philip W. Handley, "The Lightweight ACM Trainer," unpublished paper for the USAF Air Command and Staff College, Maxwell AFB, Alabama, May 1974, M-U 35582–7, pp. 26–27.

19. Henderson interview.

20. *Ibid.*

21. *Ibid.*

CHAPTER 9

✪

Red Flag

When you saw a buddy die in combat, he may not have learned much, but you did![1]

The Fighter Mafia

The basement of the Pentagon is another world. Exposed pipes stretch along hallway ceilings, mice scamper among dark corners, and each year the "spring floods" spread muddy puddles across office floors, forcing officers to walk across boards on the floors to keep their feet dry as they move from desk to desk conducting the highest levels of Air Force business. Many Pentagon workers are unaware that the basement offices exist, and those who do hesitate to venture into the confusing maze of rooms where the only recognizable landmark is a purple water fountain. Nonetheless, in the 1970s, the basement was home to the Air Force Directorate of Operations, the two-star general in charge of flight operations, weapons, tactics, and training.

Air Force officers selected for Pentagon duty are considered to be the best and the brightest the service has to offer. Not only are they experts in their particular field, but they are innovators with reputations for fearlessly pursuing their goals. The tour of duty is normally four years. The officers who do the work are called action officers, and they are usually young majors. Each action officer is assigned several programs to monitor, and each one spends time walking the halls of the Pentagon developing solutions to problems and proposing improvements with their counterparts in other offices. An action officer's lifeblood is the trust he builds with other action officers from the different directorates of logistics, personnel, intelligence, and budget. Informal networks of action officers form strong bonds as they cope with the intense heat of the Pentagon pressure cooker. Officers working toward a common goal are a formidable force because they are smart, focused, tenacious, and often fearless—not so concerned with the careerism too frequently found in the Pentagon. A common nickname for them is "The Iron Majors." Sometimes a group of iron majors and their allies becomes so persuasive and efficient that it achieves a legendary reputation. One such group was called the Fighter Mafia.

Although the Fighter Mafia's influence and productivity rose and fell as new action officers arrived and old members returned to line units, a particularly fruitful period came in the early 1970s when the Fighter Mafia's center of power was in the Directorate of Operations' tactics branch. Several action officers in that branch went on to great achievements during the following twenty years. The branch chief, James R. Brown, rose to three-star rank. John Vickery, a young captain on a special tour at the Pentagon, became a full colonel and commanded the Warrior Preparation Center in USAFE. John Corder became a wing commander and later commanded the Tactical Air Warfare Center as a two-star general. Chuck Horner commanded coalition air forces during Desert Storm and ultimately retired as a full general. And then there was Moody Suter.

Brown, Suter's boss, said of him, "He was capable of pure thought. He had 1,000 ideas a day."[2] Nonetheless, Suter needed others, particularly the Fighter Mafia, to give his ideas a sanity check. The tactics branch was just the place to do it because it was filled with bright articulate officers, all Vietnam veteran fighter pilots, who would shoot down 999 of Suter's ideas. However, when a good one came along, everyone helped the intellectual Suter refine the concept into something usable. Brown fondly recalls that Suter needed help at times. "We would wait until Moody left the office on a trip and then clean out his coffee cup. It looked like a science project was growing in it!"[3]

The Concept

Jim Brown kept a grease board* on his office wall where he scribbled ideas and projects. Frequently the action officers would gather there to discuss ideas and exchange information. During these sessions, a common theme of discussion was the high casualty rate among inexperienced pilots at the beginning of their combat tours. Suter had found several studies that indicated the loss rates were highest during the first ten combat sorties. Once a pilot survived the first ten, his chances of surviving the rest of his tour improved and remained constant. As the Fighter Mafia chewed on this point, a consensus developed that training was the key to getting pilots through those first ten missions. They concluded that a realistic training exercise, which closely replicated actual combat, was the answer. If the exercise lasted two weeks, each participant could fly those "first ten" missions before he ever got into actual war.

During one of the discussions, someone suggested the exercise might be used to conduct operational readiness inspections or even to test new weapons. The suggestion met with an immediate chorus of derisive comments. The exercise, for which they still did not have a name, must be only for training. If the Air Force were to conduct ORIs during the exercise, the whole idea of learning would stop. Commanders would insist that their pilots fly in order to pass rather than to learn. Instead of units looking forward to the exercise, they would come to dread it. Testing new weapons during the exercise was out as well. Test programs

---

* A large plastic-covered board upon which one writes with a grease pencil. It was a ubiquitous fixture in Air Force offices at that time.

required specific events with strict controls. In order to fill in a test matrix, the crews would be told what to do rather than learning what to do. Evaluating and testing were incompatible with training, and the objective was realistic war scenarios designed to blood the warriors.

This type of exercise was unprecedented in peacetime, and, in fact, the track record of the Air Force in maintaining high levels of combat proficiency following a war was not good. In a briefing to the Kansas Air National Guard in 1977, Lt. Gen. James D. Hughes showed charts that indicated sharp rises in fighting proficiency during World War II and Korea and sharp declines immediately afterward. In Vietnam, the trend occurred twice, after Rolling Thunder and again following Linebacker.[4]

Where to conduct such an exercise had an easy answer, the vast gunnery range—six million acres—at Nellis Air Force Base, Nevada. A large section of southern Nevada, approximately eighty miles wide by forty miles long, was already available.[5] The area was virtually unpopulated desert and mountains, and the airspace over it was restricted from use by civilian aircraft. It was only five minutes flying time from Nellis into the ranges, and the area had the added virtue of enjoying clear skies most of the year. Although the ramp space at Nellis was crowded with jets permanently assigned there, a small base at Indian Springs was only a few miles to the west. The thinkers envisioned units from TAC flying to Indian Springs and operating there for two weeks, while the Aggressors flew out of Nellis to provide enemy, or Red, fighter defenses.

Despite the huge chunk of airspace dedicated to it, the Nellis ranges were not well equipped with targets or simulated enemy defenses. In fact, there was very little of either. Tom Hall, a Fighter Mafia action officer, remembers one target that was nothing more than a few 50-gallon barrels stacked on top of each other in the middle of the mountains to simulate a "missile launch facility." "That was an indicator," he said, "of the level of investment that had been made in the ranges."[6]

Fighting the Good Fight

The task of putting the concept on paper fell to John Vickery, whom Brown calls "an unsung hero" of the Red Flag effort.[7] The young captain, by far the youngest officer in the tactics branch, had a way with words. He produced a concept paper that outlined the scheme logically and convincingly. Every staff package* that circulated through the Pentagon for coordination used Vickery's paper or a version of it to articulate the concept and its implementation.

---

* A package is a folder that contains all pertinent information on a topic. The package is coordinated with other offices starting at the bottom of the chain of command. Ultimately, it ends up on the desk of the approving official, who either approves or disapproves the project.

Capt. John Vickery strapped into the cockpit of a 555th Tactical Fighter Squadron F–4D.
Courtesy of John Vickery.

Suter, the skilled briefer, took the lead in convincing the Air Staff that the concept was sound. In a personal letter he wrote that

It [Red Flag] was the idea of the line jocks* [air crews]...The concept entailed a huge project with a lot of work, risk and money required—and the results may never be measured...initial briefings were at the action officer level to shake the bugs out and learn to answer the hard questions. Next the one and two star level to find out why it wouldn't work and finally the three star level for approval to take it to TAC.[8]

Suter was probably understating the hard work it took to convince the Air Staff that the concept was worthwhile. He gained the approval of every level and every office until he came to the three-star general who was in charge of Air Force budgets. The general said no. He could not and would not reprogram the money to conduct the exercise and told Suter it would never happen while he was in charge of the money. Suter, uncharacteristically dejected, came back to his office and threw the package into a drawer in disgust. The general, a veteran of Pentagon politics, had also warned Suter not to try an end run around him by taking the plan to TAC and using them to bring pressure to bear on the budget. He further cautioned Suter not to try to go around him to get to the Air Force chief of staff, either. Since he had been warned, Suter knew that to do so could mean the end of his career. He was not that worried about his career, but he was an honorable man and a soldier. The general had ordered him not to pursue the project directly to TAC, and he would honor the request. Suter was out of air-speed, altitude, and ideas.

A few days later, Suter, Vickery, and some others of the Fighter Mafia were having a beer after work at a bar near the Pentagon. Included in their group was Keith Ferris, the famous aviation artist. Ferris was friendly with many of the Fighter Mafia and a member in his own right. When Suter related the dead end he had hit, Ferris made a suggestion. He said he had a friend on the Army staff who worked air defense issues.* Maybe they would be interested. The next day Suter started working his briefing through the Army staff at the Pentagon. They were very excited about the idea. It might be a chance for them to train their air defense crews against a variety of targets coming at them in large numbers. After several days of briefings, Suter found himself before the Army chief of staff pitching the concept. The general loved the idea. Within a few days, the Army chief was in a meeting that also included the Air Force chief, and he mentioned to his counterpart that he thought the concept briefing he had heard from Suter was an excellent idea. Of course, the Air Force chief, Gen. David C. Jones, knew nothing of the plan, but as soon as he returned to his office he called for Suter to give him the briefing as well. Jones thought it was a great plan and told Suter to take it to TAC and brief them since it should be a TAC program. The concept was reborn.

Finally, after all the coordination process was complete and the concept had gained Air Staff approval, Suter took the briefing to Gen. Robert A. Dixon, the commander who had succeeded General Momyer. When he briefed the garrulous TAC commander, Suter followed his own three guidelines for success.

1. Prove the project will not cost any money.
2. Understand the politics that will influence the decision.
3. Know the principal players' personalities and quirks.[9]

First, he pointed out that the concept would cost little money. The ranges were already there. The Aggressors were in place and had been successful for two years. Threat simulators were available if they undertook a consolidation effort to gather then at the Nellis ranges. Money to pay for the cost of deploying to Nellis might come from other exercises that were not so effective.

Second, the politics were right. Congress and the media were clamoring for improved combat effectiveness in light of perceived military shortcomings in Vietnam.

At the conclusion of the briefing, Dixon and his staff asked several questions, all of which Suter answered to their satisfaction. Finally, Dixon asked the questions Suter knew were coming and had prepared for under point 3.

General Dixon: "Whose program will this be?
Major Suter: "Yours, sir."
General Dixon: "Who will get credit for it?"
Major Suter: "You will, sir."[10]

---

* The Army is the lead service for air defense missiles and artillery. Thus, the Army's Patriot missiles were defending Saudi Arabia and Israel against Scud missiles fired from Iraq during Desert Storm.

General Dixon named the exercise Red Flag. In May 1977 TAC won the Collier Trophy for the outstanding achievement in aviation for the year for its accomplishments with Red Flag. TAC accepted the award at a lavish affair in Las Vegas, Nevada. No one from the Fighter Mafia was invited. Someone scrounged a few tickets, and they sat in the back of the huge banquet room. When Dixon gave his acceptance speech, no mention was made of Moody Suter or the other mafiosos who helped him.[11]

Red Forces

If the objective of Red Flag was to get the first ten combat missions complete before the actual shooting started, then Red force defenses had to be as realistic as possible. The Soviets employed, and sold to their allies, an integrated air defense system that included MiGs, SAMs, AAA, and GCI. Long-range early warning radars initially picked up, or acquired, attackers. Then each target or target groups were handed off to a specific part of the IADS. Long-range SAMs engaged some, while MiGs targeted others. Short-range SAMs and AAA defended sensitive areas such as airfields, cities, industrial areas, rail yards, and bridges. Much of the Soviets' AAA was controlled by radars that aimed the guns for better accuracy. The Soviets were partial to SAMs and had many types, all of which overlapped in their coverage of the battle arena.

The task of the Red Flag planners was to equip the ranges with SAM and AAA systems that could track the Blue forces and make them think, as realistically as possible, that they were being engaged by the IADS. Of course, it was impossible to shoot real SAMs or bullets at the fighters, but they could activate the fighters' radar warning receivers (RWRs) and give them the same indications of an actual Soviet radar tracking them. The radar warning receivers were installed during Vietnam when the enemy started firing Soviet-made SA–2s at the U.S. fighters. The RWR was a small, circular scope, or screen, in the cockpit that showed the direction and strength of the radar that was tracking the airplane. The system also put a series of tones into the pilot's headset that indicated which type of radar was tracking him. Many Vietnam War pilots considered the RWR as nothing more than a nuisance, another piece of information that complicated an already confusing environment. They relied on their eyes to see the SAM and outmaneuver it. However, the Warsaw Pact possessed many types of SAMs, and the new generation of pilots and WSOs were learning to depend on RWR and on-board jammers to help them defend against the missiles and bullets from radar-guided systems. Several "threat emitters" were available throughout the Air Force at different training sites. Suter and the others proposed gathering them all onto the Nellis ranges to replicate the thick defenses of a Soviet IADS. After considerable teeth-pulling and inspirational persistence they prevailed, and many of the assets were moved to Nellis.

The Aggressors, already a very successful program with the line jocks, were in place, and by 1975 they were flying their shiny new F–5s. They would provide the MiG portion of the IADS for every Red Flag.

The First Ten Missions

On July 15, 1975, General Dixon received his marching orders from the chief of staff to implement Red Flag, and Dixon wasted no time. He wrote on the correspondence from the Pentagon, " Now let's get it laid out and in a briefing we can use as the model for the project."[12] He further directed that the first exercise take place before the end of the year.

In December an F–4 squadron from Holloman Air Force Base, New Mexico, arrived at Nellis to participate in Red Flag 75–1. As originally conceived by the Fighter Mafia at the Pentagon, the exercise lasted two weeks. Developing the mission scenarios and supporting the participants fell to a handful of young captains who had been diverted from flying assignments to serve as the Red Flag staff. All were Vietnam veterans and either F–4 pilots or WSOs. General Dixon had tasked the Tactical Fighter Weapons Center at Nellis to be the commanding agency for Red Flag, and the center commander had further delegated authority for setting up the operation to his deputy, Brig. Gen. Robinson Risner. Risner, a highly respected fighter pilot, was revered throughout the fighter force for his incredible leadership as a senior Air Force prisoner of war in the Hanoi prison camps. He "flew top cover" for the young captains who worked tirelessly to plan the exercise.

The Red Flag staff set up operations in an old building that had no plumbing and few other amenities. There Jack Lefforge, Jack Ihle, Stump Bowen, and Chuck Corder built the framework and designed the scenarios for the exercise. Since the western half of the Nellis ranges contained a majority of the few tactical targets then available, they made that area the Red territory. Blue forces would take off from Nellis, fly north into the eastern half of the ranges, then turn west and ingress to the target area across an imaginary border. Red forces would fly west out of Nellis, then north to the western half of the ranges, and defend their "homeland." A few threat simulators were available to track Blue forces with their radars to simulate enemy SAMs and AAA.

The Red Flag staff used the same building block approach established by the Fighter Weapons School to lay out the missions. The first few Red Flag sorties were flown as four-ships, the basic fighting unit, to targets that were not difficult to find. Only one or two Aggressors defended the targets, and they were limited in the attacks they could make on the Blue forces. During the second week, though, the missions started to build in intensity. Larger attack packages thundered westward into Red territory, escorted by fighters looking to kill the Aggressors. Tacticians integrated aircraft capable of jamming the Red radars into the strike force. By the end of the second week, it was all-out war with the Blue force throwing everything they could at the targets while the Red force defended in full strength.[13]

The exercise had two "goes," one in the morning and one in the afternoon. Crews flew once a day with the nonflying half of the day devoted to planning the next mission. At some point during their two-week stay, the crews were encouraged to visit Red Flag's Threat Training Facility. John Corder, the Pentagon action officer from the tactics branch, had visited Israel following the 1973 Arab-Israeli War. There he was astounded to see all the Soviet equipment the Israelis had captured. As his part of the Red Flag concept, he made arrangements with the U.S. Air Force and the U.S. State Department to have representative pieces of that captured equipment shipped to Nellis. There it was put in an area behind a fence and away from prying eyes. Red Flag crews visited the Threat Training Facility to inspect AAA guns, missiles, radars, and MiG cockpits. Some called it a show and tell. The pilots and WSOs got a firsthand look at what they would be up against in a shooting war with the Soviets.

After every mission, the entire package assembled in a large auditorium to debrief the events of their mission. Each flight leader stood in front of the other participants and recounted the successes and failures of his mission. The tone of these debriefings quickly became brutally honest. An experienced Vietnam veteran wrote, "We are not trying to relearn all the [Vietnam] lessons. We are trying to do some good realistic training for the next war."[14]

Following the Blue flight leaders, the Aggressor flight leader presented his side of the story. He evaluated the formations, tactics, and maneuvers he and his flight mates had seen and made suggestions for improvements. He might show gun camera film of Blue pilots defending against his attack.* He also debriefed errors he and the Red Forces made—a clue that the Blue forces would likely not see the same mistake the next day.

The final debriefing was from the Red Flag staff. They told the Blue forces exactly where their bombs had hit and what the estimated damage was. They showed videotape from cameras attached to the AAA guns that showed the crews the effectiveness of their evasive maneuvers, "jinking." Video cameras on the range taped the jets in their bombing passes, and sometimes the aircraft recovered low enough to be damaged by frag from their own bombs, had they been carrying live ordnance. Crews seldom, if ever, had the opportunity to drop live ordnance at their home bases because there were very few ranges that permitted it. Therefore, some crews did not fully appreciate the danger from their own frag. The video cameras drove home the point in living black and white.

These debriefings became nearly as important as the flying. The credo was honesty. If it was screwed up, say so. Learn from it and move on. When General

---

* It took two hours to send the film to the photo lab for developing and get it back to the Red Flag area. The film was always available the next day for the Blue pilots to view.

F–5s in flight as part of the testing programs at Nellis. *Official USAF photo.*

Dixon was asked how he viewed the training at Red Flag, he responded:

> Aircrews are being given a chance to try their ideas, to fly missions the way they think war should be fought, and to learn from their own mistakes…men learn a lot more from mistakes than they do from rhetoric.[15]

Bigger Really Is Better

Red Flag expanded dramatically over the next several years. The exercises were so successful that everyone wanted in on the act, and TAC was more than glad to accommodate them. Strategic Air Command B–52s flew from their home bases, dropped bombs, and then returned home. Military Airlift Command (MAC) C–141s, C–130s, and, later, C–5s made cargo drops while attempting to evade persistent Red forces. Air refueling tankers orbited in the eastern and western reaches of the ranges and refueled Red and Blue forces. Rescue forces conducted search and rescue (SAR) missions to pick up crewmen who had been "shot down" in Red territory. Forward air controllers directed strikes in support of Army troops. Between 1975 and 1980, every major aircraft in the U.S. Air Force, Navy, Army, Air National Guard, and Marines flew in Red Flag. It was common for twenty different types of aircraft to fly in a single exercise.[16]

Air Force units from Europe started attending Red Flag, and the Pacific forces started their own, similar exercise called Cape Thunder at Clark in the Philippines in 1976. Canada initiated Maple Flag at Cold Lake in 1978. Allied nations participated regularly in all three exercises.

The objective of getting a pilot his first ten combat missions was being achieved in spades. In 1976, the first full year of Red Flag, seven exercises were accomplished, and 2,105 aircrews were trained. In 1977, 6,577 more completed the course. By 1980, over 24,000 pilots, WSOs, navigators, load masters, boomers,* and other fliers had sweated their way through some of the most realistic training any aviator had ever seen.[17]

Lessons Learned

At the end of each mission debriefing, each flight leader related the lessons he and his flight learned. Then, at the end of each Red Flag, the staff compiled a report that reviewed the objectives, results, and lessons learned for the exercise. Every flying unit in the Air Force received copies of every Red Flag report. A unit scheduled for Red Flag often used the lessons learned to help them prepare for their trip to Nellis. Frequently the lessons learned had Air Force-wide implications, and sometimes they had some surprising results.

The B–52, America's 1950s vintage bomber, is an enormous airplane with eight engines. When they came to Red Flag for the first time, the B–52s entered the Nellis ranges at high altitude in a three-ship formation, trailing enormous white contrails for miles behind them. The Aggressors, who had a tally on these contrails from more than fifty miles away, shot all of them down. When the B–52 flight leader was asked why he did not change his altitude when he knew he was producing contrails, he replied that he was flying at the altitude selected by his headquarters. It never occurred to him to change altitudes. He had been trained in the strategic bombing mentality, wherein the mission was planned at the headquarters, and a good pilot would execute the plan perfectly. Flexibility was not an option. Further, the B–52 pilot assumed that his fighter escort could always protect him. After the B–52s got their teeth kicked in a few times, they changed the way they operated. First, they started landing after the mission at a nearby base, so that they could come to the debriefings and join in the planning for the next day's mission. There they received the same feedback as the fighter crews, and they learned each other's operating needs.[18] It did not take long for them to start working as a team, using different tactics on different days to foil the Red defenses.

The lessons learned by the transport, or airlift, pilots were no less dramatic and made their airplanes look quite different. At their first Red Flag, the airlifters flew into the drop area in a long string of C–141s. The C–141 was painted white, and the string formation they flew is what they always flew when they were delivering troops or cargo via parachutes to the ground. Of course, the Aggressors' hot knives went through them like butter. It was not as though the Blue fighter crews were totally inept. They shot down Aggressors regularly, but the C–141s were so bright and so close together that the Aggressors had no trouble keeping track of where they were. Thus, the Aggressors could plan their attacks to avoid the

---

* An enlisted man or woman who controls the refueling boom, or probe, on an air refueling tanker.

fighter escort while always knowing exactly the location of the C–141s. The Military Airlift Command immediately started a program to camouflage the C–141, and soon the jets appeared around the world sporting a camouflage paint scheme similar to the fighters that participated in Red Flag.

When Red Flag began, the Air Force did not possess any aircraft that could penetrate enemy defenses and jam enemy radar systems, but the Navy did. The Air Force quickly learned the value of a penetrating jammer at Red Flag as soon as the Navy brought their EA–6s to the party. The Air Force responded by building a jammer version of the F–111 medium bomber called the EF–111.

The goal of Red Flag was to present an adversary to the Air Force that was as realistic as possible, and planners used the high-threat European scenario as their model. Aggressors and Red defenses used Soviet tactics and replicated Soviet equipment, and Blue forces used tactics and plans tailored to fighting against the Warsaw Pact. However, everyone quickly learned that the successful warrior fights with what he has available at the moment. In Europe the crews planned to fly low to avoid enemy radar, and there was nothing wrong with that plan. In fact, using fighter pilot logic, if low was good, then lower was even better. However, flying very low over the desert of Nevada was not always a good thing. The Aggressors learned quickly, and the Blue pilots nearly as quickly, that the low-flying jets cast distinct black shadows on the light desert background, especially over the many dry lake beds on the Nellis ranges. The black shadow was a dead giveaway of the Blue fighters' positions. The Aggressors hawked the suspected attack routes at medium altitude, where they could conserve fuel and see many miles until they spied the shadows of an ingressing flight; then they swooped into the attack.

Flying in Red Flag also required the fighter crew to think differently about low-level navigation. At their home units and local flying areas, the fighter jocks practiced low-level navigation on a few approved routes. They could fly below 1,000 feet only on these routes because the noise from the thundering jets was a nuisance to many Americans who did not believe that jet noise was the sound of freedom. The crews got to know these routes very well since they flew them over and over again. Moreover, the routes were only three miles wide, so the pilots had to adhere closely to the black lines on their maps that delineated the course. Many TAC units had a secondary mission of nuclear weapons delivery at their deployment bases in Europe and Korea.* Nuclear weapons missions required precise timing of the bomb delivery, so that a blast scheduled a minute or two before or after they passed a certain point would not fry a friendly crew. Therefore, the F–4 jocks took great pride in their ability to navigate exactly down the black line within a few seconds of their predicted time. They learned a different lesson at Red Flag. When an Aggressor jumped into the middle of their formation, and

---

* Every TAC squadron was assigned an overseas base to which they would deploy in wartime.

they took evasive action, black lines and timing within seconds went out the window. So did staying within a three-mile-wide low-level corridor. They not only had to plan on being forced off course at some time; they also had to learn how to reorient themselves and still get to the target.

Once they arrived at the target, the crews dropped practice bombs on their aim points. However, they only were simulating dropping live ordnance. Sometime during each Red Flag exercise, each crew had the opportunity to drop real bombs, usually a load of 500-pound, MK–82 general purpose bombs. The live ordnance drop was a highlight of Red Flag because many crews did not have combat experience, and the numbers of those who did decreased every year. Since nearly all fighter bases had no place to drop live bombs, the mission at Red Flag added a whole new set of problems for the jocks. Not the least of these problems was planning for a greatly extended takeoff roll and the danger of an engine failure immediately after takeoff. Most had to dig into the books to review the procedure to jettison bombs. They had to take into account the added gross weight as they maneuvered through the attack phase. Most important, they had to plan precise delivery parameters, or risk flying through flying bomb fragments from their own deliveries. If the pilot was a little shallow or slow, he could "press," or fly closer to the target with a practice bomb to get a good score. With a live MK–82, though, such a practice was hazardous at best and deadly at the worst.

The Red Flag experience was full of lessons learned. Many were learned, forgotten, and relearned as the cycle of training and new crews ebbed and flowed through Nellis in search of the proficiency and knowledge that would keep them alive when the next war came.

Not Without a Price

Training 6,000 aircrews a year in the most demanding exercise most had ever seen was not cost free. During the first four years of Red Flag, 24 aircraft were lost. Some smacked into the ground, while others smacked into each other. In 1979 the Air Force accident rate for all its aircraft types together was 2.8 crashes per 100,000 hours of flying time. The TAC rate, a command that flew nearly all fighter aircraft, was 6.3. At Red Flag, the rate was an astonishing 21.8 for its first four years of operation. Still, the Air Force pressed on with the exercise, which is no less demanding today. One officer recalled a discussion at the Pentagon concerning flying accidents and the exercises at Nellis. When the vice chief of staff worried aloud about accidents, Lt. Gen. Joseph Wilson, the chief of operations, exclaimed, "At least we'll lose 'em doing smart things; right now we're losing them doing dumb things!"[19]

---

1. Joel T. Hall, interview with author, Las Vegas, Nevada, April 12, 1999.

2. James R. Brown, telephone interview with author, April 26, 1999.

3. *Ibid.*

4. Ronald L. Rusing, "Prepare the Fighter Force—Red Flag/Composite Force," thesis presented to the U.S. Army Command and General Staff College, June 11, 1980, p. 2.

5. *Ibid.*, p. 13.

6. Hall interview.

7. Brown interview.

8. Rusing paper, p. 9.

9. John Vickery, telephone interview with author, April 15, 1999.

10. *Ibid.;* Brown interview.

11. *Ibid.*

12. Rusing thesis, p. 18.

13. Jack A. Lefforge, telephone interview with author, April 28, 1999.

14. Rusing thesis, p. 25.

15. *Ibid.*, p. 25.

16. *Ibid.*, p. 26.

17. *Ibid.*, p. 22.

18. Lefforge interview.

19. Dawson R. (Randy) O'Neill, e-mail to author, April 28, 1999.

CHAPTER 10

✪

Measuring Combat Capability

If it ain't on film, it ain't! [1]

Gun Cameras

Everyone interested in U.S. military history has seen the grainy, flickering, black-and-white film of the German Me 109 pilot or Japanese Zero pilot dead center in the American fighter's sights. The film jitters as the firing machine guns shake the airplane. Tracers claw through the sky, striking in flashes along the enemy plane's wings and fuselage. Small chunks fly off, then larger ones. A burst of oily flame streaks back from the engine, followed by a cataclysmic blast as the enemy fighter explodes. The use of gun cameras to document aerial kills is nearly as old as fighter aviation itself, but the cameras served another purpose as well. While we see only the successes on the screen, the cameras also documented the failures caused by poor marksmanship and poor positioning. In short, the missed shots on gun camera film had a good side. They allowed the pilot to look at his film after a flight and learn from it. Perhaps he had been firing from a range outside the effective reach of his guns. Perhaps he was not "tracking" the target smoothly. Perhaps he did not even have the pipper* on the target, although in the excitement of the moment he had convinced himself that he was perfectly aligned.

Despite the proven advantages of having a gun camera, the F–4, the fighter that would become the backbone of Air Force tactical aviation for more than a decade, originally did not have one. Conceived during the years before Vietnam when designers and developers thought the era of the dogfight was over, the F–4 was built to use the radar-guided Sparrow missile that could be fired beyond visual range. The designers of the F–4 reasoned that the aircraft did not need a gun for combat at close quarters. If there was no gun, then it seemed reasonable not to have a gun camera. The rear cockpit radarscope did have a camera that filmed the radar picture, allowing crews to document and learn about employing the radar, but there was nothing to document visual maneuvering and shots.

Six years after the first F–4s appeared in the inventory, a modification that added a gun camera arrived at units that were equipped with the F–4E. However, units flying the older F–4C and F–4D jets were left out. Even though the cameras were delivered over the next two years to the E-model units, an entire

---

* The small dot in the center that is the true aiming index of the gunsight.

Lt. Tom Owens stands between two AIM–9B Sidewinders loaded under the wing of an F–4, ready for combat.
Courtesy of Sherrard Owens.

generation of fighter pilots had never flown with a gun camera. Many others would never see a gun camera until they converted to the new generation of fighters that succeeded the F–4.

Experienced fighter pilots will say, "No one can lie to himself better than a fighter pilot about to pull the trigger." The task of getting the airplane into a firing position is so demanding that at the moment of truth, when he pulls the trigger to shoot a missile or presses the pickle button to drop a bomb, his mind tells him that the pipper is exactly on the target when it really is not. The gun camera modification made the point "loud 'n' clear" to Phantom pilots. A flight leader would hear his young wingman say in the flight debriefing that it was a mystery why his bullets went to the left of the target. He was certain that he had the pipper directly on the practice strafe panel as he squeezed the trigger. They might all scratch their heads and wonder if the winds were really as reported, or if perhaps the gun was not properly bore sighted.* The next day, when the camera film came back from the photo lab, the cold reality was there for all to see. The pilot had the pipper tracking the target until a half-second before he fired, but then it drifted ten feet left of the target—exactly where the bullets had hit.

If gun camera film was a rude awakening for the pilots after their bombing and strafing missions, it was a shock to see it after an air combat training sortie. Pilots could assess several parameters on the F–4 film. First, the gunsight itself was displayed, a solid, red outer circle that was 50 mils in diameter with a segmented red circle 25 mils in diameter inside it. At the very center was a 2 mil red dot, the pipper. A pilot could determine the range to the target one of two ways from the film. If his radar was tracking the target, a sliding bar appeared on the

---

* The maintenance process of aligning the gun with the gunsight.

inside of the outer circle to tell him how far away he was. In the case of a Sidewinder missile shot or a gun shot, though, he often did not have a radar lock on the target. Without radar ranging, the range assessment process was more difficult. The pilot had to freeze the film and measure the length and width of the projected image on the small movie screen. Either way, the film showed his range and angle off the moment he simulated firing. The simulated firing itself was documented by a bright "witness mark" that showed on the side of the film whenever the trigger or pickle button activated.

Film review, as it was called, showed many pilots that they were using poor technique and taking undisciplined shots. This was not a new phenomenon in fighter aviation and combat. Almost half the Sidewinders launched by United States pilots during Rolling Thunder were fired out of parameters.[2] Other missed shots resulted from a pilot setting up switches incorrectly, documented by the lack of a fire signal, or witness mark, on the film. Fumbled switches were nothing new in aerial combat either. A Japanese fighter pilot, who ultimately had sixty kills during World War II, said of his first engagement:

> One of the planes attacked me....All my careful plans of what I would do in my first combat evaporated....I failed to see anything on the sides or behind me. I finally rolled in behind an enemy fighter and discovered I had not armed my guns.[3]

With gun cameras documenting the shot discipline necessary to be successful in combat, the fighter force attacked the problem with what can only by described as fanaticism. The leaders in the movement were the instructors at the Fighter Weapons School who inculcated every student with the burning desire to document and assess every attempted ordnance delivery. The weapons school graduates returned to their units and, with a missionary zeal, developed detailed shot analysis programs that examined every shot down to a gnat's eyelash.

An example of the emphasis put on documentation was the penalty devised by Capt. Joe Bob Phillips and Capt. Ron Keys for the GAT 5/6 weapons school graduation exercise. A pilot who called a kill on another aircraft during one of these missions but could not prove it on film had to pay five dollars into a kitty. Conversely, any pilot who was called killed but did not leave the fight had to pay five dollars. At the end of the two-week exercise, the money was spent on a party for all participants. For the time, this was not an insignificant sum; however, the sting of embarrassment was worse than the money lost. Every pilot concentrated hard on his parameters: range, angle off, pipper placement, and tracking time. The WSOs, who also had to throw money into the kitty, became adept at making key reminders during crucial moments. For example, the Phantom's radar needed four seconds of settling time from the time it locked on until it was giving enough information to the Sparrow missile to be accurate. WSOs became talking clocks.

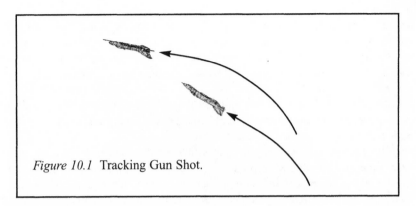

Figure 10.1 Tracking Gun Shot.

Many would lock up the target, then slowly say, "Locked...1...2...3...4, shoot, shoot, shoot" to help insure a valid shot.

Such fanatical attention to detail influenced tactics and training in many ways. There are two basic kinds of gun shots a fighter may attempt against a maneuvering, or turning, adversary. The most accurate is the tracking shot where the attacker camps inside the defender's turn at close range and matches his turn rate, radius, and g. If the pilot does it properly, then his pipper will settle on the target for several seconds, and he can squeeze off a long burst and hammer the target hard. (Fig 10.1)

However, there are circumstances where the attacker cannot or does not want to stabilize inside the defender's turn for a tracking shot. When a less maneuverable fighter, like the F–4 attacks an agile one like the MiG–21 or F–5, the wise Phantom pilot remembers Boyd's EM studies and stays fast. If he does so, he will more frequently be presented with the opportunity for a snap shot, what the World War II and Korea pilots called a high deflection shot. In the snap shot, the attacker simply pulls his nose well in front of the defender to establish lead, then puts out a steady stream of bullets for the defender to fly through. (Fig 10.2)

Before the F–4 received its gun camera, crews saw little value in snap shots because they were not really sure where the bullets might be going. However, once they saw their pipper on a snap shot march down the length of an F–5 fuselage, they started to get the picture. When added to the F–4's lack of turning ability against the MiG family, as represented by the Aggressor F–5, the snap shot, or high-angle gun shot, became more and more appealing. The trick was to get in the same plane of motion as the defender, then time the stream of bullets to coincide with his arrival at the same point in space. While the snap shot was not nearly as deadly as a tracking shot, a smooth, controlled tracking shot seldom presented itself if the adversary had a tally, the usual case against the big, blocky F–4 with its smoky engines.

As units got their gun cameras, they discovered problems with the tracking shots as well. In order for a tracking gun shot to be valid, the pipper had to be on

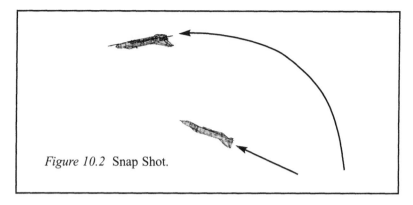

Figure 10.2 Snap Shot.

the adversary for one second. The film ran at 24 frames per second, so the film assessor could count each frame as the shot progressed. Pilots discovered that their tracking was lousy and that it took more concentration to complete the demanding task than they thought. So several units devised tracking exercises that they flew to and from their working areas. One aircraft would maneuver in gentle acrobatics while the other practiced tracking him with the gunsight. As the exercise progressed, the leader would maneuver more and more aggressively to present the tracker with a more challenging problem.

No idea is a good idea unless someone does not like it, and high-angle gun shot technique was no exception. The safety offices at TAC expressed concern that the slashing gun attacks were dangerous. They did not like the idea that the attacker had to pull his nose so far out in front of the defender. They saw the danger of a midair collision. The debate was put to rest when Gen. Robert Dixon, the TAC commander, flew in the back seat of an Aggressor T–38 while the weapons school commander, Lt. Col. Larry Keith, and his wingman, Capt. Bill Sakahara, made "75 high-angle gun passes" on Dixon's jet. After the mission, Dixon said he saw no danger in the passes. The technique survived, and tactics took another step forward.[4]

F–4 pilots were not the only ones to experience the gun camera epiphany. The Aggressor T–38, a trainer, had no gun camera either. As the new F–5, which did have a gun camera, arrived at their squadrons, Aggressor pilots started to use it. However, by the time the F–5 arrived, the Aggressors had been in operation nearly three years, and because of their extensive training and total immersion in DACT they had become the best dogfighters in the Air Force. In the minds of the F–4 pilots, especially the weapons school, the Aggressors copped an attitude. "We don't need to show our film; if I say I took the shot at 2,000 feet, then it was 2,000 feet." Nonetheless, everyone else was showing their film and honoring the five dollar rule, and it was not long before the Aggressors were bringing theirs to the debriefings as well. They were far better than the F–4 crews had been before cameras, but even with all their experience and training, they found they were taking some bad shots, too.[5]

In the Circle

In their quest to improve air-to-air training, pilots wanted real-time feedback so that they could know immediately if their shots counted. Kill removal, the process of removing "dead" aircraft from a fight, they believed, was the key to tactics validation because it more closely replicated actual combat conditions. But implementing kill removal was not easy. In a DACT mission, adversaries flew on separate frequencies, so that their opponents could not base key defensive reactions on overheard radio calls. For instance, if an Aggressor flight leader heard the F–4 flight leader tell half his flight to deploy west, it was hard for the Aggressor flight leader to keep that out of his mind. As a good training aid, he would not react to the call, but he heard it. Therefore, it was part of the big picture of the battle in his mind and increased his awareness of what was happening. Thus, each side had its own radio frequency so the other could not eavesdrop, even inadvertently.

Separate frequencies, however, had a negative side, and that was kill removal. If an F–4 shot an F–5, he had to call the kill on his own frequency. Then another person, usually the F–4 GCI controller, had to pass the kill call to the Aggressor controller sitting beside him, who in turn relayed the kill call on the Aggressor frequency. Pilots tried to make their kill calls specific by using their call sign, the type of shot, the type aircraft shot, the target's altitude, and the target's maneuver. For example, "Noway 1, Fox 2, kill, F–5, 15,000 feet, left turn." His GCI controller, who was also busily engaged in the fight, then had to repeat that to the Aggressor controller, who then repeated it on the air to the Aggressors. It was like the parlor game where one person whispers something, and the whispered something is circulated around the player's circle. By the time it gets back to the originator, it bears no resemblance to the original comment. So kill removal was very difficult to do consistently, yet it had a huge impact on the outcome of the fight. Often the F–4 crews would fight outnumbered, so they planned their tactics to thin the adversary ranks as quickly as possible. If players did not leave the fight, or if the wrong ones left, the outcome was meaningless.

The solution to such problems and others was the addition of a new system at Nellis called the air combat maneuvering and instrumentation (ACMI) range. The ACMI range consisted of three main components. Each aircraft on the range carried a pod the same size as a Sidewinder on a standard Sidewinder rail. The pod measured aircraft airspeed, altitude, g, and other parameters that it transmitted to a series of ground stations around the range. These stations then relayed the information to a central computer that could measure within a few feet the relative position of each aircraft to all other aircraft on the range. The computer also displayed each aircraft as a small F–4 or F–5 shaped aircraft on a large display screen.

Nellis constructed the ACMI range a few minutes flying time west of the base. The area where the pods were effective was a circle thirty miles in diameter that reached up to as high as the jets could fly. In a fight between four F–5s and four

F–4s, for example, each aircraft carried a pod. The F–5 flight started on one side of the circle and the F–4 flight on the other. At the "fight's on" call the opponents started at each other. The display on the ground showed the aircraft headed at each other. When one jet shot at another, a missile streaked away from the aircraft on the display. If it was fired within parameters, it killed the target and a schematic coffin appeared over the victim. An impartial observer in front of the display board, who had access to both teams' frequencies, transmitted "Three, you're dead," and number three would leave the fight quickly.

When the crews returned to the debriefing, they met in the ACMI room and replayed each fight. As the rerun progressed, each pilot could see all the flight parameters of every other aircraft in the fight. They could see every shot, the parameters of every shot, and the result. It was common for pilots to lose track of adversaries and even other flight members in the stress, confusion, and breathtaking speeds of a roiling, swirling, twirling dogfight. When they got back to the debrief, though, everything became perfectly clear. The F–5 that they thought had separated to the west really had sliced back and shot down poor Blue Four* before anyone realized what had happened.

The crews could stop or reverse the tape at any time, and the computer could flip, rotate, or tilt the fight so everyone could see the spatial relationships of every player. The reason no one saw that F–4 was because he was 8,000 feet below the fight, pitching up into it. There was even a cockpit view that showed what a pilot was seeing out his windscreen at the moment he took a shot or decided to blunder off into the sunset, out of ideas and airspeed.

The potential for ACMI was staggering to the crews who flew on the range. For the first time in the history of Air Force fighter aviation† they could get accurate, timely kill removal. The learning did not stop there, however. They soon discovered the value of using the ACMI to teach the basics of dogfighting.

The traditional way to teach dogfighting was with hands and a chalkboard. There is a reason fighter pilots are notorious for talking with their hands. When instructors stand before their charges in a flight briefing, they constantly use their hands to explain the relationship of the aircraft expected on the mission. If the instructor is right-handed, the left hand is always the defender and the right the attacker. Left arm in a slight curve to show the hand's previous flight path, the instructor maneuvers his right hand on the attack, digging deep inside the defender's turn or zooming high to the hapless left hand's six o'clock. One fighter weapons school instructor even went so far as to wet a flying glove with lighter fluid and "flame" his left hand with a cigarette lighter at the moment of victory.

---

* Blue Four refers to the number four man in a four-ship fighter formation. Since he was the "tail-end charlie," and often the most inexperienced pilot, he was the most vulnerable to attack in the old Fluid Four system.

† The Navy bought the system before the Air Force.

Lt. Col. Hugh Moreland rolls his right hand to an advantage over his helpless left hand as Capt. R. T. Newell critiques the move.
Courtesy of Karen Moreland.

Another instructor, Hugh Moreland, had broken his left hand in a high school football game; he could flex it backward nearly ninety degrees, thereby showing his left hand doing an incredible "break turn." The other important teaching tool was an everyday chalkboard with its complement of colored chalk. Every fighter briefing room in the Air Force had them, and instructors had to learn how to draw the lines three dimensionally in order to represent what was expected to happen, and, after the fight, what did happen.

While instructing in this time-honored tradition continued, the added benefit from ACMI was enormous. After the fight, an instructor could show his students the exact relationships of the aircraft. The ACMI had a trail function that would display a line behind the aircraft, which showed where they had been and even how big or small their turn radii were. If the student was trying unsuccessfully to turn inside his adversary, the ACMI showed how his turn was bigger than he wanted. The instructor could then reference his airspeed on the performance screen and point out that the young man was far too fast to make a turn that tightly. If he slowed down to his quickest, tightest turn speed he could make the corner. These graphic representations accelerated learning dramatically. Every instructor learned that a basic maneuvers mission flown on ACMI was worth several flown in the traditional airspace, where only the instructor's hands and chalkboard were available to reconstruct the fight and determine its learning outcomes. As the lessons of the 1970s sped toward the hope of the 1980s, Air Force ACMI and its older sister, the Navy ACMR (air combat maneuvering range), sprang up at a few locations in the United States and Europe to support the blossoming DACT program. By the end of the decade, USAF, USN, and United States Marine Corps (USMC) fighters were engaging each other in vibrant, challenging, and meaningful mock combat where every turn and every swirl brought them closer to their goal of an unbeatable air supremacy force.

1. Source unknown. Common statement of fighter pilots of the 1970s.

2. Project Red Baron II, p. 18.

3. Letter, 1st Tactical Fighter Training Squadron commander to all instructor pilots, January 6, 1988, p. 3.

4. Brig. Gen. Larry R. Keith, USAF (Ret.), telephone interview with author, March 31, 1999.

5. Col. Hugh Moreland, USAF (Ret.), telephone interview with author, March 4, 1999.

CHAPTER 11

✪

The Nellis Ranges

Real-time feedback is an essential for learning.

As Red Flag got underway, the Nellis bombing ranges were not much more than 6,000,000 acres of desert, scrub brush, and mountains north of the base. A few practice targets were scraped into the ground, but most of them, and all the significant ones, were nuclear bomb practice targets consisting of large bull's-eyes in the desert. There were a few tactical targets scattered across the vast acreage, but they were haphazard and of little use to a large exercise like Red Flag.

The Nellis ranges were not the only ones in the western United States. The Navy had ranges to the south at Yuma, Arizona, and to the northwest in Fallon, Nevada. The Air Force controlled a large military reservation southwest of Salt Lake City, Utah. Even the Army had training ranges southwest of Nellis at Fort Irwin, California. A presidential blue ribbon panel investigated the utilization, manning, and future of all these ranges in 1969 and came to several conclusions. Two were destined to impact heavily on the future development of the Nellis ranges.

The panel recommended that the services investigate the possibility of linking all the ranges under one command to coordinate their efforts and act as a central point for budgetary decisions. The panel also pointed out that the Air Force did not have a formalized policy, or even a written requirement, for the Nellis ranges. The panel envisioned an enormous training complex in the western states that could accommodate all the services' air and ground training under one agency.

After much massaging and politicking, the armed services adopted the concept, and it became known as the continental operation ranges (COR). However, no idea that involved money went unchallenged. There was another large range near Eglin Air Force Base in the Florida panhandle. Not only were the Eglin ranges home to much of the Air Force development testing, but they were also in the home district of Congressman Robert Sikes, who was one of the most influential House members on military matters. Sikes did not see the value of COR, and it died before it was born.[1]

Nonetheless, the presidential blue ribbon panel spurred the Air Force to act on validating and formalizing its need for the Nellis ranges. Two officers on the Air Staff, Bob Fay and Moody Suter, were assigned the task of writing a requirement for operational capability (ROC). They produced ROC 76–1, and it outlined a range complex that would provide the training ground for Suter's Red Flag concept.[2]

The key points of ROC 76–1 were that the ranges should provide realistic targets, an integrated air defense system, and real-time feedback to the exercise crews. Target construction was not easy. Work crews had to drive many miles to remote locations, usually on the weekend, so that they did not interfere with attack missions during the week. Bulldozers bladed airfields into the desert floor to duplicate the runway, taxiway, and parking apron layout of a typical Warsaw Pact airfield, and work crews sprinkled the ground with the battered hulks of old aircraft, while telephone poles put end to end simulated fuel supply lines. Workers also built an industrial complex and used more telephone poles to lay "railroad tracks" into and out of the simulated factory area. AAA gun pits dug around the complex allowed flak suppression attackers to see an actual target. Along an imaginary line where the Red Flag crews entered enemy territory, columns of Red and Blue "armor" faced each other in battle, simulating the forward edge of the battle area (FEBA). To make the training as realistic as possible, the targets were actual size. Airfield runways were the same length as Soviet ones, and the industrial area sprawled across many acres. Duplicating the actual target size allowed attackers to use different aiming points on the targets simultaneously, which was the same way they planned to do it in actual combat. After two years of hard work, the target arrays were as realistic as possible, considering the blistering heat and blasting desert winds facing the construction crews.

Building a target complex on the ground was only part of the equation in making Red Flag realistic combat training, and assembling an IADS proved a more difficult proposition. The eyes of an integrated system are its long-range acquisition radars that provide early warning to the terminal threat SAMs and AAA. The early warning radars also give GCI controllers the information they need to vector fighters toward the attackers. Although the Aggressors did not have their own radar, they made arrangements to use civilian air traffic control radars operated by the Federal Aviation Administration, and Aggressor GCI controllers quickly established their reputation for excellent control.

Gathering a system of SAMs and AAA to defend the targets turned into a bureaucratic brawl. When Red Flag began, there was a system of terminal threats, SAMs and AAA, in the northeast corner of the Nellis ranges in an area called Caliente. Some of these radars were actual Soviet equipment the Air Force had purchased from allies, while others were threat replicates—kluged transmitting systems that put a signal on the air with the same electronic signature as Soviet systems. Wild Weasel crews trained on the Caliente complex, while flying specially modified F–105 and F–4 aircraft that were built to seek and destroy enemy ground radars. Proponents of Red Flag saw the complex as a partial answer to their problem. All they had to do was move the system to the west end of the ranges and locate it with the bombing targets. Proponents of the Wild Weasel mission resisted. They were fearful that if the threat radars became part of Red Flag, EW (electronic warfare) training would suffer because the Wild Weasel units would not have a high enough priority to book range time for their training. The Red Flag advocates used honey rather than vinegar and convinced the Weasels that putting the complexes together would provide even better training.

Since the Red Flag missions used only two hours in the morning and two hours in the afternoon, the Wild Weasels would have plenty of range time available for basic training.

The Fighter Mafia at the Pentagon also went after the threat assets that were spread around the country in bits and pieces. Although they met moderate resistance, they persevered and slowly gathered a modest threat array in the western reaches of the ranges. When Red Flag attackers winged through the valleys and popped up to attack the airfields and other targets, SAM and AAA radars locked onto their aircraft and tracked them through evasive maneuvers. One invention that greatly aided the training of the Red Flag crews was the addition of video cameras to the tracking radars. Red gunners who saw attackers tracked the jets with the guns, while the video camera filmed every move the pilots made as they tried to avoid being shot. The Red Flag staff brought these videos to the debriefing, so that everyone could watch and learn the effectiveness, or lack thereof, of jinking to avoid enemy fire.

Not all efforts at providing realistic training and feedback were so elaborate. One member of the Red Flag staff went to a hill on the ranges that was just outside the zone where crews could drop their bombs. He took with him everyday Fourth of July rockets. As fighters whistled over his head, he fired a rocket that produced a small white smoke trail into the sky. Since the planes were at low altitude, a fighter formation with strong lookout procedures was able to see the little rockets, and call them out to other fighters. Ultimately, a contract was awarded to a company to produce a Styrofoam* rocket that was much larger and put out a very big smoke plume, and the Smokey SAM was born. As crews ingressed and egressed the target area, they were confronted with white smoke trails from the ground that represented SAM launches, another combat problem to be anticipated and avoided.[3]

Of course, the crews needed to know where their bombs hit. Initially, bomb scoring was only possible from the air if other crews saw the bombs in front of them hit the ground. As in combat, pilots dropped their bombs and then immediately started jinking to foil enemy ground fire, so they often did not see where their bombs landed. Since most of the bombs did not have explosives and were inert, there was no big blast to hang in the sky as a clear marker to success or failure. Once again the technology of video cameras and tapes solved the problem. The Air Force purchased a television optical scoring system (TOSS) to score the bombs. TOSS consisted of two video cameras on high ground a safe distance from the target, so their lines of sight met at a 90-degree angle. The cameras were wired to video recorders that began recording before the attackers dropped their bombs. Since the cameras saw the impacts immediately, it was a quick and easy matter to determine the exact center of impact from where the two lines of sight

---

* So that no damage would occur to an aircraft that might inadvertently run into one.

crossed. At the Red Flag debriefing, every crew was given a score for their bombs, down to the meter, and the best hits were shown in the mass debriefing. As mentioned earlier, those videos sometimes showed crews pulling out too low from their passes, so low that they would have been fragged if the bombs were real.

Suter Hall

While new pilots still learn the basics of bombing and gunnery on controlled ranges with bull's-eye circles on the ground and steady smooth passes, the Red Flag environment is the graduation exercise, where crews come as close to combat as possible during peacetime. There they fly ten missions designed to move them beyond the vulnerability of being a "new guy" in combat. Those missions are designed to keep them and their aircraft flying and winning the next war. When they plan a Red Flag mission, it is a team effort. Bombers will drop cruise missiles to take out enemy defenses. Fighters will sweep the skies clear of enemy aircraft. Jammers will jam enemy defenses. Search and rescue forces stand by to find and save the unfortunate ones. Tankers refuel everybody. Army, Navy and allied aircraft play their parts as well. As Moody Suter said in his Red Flag briefing, "We have to learn to fight as a team."[4]

Red Flag participants come from many airplanes and all the services. On the first day of a Red Flag, though, they share one common experience. As they enter the enormous building that is now the home of Red Flag, they walk past black, block letters on the wall beside the main entrance that simply say, SUTER HALL.

---

1. Joel T. Hall, interview with author, Las Vegas, Nevada, April 12, 1999.
2. *Ibid.*
3. Jack A. Lefforge, telephone interview with author, April 28, 1999.
4. Hall interview.

PART IV

KILLING THE TARGET

CHAPTER 12

✪

Mud Beaters

You'll believe a bomb can fly!

By the end of the Vietnam War, the U.S. Air Force was deeply committed to its love affair with laser-guided bombs, a fascination that continues today. The Air Force develops many ideas for weapons. Most never advance beyond the conceptual stage, a few reach the field as operational systems, but only a handful have an immediate and forceful impact on combat capability. Deadly lethal and relatively cheap, the LGB is a weapon superstar that has had an impact rarely seen in history.

The quest for precision bombing is nearly as old as aviation. Although World War I pilots started bombing by throwing weapons from their open cockpits, hoping that the bombs would explode close to the enemy, airmen soon began looking into ways to attain better accuracy. One of the most famous aiming devices developed during the years after World War I was the Norden bombsight. The Norden bombsight improved bombing accuracy but was by no means a precision device. During World War II, advances in radio control made it possible to develop the first true precision systems.

In his monograph, *The Quest for Surgical Strike, the USAF and Laser Guided Bombs,* David R. Mets tells the story of a German attack against an Italian navy ship, using an early precision-guided munition. Although Italy began the war as a German ally, by 1943 Italy had defected from the Axis, and its navy was in full retreat to escape the Luftwaffe. Mets writes that

> When the Germans decided that their Allies were defecting, they were ready with a special bomber unit temporarily based in Sardinia. The unit, led by Major Bernhard Jope, overtook the Italian Navy just south of Corsica. He approached at altitudes above 15,000 feet, safe from most antiaircraft fire. The Italians spotted the approaching Luftwaffe but only tardily recognized them as attackers. The Italian sailors went into the defensive tactics that had temporarily proved successful for the Japanese at Midway the previous year (throwing their rudders hard over), certain that most of the bombs coming down from high altitude could not hit a speeding target in a hard turn. Were the Germans to either dive on the *Roma* or descend for a torpedo attack, both sides knew that the problem for the Italian gunners would be greatly simplified. Neither the azimuth nor the elevation of the airplanes would be changing. All the gunners would have to do would be to hold their barrels steady and keep shooting until the attackers flew into the range of the projectiles.

But Jope's pilots did not descend. As soon as their weapons were released, they pulled back the throttles and extended the airplanes' flaps, and maintained their altitude. They did this because the weapon was no ordinary bomb. Rather, it was the "Fritz X," and it was necessary to get it out in front of the airplane so that the bombardier could see the flare in its tail. Once he had spotted it, he could then use a joystick, much like the one in small airplanes, to guide the bomb toward its target far below. Using his eyes as sensors, the bombardier could automatically send signals via radio merely by moving his stick. The receiver in the tail of the weapon passed these right-left-up-down instructions to the control surfaces of the bomb. Too, the bomb had a gyroscopic system that transmitted stabilizing signals to the control surfaces to prevent rolling.

The first Fritz launched at the twisting *Roma* was directed by Sergeant Oscar Huhn. It was necessary for the pilot to maintain nearly straight and level flight, although at 18,000 feet they were not all that vulnerable to the antiaircraft fire being put up by the ships. Even at its terminal speed of 625 mph, it would take the Fritz X the better part of a minute to make its descent. But for all the *Roma's* twisting and turning, it could not escape. Huhn radioed his instructions to the bomb, and it pursued the ship. Finally, at 1540 the bomb smashed into the foredeck of the battleship. The warhead was fabricated from an armor-piercing bomb, and the weight of the weapons exceeded 3,000 pounds. Since it needed a heavy metal casing to penetrate the armored decks of the battleship, only a fraction of that could be explosive. Necessarily, it had a delayed action fuze to permit the weapons to get inside the target before its 660 pounds of explosive detonated. The first Fritz went all the way through the *Roma* and detonated immediately beneath its hull, and the second one detonated within her vital spaces. A fire was started and much water was coming aboard. The situation was desperate, and the Italian sailors knew they would have to abandon their vessel. But the fire spread to the magazine too fast, and the explosion took her to the bottom with more than a thousand of her crew, including the admiral in command of the task force. Sergeant Huhn got the Iron Cross for his precision work.[1]

Despite the obvious utility of precision-guided munitions, efforts to develop better systems languished during the years between the wars in Korea and Vietnam as the Air Force focused its efforts on nuclear weapons and delivery systems for them. Research centers at Eglin Air Force Base, Florida, and Inglewood, California, concentrated on the development and improvement of intercontinental ballistic missiles and nuclear warheads. However, as national defense policy moved away from "massive retaliation" towards "flexible response," engineers began looking into ways to improve conventional weapons.

Efforts by Navy engineers produced two guided weapons that showed promise. The first was the Bullpup, a rocket-powered, radio-controlled monstrosity that weighed over a ton. Neither Air Force nor Navy pilots liked the

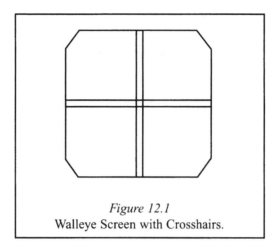

Figure 12.1
Walleye Screen with Crosshairs.

Bullpup when they used it in combat in Vietnam. Launching the missile was an adventure in itself. The huge rocket motor shook the cockpit floorboards as it rumbled away from the fighter, and the exhaust was infamous for snuffing out the jet's engine. Once the missile was clear of the shooter, the pilot had to steer it to the target by watching a flare in its tail and sending controlling signals by moving a small joystick in the cockpit in much the same manner as Sergeant Huhn had done with the Fritz X two decades earlier. During the time the pilot was guiding the missile, a process that could take nearly a minute, he had to focus all his attention on keeping it in sight and guiding it. This meant that he had no time for evasive maneuvering against enemy gunners who were intently trying to shoot him down. Finally, the Bullpup's warhead, designed to penetrate enemy ships, was not effective against the land targets in Vietnam.

Another weapon developed by the Navy and used by the Air Force, like the Bullpup, was the Walleye. The Walleye marked a change from early guided bombs because it featured a new technology, the optical tracker. A small television camera mounted inside a clear, glass dome on the nose of the Walleye gave the aircrew a black-and-white picture on their cockpit screens, while a cheap computer generated a tracking gate over the television picture. (Fig. 12.1)

The bomb's computer analyzed black-and-white contrast inside the small box formed by the crosshairs. In the case of an F–4 crew, the pilot pointed the bomb at the target, so that the WSO could see the target in the television picture. The crew moved the airplane in small increments, as directed by the WSO, until the target was exactly in the crosshairs. Then by pulling the stick trigger, they commanded the optical tracker to go into a self-track mode. Next they dropped the bomb, and it guided itself to the target. All of this is much easier said than done. The main problem with the Walleye was making sure it saw the target and not some other contrasting point within the small box, or gate. A perfect target might be a black building in a snowfield. When analyzing the contrast within the gate,

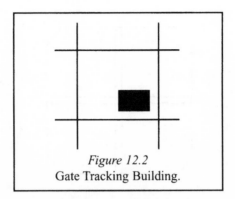

Figure 12.2
Gate Tracking Building.

the computer could easily distinguish where the edge of the contrast started and track that point. Figure 12.2 shows an expanded view of the gate and the black building in the snowfield.

Unfortunately, for the USAF and USN pilots, there were never enough black buildings on snowfields to attack. Against more typical target, the optical trackers fell victim to clutter, such as trees, bushes, other buildings, or billboards that the tracker might "glom onto." The most difficult clutter problem, however, was posed by target shadows. A small tan building in a brown grass field in the late afternoon might cast a long black shadow that the tracker liked a lot better than the building.

In addition to guidance problems, crews also discovered shortcomings in the explosive punch of the Walleye. Like the Bullpup, the Walleye warhead had been developed for attacking ships, and consequently its warhead was of marginal utility against land targets.

To remedy the problems that they found with the bombs developed by the Navy, the Air Force began its own program to produce a TV-guided bomb. Called the GBU–8 HOBOS (homing optical bomb system), it was built using an optical tracker mounted to the nose of a standard MK–84, 2,000-pound bomb body. The GBU–8 warhead was a great improvement, but getting the tracker locked to the proper point on the target proved just as difficult as with the Navy Walleye.

No matter how impressive these weapons appeared on paper or on the test ranges, their shortcomings were vividly revealed in the harsh reality of combat. On April 3, 1965, U.S. Air Force and Navy pilots began a campaign to drop the Thanh Hoa rail and highway bridge near Hanoi. This bridge was a main north-south thoroughfare leading out of Hanoi. Most of the men and equipment bound for South Vietnam crossed the bridge, making it an obvious target of great military importance. On that day, forty-six F–105s based in Thailand attacked the bridge with Bullpups and 750-pound bombs. Those Bullpups that guided successfully "bounced off" the bridge, and the standard bombs fared no better. When the dust cleared, the bridge still stood. Over the next three years, another 869 missions were flown against the bridge, with similar results, at the cost of eleven aircraft.[2]

Pave Way*

Coincident with the Thanh Hoa attacks a group of Air Force officers and Army scientists were trading information about a concept to guide Army artillery with laser beams. Col. Joseph Davis, Jr., from a small detachment at Eglin Air Force Base, had seen a laser demonstration and discussed the potential of using laser guidance for bombs with David J. Salonimer and Norman Bell from the U.S. Army Missile Command in Huntsville, Alabama. Salonimer got a small amount of Army money for Texas Instruments (TI) to develop a laser-guided rocket from an existing Air Force missile, the Shrike,† but the concept did not pan out. Davis, though, was impressed with the possibilities for a laser-guided bomb. He approached a TI engineer, Weldon Word, and asked him to draw up a plan to develop a laser guidance device for a bomb. He told Word that a plan for less than $100,000 could be approved without going through the Air Force's stifling bureaucracy. In the spring of 1965, Word came up with a hastily constructed development plan that would cost $99,000 over a six-month period.[3]

Another proposal was submitted from North American, but Colonel Davis liked the Texas Instruments plan because their solution was less complex. The TI concept, developed by aeronautical engineer Richard Johnson, proposed a guidance kit bolted to the nose of a standard Air Force bomb body with a stabilizing fins kit bolted to the tail. The guidance kit on the nose consisted of three main sections: a laser seeker, a guidance computer, and four small, movable canards, or wings. The idea was simple. An invisible laser beam shot at the target would reflect laser energy. The laser seeker on the nose of the bomb would focus the reflected laser energy through a small dome onto a laser sensor that was divided into two halves. Word and his team had neither the time nor the money to put a gyroscope in the bomb that would tell it if it was upside down or not, so they planned to let the bomb roll slowly as it flew toward the laser "spot" on the target. If the reflected laser energy were focused on one half of the sensor, then the computer would command the flight controls to correct in that direction. Since the bomb was rolling anyway, it really did not matter which way was up, down, left, or right; it just made corrections to keep the sensor centered. In order to keep the system simple, and cheap, the flight controls had only two positions, neutral and full deflection. Therefore, if the bomb needed to correct down, the flight controls deflected full down until the computer saw a need to correct up, and then the controls would deflect full up. Such a scheme is nicknamed "bang-bang" guidance because the controls bang from full deflection to neutral to full deflection.

---

* Pave is an acronym for precision avionics vectoring equipment. The initial laser-guided bomb program was nicknamed Pave Way, which finally became Paveway and is used to describe the entire family of laser-guided bombs. Other laser systems, such as the designator family, were nicknamed Pave Spike, Pave Tack, and Pave Nail.

†The Shrike was a missile designed to be fired at SAM radars. The missile could home in on the source of the radar and hit it—in military jargon, an antiradiation missile.

Fisheye view of maintenance workers of the 8th Tactical Fighter Wing at work on an F–4, readying it for combat. *Official USAF photo.*

Despite some problems with processing the reflected laser energy, the Air Force started dropping laser-guided bombs just six months after Word made his proposal. By May 1968 the Air Force was ready to try dropping LGBs in combat. However, President Lyndon B. Johnson ordered a bombing halt over North Vietnam before the system could be used in the war. During the next four years, the 8th Tactical Fighter Wing (TFW), Wolfpack, flying out of Ubon Royal Thai Air Base, Thailand, dropped the new bombs against any small, or "point," targets they could find—trucks, small bridges, antiaircraft guns, and choke points on roads along the Ho Chi Minh Trail running through Laos into South Vietnam.

The Wolfpack dropped the first LGB in combat on May 23, 1968, with guidance kits and fins bolted to World War II-vintage M–117 750-pound bombs. Statistically, the results were not impressive. The first two bombs missed their targets by wide margins. It is unclear why the first one missed, but the second attempt missed because the pilot did not drop it where the illuminator aircraft was aiming the laser. Such a breakdown in communications between the bomber and the illuminator, who had to circle the target in a left-hand turn to keep the spot on the target, were common. Nevertheless, the crews improved their procedures, and bombs started shacking the targets some of the time. Of the first thirty-five bombs dropped, the average miss distance was beyond that needed to destroy a truck, but in this case, the statistics about the accuracy of the bombs was misleading.

More than making up for the mediocre statistical average was the fact that half of the bombs were direct hits.[4] This was astounding to pilots accustomed to the difficulty of dropping manual dive bombs in the pressure cooker of combat, where a dive error of only two or three degrees meant a clean miss of the target. The implications of a system that would shack the target half the time were not missed at any level of the Air Force. With such results, a much smaller strike force could be sent into the battle, thus reducing risk and lowering losses dramatically. The planes could hit many more targets per bombing raid. The potential was unprecedented, and everyone knew it. Research and development engineers burned the midnight oil to improve on the Paveway system.

Pave Knife

The obvious shortcoming of the whole system was the Zot designator. The small black box mounted to an F–4 rear cockpit canopy rail was adequate to lase targets for the attackers, but the constant left turn at a steady altitude made the designating aircraft a sitting duck for antiaircraft fire and MiGs. Because the designator aircraft could not lase for its own bombs, there had to be precise timing and communication between the bomber and the designator aircraft to make sure the laser spot was on the target throughout the entire time the bomb was falling.

The answer to all these problems came to the combat crews in the form of a large, heavy pod, nicknamed Pave Knife. The pod was designed for carriage under the F–4 wing on a pylon normally used to carry bombs. Although it was bulky and slowed down the F–4, it had one feature that dramatically improved LGB capability: the designator was mounted in a gimbaled turret in the front of the pod. Also in the turret was a small television camera that sent a black-and-white picture to the WSO. By using his radar control handle as a joystick, the WSO could move the turret through the hemisphere beneath the aircraft. Therefore, crews could designate the target for their own bombs. The pilot rolled in on the attack pass and put his pipper on the target. As soon as the WSO saw the target in the TV picture, he took command of the pod and used his radar control handle to keep the aiming index for the laser on the target. The pilot then dropped the LGB in the same way as he would normally do in a dive bomb pass, while the WSO kept tracking the target. As the pilot pulled out of his dive, the turret continued to swivel underneath the jet as the WSO tracked the target until the bomb hit. Of course, the system could also be used to designate a target for other bombers as well. However, with the slewable Pave Knife pod, the designator aircraft was not restricted to a constant left-hand turn. The new system allowed the pilot to fly anyplace he needed as long as the hemisphere below his aircraft was facing the target.

Another improvement to the LGB system was the production of guidance kits that could be bolted to the newer MK–84, 2,000-pound bomb. The Mark series of bombs came in several weights, but the ones most commonly used by the Air Force were the MK–82 500-pound bomb and the much larger MK–84. The Mark series were more aerodynamic and therefore better suited for carriage on fighters like the F–4 and A–7. When the LGB kits were added to the 2,000-pound version, they added a tremendous punch, but the biggest punch of all came from "Fat Albert," a 3,000-pound LGB. Whenever a bomber dropped his LGB, he called "Bomb gone!" over the radio to the designator, so that the designator would know that he had to be precise in his tracking as the bomb guided. However, some crews, when dropping the 3,000 pounder, would call, "Hey! Hey! Hey! Fat Albert's on the way!" in the manner of Bill Cosby doing his popular routine of that time.

During the four-year bombing pause between Rolling Thunder and Linebacker, the members of the Wolfpack honed their skills, learned the new equipment, and waited for the opportunity to show what they could really do. In 1972, when President Richard M. Nixon resumed bombing of North Vietnam, they got their chance.

F–4Cs dropping bombs over North Vietnam. *Official USAF photo.*

On the morning of May 13, 1972, a strike force of Wolfpack F–4Ds, led by Capt. D. L. Smith, attacked the Thanh Hoa rail and highway bridge with nine laser-guided Fat Alberts, fifteen 2,000-pound LGBs, and forty-eight unguided MK–82 general purpose 500-pound bombs. In one clean, precise strike they did what hundreds of previous attacks had been unable to do—drop the Thanh Hoa bridge. Later, they put the Paul Doumer Bridge, which was an equally tough target on the route between Hanoi and China, into the water.[5] In a short time, the term "surgical strike" bubbled up in Pentagon and media accounts of the war as LGBs dropped thirteen more bridges in less than a month.

The aviators were not the only ones elated with the sensational performance of LGBs. Surgical strike meant more than just killing targets; it also meant that targets could be destroyed, while minimizing or even eliminating damage to politically sensitive areas near the target. On one raid, the Wolfpack destroyed a hydroelectrical generating plant on the Long Chi reservoir without damaging the dam. Before the LGBs, the power plant had been off limits because planners feared the dam would fall victim to stray bombs, triggering killer floods through civilian areas. No longer. Surgical strike, long hoped for by military men and politicians alike, was a reality.

Pave Spike and the Warsaw Pact

If there was one weapons system that emerged as a superstar from the frustration and agony of Vietnam, it was the laser-guided bomb. However, the weapon of choice for one war might not be the right choice for the next conflict. When tactical thinkers projected themselves into a potential clash with the Warsaw Pact forces, they saw that the LGB had some significant shortcomings.

The focus of planning for most fighter units in the United States Air Force was on the Fulda Gap, a low valley running between East and West Germany near the town of Fulda. Military thinkers saw the gap as the prime site for a Warsaw Pact armored thrust into Central Europe, and war planning focused on this vital area.

Indeed wargamers and tactical thinkers constantly put Fulda under their scenario microscope and examined it so closely that it would not be understatement to classify their diligent planning as an obsession.

The magnitude of the problem the NATO forces faced as they looked across the Iron Curtain was the root of this intensity. The Warsaw Pact outnumbered NATO forces in every category—fighters, bombers, soldiers, tanks, missiles, SAMs, mess kits, and pup tents. Along the forward edge of the battle area, where the Warsaw Pact forces would be in direct contact with the NATO defenders, the battle would be intense, with armor engaging armor, and a withering fire of mobile Pact SAMs and AAA overhead. Behind this first echelon, and stretching back over several kilometers, would come the second echelon forces pressing forward to support their engaged troops in the FEBA. Air defenses for the second echelon were thought to be less intense than those over the FEBA. Nevertheless, they were extremely formidable—much more sophisticated and lethal than the air defense system over North Vietnam. For example, while the North Vietnamese had the SA–2 SAM, a large, lumbering missile that was not difficult to see and outmaneuver, the Warsaw Pact had the latest Soviet equipment, including the SA–3 and SA–6, both of which were small, fast, maneuverable, and highly effective at low altitudes. Even worse, these new systems were very mobile, and thus the Warsaw Pact forces could move them frequently. They would be very hard for Wild Weasel hunter-killer teams to find.

Another major factor was the typically lousy weather in Europe. More than half the time the ceiling was less than 3,000 feet and/or the visibility less than three miles. Such poor weather was not even close to what the crews needed to deliver the LGB. For that matter, it was less than what they needed to deliver most of the types of ordnance available to them.

Throughout the 1970s, the burden of planning to stop Ivan's juggernaut from the air fell to the F–4 and its pilots and WSOs. Although the F–111 was present in small numbers, nearly every USAF fighter base in Europe, as well as those in the United States that would supply the badly needed follow-on forces, were equipped with a version of the Phantom.* Phantom crews trained for every conceivable mission: close air support for the Army in the FEBA, interdiction in the second echelon, airfield attack, air superiority, and nuclear strike when all else failed or if the Warsaw Pact upped the ante to total war. They had to be jacks-of-all-trades.

When the aviators viewed the Soviet system of overlapping fields of fire for their SAMs, MiGs, and AAA, as well as the poor weather, the only plausible way to stay alive was to go low—very low to fly under the Soviets' radar coverage to

---

* The F–4, in either squadron or wing strength, was based in the United Kingdom at Bentwaters, Woodbridge, Lakenheath, and Alconbury; in West Germany at Ramstein, Spangdahlem, Hahn, Bitburg, and Zweibruken; in Holland at Soesterberg; and in Spain at Torrejon.

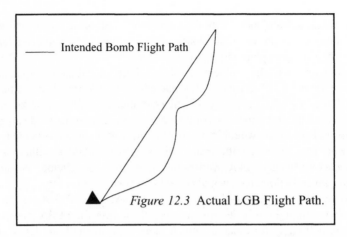

Figure 12.3 Actual LGB Flight Path.

avoid detection. Flying low was the easy part, because sooner or later someone had to kill the targets, and the LGB/Pave Knife system did not perform well at low altitude.

Although the LGB performed well when the bomb was dropped from medium altitudes and a steep dive, it had serious shortcomings at low altitude. From medium altitude, the bang-bang flight control system worked adequately because the bomb had plenty of energy to correct back to a collision course with the target. After the bomb made its first "down" correction, the added effect of gravity made it difficult for it to correct "up" to the line-of-sight to the target. Each subsequent down correction put the bomb further below its intended flight path. In addition, the full deflection of the control surfaces and their constant corrections slowed the bomb down as it fell, so it had less speed and, therefore, less ability to get back on course. If the bomb was below course just before impact, it hit short, where most of the misses occurred. (Fig. 12.3)

The sag of the bomb flight path below the intended flight path was even more exaggerated when the bomb was dropped from shallow dive angles and low altitude. Gravity became the bomb's worst enemy at low altitude by continually pulling it lower and lower. As it struggled to maintain its flight path, the bomb slowed down dramatically and sometimes stalled before it could get to the target. (Fig. 12.4)

Exacerbating the LGB low-altitude problem was the sheer size of the Pave Knife pod that had been used so successfully during Linebacker. The bulky pod performed well during dive deliveries and was usable at low altitude, but its tremendous size slowed the F–4's top-end speed and restricted maneuverability, both liabilities in the predicted dense defenses of the Warsaw Pact. Plus, the Pave Knife pod could only be carried on one of the three weapons pylons on the F–4, a pylon better used to carry a bomb.

Almost before the Pave Knife came on the scene, the Air Force was already at work on a better laser-designator pod, the third one in less than five years. The new pod was nicknamed Pave Spike, and it was much smaller, designed for carriage

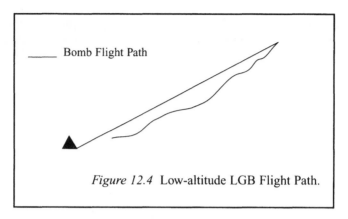

Figure 12.4 Low-altitude LGB Flight Path.

on the left, forward AIM–7 Sparrow missile station of the F–4. Because it was smaller and nestled into the semisubmerged Sparrow station, it did not restrict F–4 speed or maneuverability, nor did it occupy a precious weapons pylon. The F–4 still had three Sparrow stations in which it could carry the usual radar-guided missiles. Pave Spike, like Pave Knife, had a clear dome nose through which a television camera viewed the target area, and through which the laser could fire to designate the target. The entire nose assembly gimbaled to look throughout the hemisphere below the jet.[6]

Pave Spike and Low-altitude Attack

By 1976 the F–4 Fighter Weapons School squadron, the 414th FWSq at Nellis, was flying its F–4E fighters with the new Pave Spike pod and learning how to employ the system throughout its performance envelope. The pod was on the leading edge of technology for the day and had several operating modes and bombing options. Initially, the pod came with very sketchy operating instructions that were virtually useless to the often frustrated weapons school instructors. One instructor observed that he now had two complex operating systems to understand, and neither had come with an instruction book—his Pave Spike pod and his wife. Nonetheless, he continued, both were superb and well worth the effort.[7]

The main source of consternation proved to be the acquisition modes. The system offered the crew three options to acquire, or see, the target in the pod's television picture. In the most basic mode, the pod looked straight ahead, at the same location as the pilot's pipper on his gunsight. The pilot pointed the gunsight at the target, the WSO saw it in the TV picture, and, after taking command of the pod, tracked the target with his radar control handle. This mode was called 12-acquire or 12-vis because the pod looked at the visual point at the jet's 12 o'clock. A second acquisition mode was 9-acquire, or 9-vis. In this mode, the pod looked directly left of the aircraft at 9 o'clock. This mode enabled the crew to point the pod at the target before they rolled in on the attack if the target was on the left side of the airplane.* The third mode, weapons release computer system acquire, was at once the most useful and the most difficult to use because of its complexity. During their mission planning, the crew measured the distance between a point that was easy to find and their intended target. As they approached the target, the crew could fly over the preplanned point, whereupon the WSO pushed a button that commanded the pod to look directly at the target over the premeasured distance.

All of these modes were particularly useful if the crews planned to fly at low altitude to the target, then pop up to higher altitudes to drop their LGB. In fact, a proficient crew might plan to use all three, each one as a backup for the other, during the attack. As the attackers zipped toward the target, they would plan to have the target offset to their left side. First, they would fly over a known point and insert the WRCS offsets to slave the pod toward the target. Then, at a specific distance from the target, the pilot would select full afterburner and start a 20- or 30-degree climb, while visually scanning out the left side for the target. If the WRCS acquire worked perfectly, then the WSO would see the target in the picture. If not, and the pilot saw the target visually, he would tell the WSO to put the pod in 9-acquire to find the target. If that worked, fine, but if it did not, then the pilot would start a left roll in and put his pipper on the target, after telling the WSO to change acquisition modes again to the 12-acquire option.

Needless to say, the chance of double dribbling the switches during all these changes was very high. The crew had to know the system intimately and have their coordination and intercom calls down pat. At times, the pod seemed to have a mind of its own. If the crew activated one of several switches out of its proper sequence, the pod got confused and went into what the crews called the "idiot mode," in which it wandered aimlessly around the sky or ground waiting for a frustrated WSO or angry pilot to discover the error.

Despite the lack of technical manuals, and the pod's sometimes cantankerous performance, the Nellis crews at the 414th FWSq and the 422d Test and Evaluation Squadron gradually mastered Pave Spike and its quirks. In areas where the pod and its leading edge technology were lacking, they found simple accommodations. For example, there was no aiming reference out the left side of the airplane with which to point the pod when it was in 9-acquire, so the crews improvised. As they sat at the end of the runway before takeoff, the WSO would put the pod in 9-acquire so it was looking left of the airplane. The pilot looked at his TV picture to see where the pod was looking; then he would look through the left side of the canopy at the same point. With his left eye closed, he then drew a half-dollar-sized circle on the inside of the canopy around the point with a grease pencil. He then repeated the process with his right eye closed. When he opened

---

*At this point the reader might ask, "Don't they do anything in right-hand turns?" The answer: not unless they have to.

both eyes, the circles appeared as one black circle around the same point at which the pod was looking. Later, during the attack, with the pod in 9-acquire, he looked through the circles and flew the jet to superimpose them over the target, thus allowing the WSO to see the target in his TV picture. It was a five-cent fix to a multithousand-dollar problem.

Still, the problem of dropping LGBs from altitudes below enemy radar coverage and the weather persisted. Two improvements, one in the LGB and one in tactics, solved the problem and solidified the position of LGB attacks, even in the low-altitude arena.

The improvement to the LGB came in the form of a redesigned kit that bolted to the rear of the bomb. The original LGB, or LGB I, had large, immovable fins in the back to give it stability in flight. The fins were so large that the F–4 wing weapons pylons could carry only one bomb loaded directly to the pylon. The newer version, LGB II, had rear fins that folded together, thus decreasing the diameter of the assembly enough so that a triple ejector rack could carry two 500-pound LGB on the TER loaded to a weapons pylon. Thus, an option was available to the crews when they planned attacks. They could load one 2,000-pound LGB directly onto each wing pylon or four 500-pounders, two on the TERs under each wing. The guidance units at the front of the LGB II were improved as well. A better microchip processor improved the guidance logic and reduced mechanical failure. Also, a code was added to each bomb so that it would guide only on its designator's laser, and not on some other laser that might be designating a nearby target.[8]

The improvement in tactics came from the terminal guidance flight within the FWS. The TG flight taught the portions of the weapons school curriculum that focused on precision-guided munitions. Captains John Craig, Steve Heaps, Jack Sornberger, and Tim Kinnan developed a low-altitude loft delivery that was reliable and relatively easy to use. Loft deliveries were common in fighter tactics. In a loft delivery, the fighter flew low and fast toward the target until he was about five miles from it. Then, the pilot selected full power to maintain his speed, pulled up to a steep climb, and released his weapon. The weapon continued to climb, then arced over toward the target, while the fighter turned away and started his escape maneuver back down to low altitude. The bomb, depending on its size and weight, could travel about five miles during a loft delivery, so the maneuver was particularly effective when the weapon was a nuclear bomb. A loft was the least accurate of deliveries, but with a big enough warhead, miss distance was not much of a factor. The TG flight was experimenting with loft deliveries and the Pave Spike pod. They could loft an LGB from a few miles away, then designate the target as they turned away, in a slicing descent, to low altitude. The major disadvantage to the steep climb in the loft delivery, though, was the long time the airplane was exposed to enemy radars. Gradually, the instructors started moving the release closer and lower to the target, experimenting with shallower release angles and lower release altitudes. They used an automatic release feature in the WRCS to let the computer release the bomb at precisely the right moment.

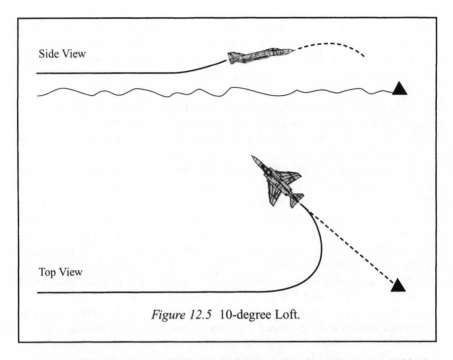

Figure 12.5 10-degree Loft.

They finally settled on a 10-degree loft, two miles from the target. With the pod in 12-acquire, the crew flew directly at the target at very low altitude. As soon as the WSO saw the target in his TV, he took command of the pod and started lasing the target. A cockpit indicator displayed exact laser range to the target, and, at precisely two miles from the target, the pilot depressed the pickle button and pulled sharply up. The computer would then release the bomb at 10 degrees of climb. The whole pull-up and release process took only two seconds. Immediately after the bomb came off, the pilot would start a 6-g turn away from the target and back to low altitude, while the WSO lased the target until the bomb hit. (Fig. 12.5)

After they had refined their tactic, the pilots and WSOs knew they had a delivery that they could do at low altitude, and not fly up into the enemy radars, or up into low ceilings that could befuddle the laser. Further, they did not have to overfly the target, a more dangerous path than the hard turn away. Since the delivery used only the 12-acquire mode, there was less chance of inadvertently putting the pod into its notorious idiot mode. However, there was a problem. It was still a low-altitude delivery even though they were lofting the bombs up a bit, and the LGB still had a tendency to hit short. They partially solved this problem by carrying four of the new, 500-pound LGB II with the folding rear wings. If one, or even two of the bombs hit short, there were still the others to shack the target.

In December 1978 the 414th FWSq got the opportunity to demonstrate how the Pave Spike pod and the new LGB could perform at low altitude. The Air

Force hosted a precision-guided munitions firepower demonstration for the secretary of defense to showcase improvements in precision munitions. Of course, USAF officials did not want any chance of a miss in this very important demonstration, so they initially requested that the 414th FWSq drop via a medium-altitude diving LGB delivery. After a flurry of messages among the Pentagon, TAC, and Nellis, the fighter pilots' desire for a more realistic delivery prevailed. Capt. John Craig, the resident LGB/Pave Spike expert, and his WSO, Capt. Brad Spires, led the mission, and their wingman was Capt. Tim Kinnan and his WSO, Capt. Steve Heaps.[9] Their target was a large fuel tank, partially filled with condemned jet fuel, located at a safe distance from the reviewing stands occupied by the secretary of defense and his entourage. When Craig and Spires screamed across the desert toward the target, they took most viewers by surprise. Before the audience could recover, the quick loft of the four LGBs was over, and the flight was already heading away. All four bombs shacked the fuel tank in an enormous black-and-red fireball. Most doubts about the viability of the LGBs and Pave Spike for combat in a low-altitude war against the Warsaw Pact vanished like the two Phantoms disappearing over a nearby ridgeline.*

Newer Systems

Even though Pave Spike was a good system, it had one insurmountable short-fall—it was suited for use only during periods of good visibility during the daytime. At night, in haze, or in bad weather, the pod was virtually useless. The answer came in the form of Pave Tack, a pod that used imaging infrared (IIR) to produce a TV picture for the crew. The technology of the 1970s, however, was unable to produce a small IIR pod, and the Pave Tack was even bigger than the Pave Knife pod the Wolfpack had carried to the Thanh Hoa Bridge. Making matters worse, Pave Tack, when its turret was out during bomb deliveries, was even bigger and produced enormous drag that slowed the F–4 at the most critical time— in the target area. Only a few F–4s were modified to carry the IIR Pave Tack pod, and finally the Air Force gave up on building them for the Phantom. However, the F–111, a medium bomber, could carry the pod partially submerged in its bomb bay. Even when the pod was swiveled out for lasing, the large, powerful F–111 did not feel the drag in the same way as an F–4. Pave Tack and the F–111 made a good marriage. The Air Force soon redistributed most of the big pods from grateful F–4 units to eager F–111 squadrons.

Surgical strike is a tremendous capability for any armed force to provide its national leadership, and the U.S. military went through several kinds of systems

---

* A third jet, flown by Maj. Robert Tone and Capt. R. T. Newell, was positioned directly behind the two primary jets as a spare in case either of the lead airplanes had a mechanical problem.

before Colonel Davis and his associates started the laser-guided bomb effort with $99,000 in 1965. The concept was so successful that in less than twenty years, the Air Force developed five different designators and three versions of LGB that were fielded in large numbers. Skeptics, as well as some old school pilots who thought manual dive bombing was the only reliable way to get the job done, soon saw the truth in the opening visual graphic of laser-guided bomb academics at the FWS. When the students entered the classroom for the first day of LGB class, they saw a large, overhead projection slide on the screen. That showed a painting done for the author by Blake Morrison, the school's aviation artist who did graphics for the *Fighter Weapons Review*. Morrison's watercolor was an artistic parody of the then-popular advertising slogan for the movie *Superman*. It showed an LGB in flight toward the target, complete with a red cape flying in the wind. Beneath the bomb were the red and gold words "You'll believe a bomb can fly."

---

1. David R. Mets, *The Quest for a Surgical Strike, the United States Air Force and Laser Guided Bombs*, Office of History, Armament Division, Air Force Systems Command, Air Force Historical Research Agency (AFHRA), Maxwell AFB, Alabama, 1987, roll 41349, frame 0010.

2. Shelby G. Spires, "Guiding Light," *Air and Space*, April/May 1999, Vol. 14, No. 1, p. 66.

3. *Ibid.*, pp. 66–68.

4. History, Headquarters Pacific Air Forces, Summary, "Air Operations, Southeast Asia," HQ PACAF/DO, July 29, 1968, AFHRA, Maxwell AFB, Alabama, roll 44218, frame 0289.

5. Spires, p. 73; Mets, p. 87, frame 0102.

6. Technical Order 1F–4E-1, Flight Manual, USAF series F–4E aircraft, published under authority of the Secretary of the Air Force, October 2, 1979, pp. 5–34, fig. 5–10.

7. Gen. John P. Jumper, interview with author, Ramstein AB, Germany, February 27, 1999.

8. Mets, frame 0113.

9. Maj. Gen. Timothy A. Kinnan, interview with author, Springfield, Virginia, February 19, 1999.

CHAPTER 13

✪

Maverick: Love It or Hate It

We had the first combat kill of a tactical bush.[1]

Even though the LGB showed tremendous promise for precision guidance, the Air Force did not abandon its efforts to develop a TV-contrast tracking system like the type used in the HOBOS and the Navy Walleye. Those systems recorded the edge of contrast in their tracking gates, so besides being vulnerable to breaking lock and going stupid, they were inherently somewhat inaccurate. That inaccuracy was usually insignificant when attacking a large building with a 2,000-pound warhead, but it was an enormous problem when attacking one of the Warsaw Pact's primary threats—tanks. Killing a tank from the air is no easy task. A 500-pound LGB required a direct hit to kill one. A fifteen-foot miss might dust it off, possibly damage it, maybe give the crew inside a mild case of tinnitus, but the tank would still be usable. Of course, the same miss with a 2,000-pound LGB was a different story, but an F–4 could carry only two of them. The Air Force needed a way to destroy many tanks on every mission. NATO's worst nightmare was a steady stream of Warsaw Pact armor plunging through the Fulda Gap.

By the early 1970s the Air Force and Hughes Aircraft Company had developed and started to produce a weapon to do the job of killing large numbers of armor. It was the AGM–65A Maverick, a TV-guided, rocket-powered missile that carried a shaped-charge warhead that could penetrate even the thickest Soviet armor like a high-powered rifle through a padlock. An F–4 could carry six of the missiles in clusters of three under each wing. Like earlier optical trackers, Maverick carried a small black-and-white TV camera in its nose that presented a picture to the fighter crew.* However, the tracker was a centroid type that could expand and contract with target size. While at rest, the missile looked straight ahead in the same place as the gunsight pipper. When the F–4 pilot put his pipper on the target, the WSO took control of the TV camera in the Maverick and moved the tracking gate over the target with his radar control handle. When the WSO commanded lock on, the tracking gate would expand to track the center of the contrast, whereupon the pilot launched the missile and started his escape maneuver.

As the missile streaked toward the target, the centroid tracking gate expanded to maintain the target perfectly centered, and its accuracy was incredible, if not

---

* At first, Maverick was fitted to only the F–4 and A–7.

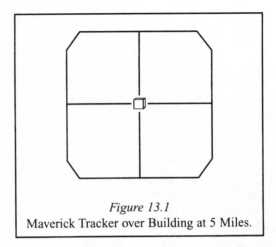

Figure 13.1
Maverick Tracker over Building at 5 Miles.

legendary.* Essentially, there was little or no miss distance. Even more impressive than the accurate guidance was the warhead performance. The warhead fuze functioned as soon as the nose of the missile touched the target so that the warhead detonated a few inches from the armored surface. The interior of the warhead was shaped to produce a superheated, hypersonic punch directly focused on the target. The results devastated a tank, rendering it a useless pile of junk in one bright flash.

The first crews to use Maverick in combat were the handpicked Rivet Haste crews who flew the newest, slatted wing, F–4E to Udorn, Thailand, just in time for the start of Linebacker II in 1972. Those newest F–4s contained the wiring and other equipment needed to employ Maverick. Capt. Hugh Moreland and his WSO, Capt. Ken Kenworthy, shot their first Maverick in combat at a truck on a road during Linebacker. The hit nearly vaporized the vehicle, and they flew home congratulating themselves on succeeding with one pass what might have taken several with dumb bombs. After they landed, however, their euphoria evaporated as quickly as the truck had. They got a severe ass chewing from their commander for shooting a $25,000 missile at a $500 truck. The next day the general commanding all Air Force efforts in Southeast Asia directed that the Mavericks would be fired only at tracked vehicles and storage caves.[2]

The training that Moreland and the other Rivet Haste crews had at Nellis taught them that Maverick, as accurate and devastating as it was, had some limitations, and the firings they made in combat brought home those lessons.

---

* Hughes Aircraft had produced the Falcon air-to-air missile a decade earlier. The Falcon, a heat-seeker, was very accurate. However, it had a small warhead and had to hit the target to explode, whereas other missiles had influence fuzes that detonated at the point of closest approach. Hughes drew on its experience with the Falcon guidance and autopilot to produce the Maverick.

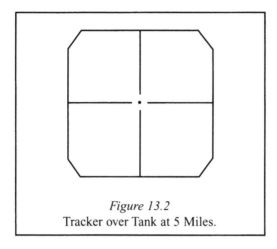

Figure 13.2
Tracker over Tank at 5 Miles.

The biggest problem was target size; the target had to be large enough for both the pilot and the video camera to see it. Small targets such as tracked vehicles were not easy to see from a jet whistling along at 500 mph. During the original Maverick tests in 1970, a test crew made several passes before the pilot could see the small armored personnel carrier that was their target. Finally, their fuel was so low that they had to return to their base with the unexpended Maverick under the wing and, presumably, their tails between their legs.[3]

Once the pilot spotted the target, he had to get close enough for the tracking gate to see the target. Some advocates touted Maverick's long-range ability, but for small targets, the crew had to get close. For example, if they wanted to shoot a building (Fig. 13.1), the missile tracker was capable of locking on and tracking from several miles away. However, from that same distance, a tracked vehicle was very small: too small (Fig. 13.2).

Not only were tank targets too small to shoot at long standoff ranges, but there was also the problem of clutter, such as unwanted shadows and foliage, in the tracking gate along with the target. One of the Rivet Haste crews had the problem graphically demonstrated to them when they launched a Maverick at what they thought was an enemy tank, only to have the missile obliterate a large leafy bush near the target. They jokingly referred to it as a tactical bush, but the point was clear—in order to kill small targets with the Maverick, they had to get close to their work.[4]

Videotape and Learning

One advantage the Rivet Haste crews had over all other Air Force fighters of the day was a video recording system. Their new F–4E carried a video recorder in a previously unused area in the spine of the jet directly behind the rear cockpit. A panel there, Door 19, covered a small empty space into which maintenance crews placed a reel-to-reel video recorder. The recorder taped everything the crews saw on their scopes, radio calls into and out of the jet, and the words the pilot and WSO said to each other on the intercom.

Each time they made a Maverick pass, they recorded it for later playback in the mission debriefing. It was as revolutionary as the gun cameras had been. They could see immediately where they had gone wrong, such as locking onto the tactical bush. By analyzing each attack, they learned the system very fast: how the tracker could slip onto a shadow nearly unnoticed; how to adjust the brightness and contrast efficiently for different visibility conditions; what distance from the target to start the pass so they did not spend vulnerable moments pointing at it from a range where lock on was not possible. They established rules of thumb for target size and launch ranges that made them much more efficient.

Maverick at Nellis

At the same time the terminal guidance flight at the F–4 weapons school was cranking up their Pave Spike training program, they were doing the same with Maverick. The Rivet Haste experience provided a baseline, and, soon, the missile was an integral part of the curriculum.

Nellis proved to be the perfect environment for learning the system. Nearly every day was clear with no restrictions as to visibility. If the pilot could see a target, the missile could as well. Tanks on the desert were much easier to see and track with the missile than were the enemy armored vehicles in the jungles of Vietnam.

Realistic training were the buzzwords, and the Air Force produced a training version of Maverick called the TGM–65A. The TGM was an actual nose section mounted on a dummy body that had neither warhead nor rocket motor. In the cockpit, the crew had exactly the same switches to throw and TV presentations as when they were carrying a real missile. Coupled with the audio-visual tape recorder (AVTR) machines that were added to all weapons school airplanes, the TGM provided a nearly perfect learning situation. The only thing missing was the actual whoosh of a missile coming off the jet at launch.

It was not long before that problem had a solution as well. When the Air Force contracted with Hughes to produce Maverick, farsighted planners included an incentive firing plan (IFP) in the contract. Under the incentive plan, the Air Force would shoot fifty missiles a year. If 90 percent hit the target, Hughes received a bonus. Nellis was allocated the lion's share of the incentive plan missiles, and soon every student attending the weapons school was shooting a live Maverick as part of the curriculum. Whenever the students were shooting, Hughes sent a representative to Nellis to observe the briefings and debriefings and to look at the videotape after each mission. TG flight instructors gave the students free rein to shoot the missiles as they thought they would shoot them in combat. Since most, if not all, viewed the European low-altitude scenario as their most likely next war, they planned a low, fast ingress with a quick pop over a ridgeline and less than five seconds of wings-level time to get the missile off. Since their targets were tank hulks in the desert, all the aim points were small and required exquisite timing and skill with the missile to succeed. At each of the firings the Hughes representative stood by nervously, wincing uncomfortably as the student crews planned their attacks with total disregard for the money at stake to the manufacturer. He need not have worried. During every year of the incentive plan, at least 90 percent of the missiles shacked their targets and Hughes got its bonus.[5]

The success of Maverick firings at Nellis was even more remarkable when another fact is considered: many of the F–4 students who came to Nellis had never used the missile. Not every unit had Maverick as a wartime tasking. For those who did, the aircraft modification to carry it moved along slowly. Thus, for many students, their first hop with the missile was during the three-ride Maverick portion of the program. All students flew in the rear cockpit for the first ride, so that WSOs and pilots alike could learn the intricacies of taking command of the missile, slewing the TV camera, and locking on to the targets. On the second ride, they learned formations and tactics. On the third, they fired the live missile on their first pass.

Clearly, they quickly learned the skills needed, and several factors were at play. The TG flight built the training program using a building block approach. They taught basic skills first, then gradually increased the complexity, but never progressed until the student demonstrated that he could accomplish the task at hand. Again, it is important to understand that this was not always the case in other training situations. The old attitude was to give credit if the student attempted the task and let him move on; there was plenty of time for him to get good at it later. This kind of training philosophy worked when pilots were flying forty hours a month before Vietnam, but after the war, when they were flying less than fifteen hours a month, it was a recipe for disaster. To the weapons school instructors, the important issue was not to push a student beyond his ability, but to carefully teach him every step of the learning process.

On the first Maverick mission with the training missile, all students flew in the rear cockpit. Instructors in the front seat started the mission by pointing at large targets, while flying slowly to teach the basics of switch movement and locking the tracker to the proper point on the target. As the student improved, the instructor picked smaller targets and flew faster, so that the student had to work faster to get the missile off before they flew inside minimum range. Then they started doing multiple launches, where they fired at two, then three, different targets on the same pass. Finally, the instructor flew them through the "Run for the Roses." The TG flight had set up a series of targets in a long, winding, slalom course through the range. As soon as one target or series of targets was shot, the instructor would pull off, and immediately another run would start. All the targets were different sizes and shapes. Altogether the run took about ten minutes of intense, high-speed, high-g maneuvering. After the mission, and its climax with the run, the students dragged themselves, exhausted and soaked with sweat, from the cockpit. However, the mission was not over. In the debriefing rooms

A–10 Thunderbolt II
firing its cannon.
Official USAF photo.

they got to see again every single pass, lock on, and shot on videotape and learn
what they had done right, what they had done wrong, and how to do it better
the next time.[6]

Yeah, but...

There was no question that Maverick worked well against targets in the unlimited visibility and high contrast of the Nevada desert. However, critics continually
pointed to the lousy weather and rugged terrain in Europe and predicted that the
missile would fail on the real battlefields. It was a difficult task for a pilot to find
tanks, let alone attack them from a couple of miles away. Maverick advocates
argued that tanks on the move toward Fulda would be much easier to spot in
enough time to line up, lock on, and shoot Maverick. Advocates further argued
that Maverick's devastating warhead was the only weapon that could consistently
kill armor. The next best weapon was Rockeye, a cluster bomb that dispensed 247
small armor-piercing bomblets over a football-field-size area. Rockeye, though,
had plenty of shortcomings of its own. The bomblets spread in a thin pattern that
put only one in each ninety square feet, and its warhead, although a shaped charge,
was about the size of a hand grenade. Plus, it was very difficult to deliver accurately because the pilot had to aim nearly fifty feet upwind for every knot of wind.
With all these shortcomings added together, a pilot could get the same result from
two Maverick passes as he would get with over thirty passes with Rockeye.

Nevertheless, some thought that the best thing said about Maverick was that
it was the least of all evils. As the controversy boiled among the crews, the Air
Force was producing two new versions of Maverick. The first, the AGM–65B,
featured a magnification of the scene in the TV camera; therefore, it was nicknamed the Scene Mag. The idea was to make the small tank-size targets bigger
in the video. It was an improvement, but not much of one.

In 1977 the 422d Test Squadron crews took the missile to Europe to test it and
the Scene Mag version in the actual glop of European flying weather.[7] The TV
version was unimpressive. However, they also had with them a third version of the

missile, the AGM–65D. The newest version had a standard Maverick body, warhead, and rocket motor, but in its nose was an imaging infrared sensor. The sensor was able to detect very small temperature differentials, and a processor turned those differences into a TV picture that the missile sent to the cockpit. The picture was a little blurry on the edges of objects under some conditions, but it gave the crew an impressive IIR view of the world. Even a tank driving along a highway has several temperature differentials among the treads, the body, the engine, the sunny side, and the shady side. The IIR produced a TV picture that was nearly identical in detail to a standard video picture. However, the IIR could do it in haze and smoke, and, even more importantly, at night. It would be several years before the IIR Maverick would enter the fighter inventory, but tests with it in the mid-1970s gave fighter crews a glimpse of a new and promising capability: night attack.

Taking to the Road

Lt. Col. Larry Keith, commander of the F–4 weapons school, had a vision of the role of the school. One of his goals was realized when the watershed issues of the *Fighter Weapons Review* laid the foundation for the building block approach to structured training. Another of his goals was to find ways for his instructors to get away from Nellis to fly and teach F–4 crews at their home bases. The advent of the new Pave Spike and Maverick systems provided just such an opportunity. During a four-year period from 1976 to 1980, instructors from Nellis traveled to every F–4 base in the Air Force to teach terminal guidance academics and to fly those systems with the operational F–4 crews.

Many critics chastised the weapons school for living in an ivory tower with no feel for the problems operational units faced. They believed that Nellis had the best crews, the best jets, the best weather, the best targets, and the best ranges. Of course, tactics worked at Nellis, they charged, Nellis does not have to deal with poor weather and ranges and inexperienced aircrews.

One of the most contentious issues was the low-altitude, line-abreast formation that the Nellis instructors flew. More than one general, thinking it dangerous, refused to let his command use the formation. One, who initialed some of his memos WGFP, for world's greatest fighter pilot, could not see how the aircraft could turn without running into each other. Keith sent two of his best instructors, Jumper and Capt. Ron Keys, to brief the general. In preparation for the confrontation, the young officers spent hours computing turn paths for every conceivable circumstance, drawing each situation carefully on graph paper, second by second, to prove to the general that a midair collision was highly improbable. After an hour of discussion, the general finally acknowledged that they might be right.[8]

During the TG road shows, the instructors taught every aspect of each system directly to the crews. Usually, the two-week deployment started with an academic session for all pilots and WSOs in an auditorium. In these sessions, the instructors explained how each step would be learned in sequence and how no aviator would be pushed to go to an advanced step until he had mastered the basics. Flying started the next day, and the instructors usually focused their efforts on training a few crews, who would then train the rest of their squadron mates.

The benefits from those training road shows were many. They gave the unit a solid training program from the first day that saved the units from making the same mistakes others had made from ignorance about the system. Also, the training visits were two-way streets. The Nellis instructors, never short on ego and opinions, learned that each base indeed had problems in training for which compensations had to be devised. Sometimes the problem was a commander who was more interested in not losing a jet than in combat capability. Some units had no reserved airspace where they could maneuver freely at low altitude. The Nellis instructors quickly learned that the perfect environment for learning they had at Nellis was unique and that despite their high ideals, compromise was a necessity.

By the end of the 1970s, Maverick and Pave Spike tactics and systems were a mature part of the F–4 fleet. For those units tasked with a TG system, it was old hat to fly line abreast at low altitude without using the radio to call their turns and to do a "Run for the Roses" exercise with Maverick.

---

1. Col. Hugh Moreland, USAF (Ret.), telephone interview with author, March 4, 1999.

2. *Ibid.*

3. Letter, HQ 4900th Test Group, Kirtland AFB, New Mexico, to FTCC, October 21, 1970, AFHRA, Maxwell AFB, Alabama, roll 39957, frame 0665.

4. Moreland interview.

5. Bob Wilson, interview with author, Las Vegas, Nevada, June 15, 1999.

6. Gen. John P. Jumper, interview with author, Ramstein AB, Germany, February 27, 1999.

7. Multi-Service Test and Evaluation, Maverick, Combat Hunter Phase III, Final Report, September 1972, AFHRA, roll 30452, frame 216.

8. Jumper interview.

CHAPTER 14

❂

Shooting Missiles

It takes fourteen consecutive miracles to get a drone into the air and a missile to hit it.[1]

Although Nellis was an exciting hub of tactics and training, it was not the only place that could lay claim to innovative thinkers and programs that increased fighter lethality. Since the 1950s, pilots had participated in a program of air-to-air missile firings over the Gulf of Mexico, where the Air Force controlled over 10,000 square miles of reserved airspace. The missile firing program went by several names over the years—Combat Pike, Combat Echo, Combat Archer—but the general program under which it fell was the weapons system evaluation program (WSEP).

WSEP was the key part of an effort to increase the lethality of the three major components of an air-to-air system: the pilot, the aircraft, and the missile. Pilots flew aircraft from their home bases to Eglin Air Force Base, Florida. After the jets landed, WSEP maintenance crews put the jets and their radars, launch rails, computers, and fire control systems (FCS)* through a rigorous inspection. Meanwhile, other WSEP technicians worked on missiles selected at random from worldwide storage locations. They removed the warheads from these missiles and installed a telemetry package in the emptied spaces. The missile was then turned over to loading crews from the visiting unit, who loaded the missile on their fighter. The pilot then took off and shot the missile at a target drone over the Gulf.

WSEP technicians evaluated every step of the process. If they discovered a fault in the missile or any aircraft system, it was recorded into the database of that aircraft or missile. If the load crew made an error in loading the missile, that error also went into the database. Chase pilots followed the shooter from takeoff to landing. If the shooter fumbled his switches or shot out of parameters, the chase pilot duly recorded the error. The telemetry package in the missile transmitted data on the missile's performance throughout the mission, including the critical parameters, during its streak toward the target drone. After the mission, other WSEP analysts pored over every detail to insure that everything slated for the database was accurate and complete.[2]

As the WSEP program progressed, trends started to emerge from the huge database, and technicians proposed changes to a missile, or an entire fire

---

* The FCS is a general term for the whole aircraft system that controls missile launch.

control system, to improve performance. It was this last step, the improvement process, that proved to be the best value in WSEP.

As discussed earlier, missile performance in the skies over North Vietnam was awful. The Air Force started a WSEP program at Clark Air Base, the Philippines, called Combat Sage, as part of the effort to improve results. Data from the Gulf of Mexico firings and ones in the Philippines, combined with pilot reports from combat, led to several new missile types in a few short years. The original AIM–9B Sidewinder, the heat-seeker most employed in combat, was blunt nosed and did not maneuver well. Its design purpose was to shoot down nonmaneuvering, large nuclear bombers headed for American shores, and it did not perform well against the small, agile MiGs flown by the North Vietnamese. Based on data from WSEP and combat firings, the Sidewinder went through several modifications until the AIM–9J emerged in the last days of the war. That newest version featured an aerodynamic nose and redesigned wings that greatly improved the missile's ability to hit the agile MiGs, especially at lower altitudes. Also, the guidance of the AIM–7 Sparrow, the F–4's radar-guided missile, was significantly changed as a result of the lessons learned from the database and combat firings.

Despite WSEP efforts, neither aircraft nor missile reliability improved towards the end of the war or in the years immediately after. During one typical deployment to the Gulf missile ranges, one F–4 unit arrived in 1975 with fewer than a third of its aircraft fully mission capable for the air-to-air mission. Crew performance was nearly as bad. Only half of the crews were able to complete the mission profile by firing their AIM–7 head-on to the drone and then maneuvering to a position behind it, where they could shoot their AIM–9.[3] Such poor performance only served to confirm the results Bill Kirk's team found during their tour of U.S. bases and the testing results they saw there.

As part of Tactical Air Command's efforts to improve combat capability, an effort that included the Aggressor squadrons and the Red Flag exercises, TAC put on the full court press to improve aircraft, missile, and aircrew reliability. Over the next two years, the missile allocation for WSEP firings tripled, and evaluations and training became more realistic for the participating aircrews.[4]

The major obstacles to realistic combat missile firings were the drone targets. The primary target was the BQM–34 Firebee, a little drone with a wingspan of only six feet. To make it show up on fighter radars like an aircraft, the drone carried a radar reflector built into its nose, but the small size of the Firebee made it difficult for pilots to see and maneuver against it for a Sidewinder shot. In addition, the little drone carried only a small fuel load, so it could not stay airborne long enough to service more than one or two shooters per drone mission, and it was restricted to subsonic speeds.

The answer to these problems came in a program to convert old fighter aircraft into target drones. The first one to be converted was the F–102, an interceptor jet that had gone out of service. Technicians under contract added radio receivers and other equipment to the cockpit of the F–102, so that pilots on the ground could fly it by remote control.*

Although the WSEP shooters staged out of Eglin, the drone operation was based at Tyndall Air Force Base, fifty miles east of Eglin and also on the Gulf Coast. The Firebee was launched from a rail out over the water, but the PQM–102, as it was known after it became a drone, had to take off and land on a regulation runway. The effort to get a full-scale drone airborne was complex. The operators stationed a large van at the end of the runway. On top of the van were two control stations, one for pitch and another for roll. They then parked the PQM–102 pointing straight down the runway, locked its brakes, started the engine, and closed the canopy. The pilots in the van, acting as a team, released the brakes, lit the afterburner, and guided it down the runway to liftoff. When it got high enough for its radio signals to be seen by other pilots in a control facility a few miles away, the pilots in the building took control of it and flew it to the Gulf ranges. There they put it through its paces while shooters launched their Sparrows and Sidewinders at it.

Usually, the PQM–102 survived the shots because the missiles had had their warhead teeth pulled in trade for the telemetry package. Nonetheless, missiles sometimes made direct hits that ripped holes through the drone. After all the shooters had expended all their missiles, a chase pilot joined up with the drone and inspected it for damage that might make it unsafe to attempt a landing. If the drone was safe to recover, the pilots in the building flew it back to the runway to a point where the van pilots could see it. The drone approached the runway with its landing gear and flaps down, as well as its arresting hook. The hook was very similar to ones used to arrest Navy aircraft landing on a carrier. The van pilots, one controlling pitch and the other roll, then landed it on the runway and guided it straight down the runway for a few hundred feet until the arresting hook snagged a cable strung across the runway. It was a touchy procedure, flying a fighter by remote control, and several were lost, most of them in the landing phase.

The process was complex and expensive compared to Firebee operations. Therefore, most WSEP shots continued to be made against the Firebees. However, the data gained from shooting at real fighter targets was invaluable.

WSEP was not the only organization that shot at the full-sized or full-scale drones, as they came to be known. Research and development organizations in the Air Force planned their efforts around shooting at these realistic targets whenever possible. A missile that missed a Firebee by a few feet might have been a hit against a full scale drone. The PQM–102 could fly more than twice as long as the

---

* The Air Force does not destroy all aircraft that reach the end of their serviceable life spans; most are flown to a facility outside Tucson, Arizona, where they are mothballed. The boneyard there holds several square miles of old aircraft parked wing to nose, awaiting a day to be reborn or be salvaged for spare parts.

small drone, thereby giving pilots many more shooting opportunities per mission. Since the PQM–102 retained most of the performance characteristics of the F–102, its speed and turning ability gave pilots an opportunity to shoot a missile at a target that approximated what they would see in combat.

In 1976 the Air Force built a special drone runway at Tyndall in a remote section of the base.[5] The end of the runway came nearly to the edge of the Gulf, so that drone takeoffs went out over the water and were recovered from over the water. By 1977 drone control systems were so improved that the controllers could fly two of them in any formation the mission scenario dictated.[6]

The supply of old F–102s was not limitless, and Tyndall took delivery of its last PQM–102 on February 24, 1982. Its replacement was the venerable F–100 in its drone version as the QF–100. The "Hun," a frontline fighter of the 1950s and 1960s, had built an impressive record in South Vietnam in its role as a close support aircraft. Many Army combat veterans recall it screaming over their heads while they were attacking enemy troops. By 1991, though, the ones that survived years of combat were all at the bottom of the Gulf of Mexico, and the third full-scale drone, the QF–106, had taken its place.

During the years of the QF–106, remarkable control system improvements greatly increased the ability of the drone flyers to provide realistic targets. The gulf range drone control upgrade system (GRDCUS) made it possible to fly four drones simultaneously. Drone controllers could fly them either independently or in any formation. Further, the addition of radio relay aircraft posted outside the range made it possible for the controllers to fly the drones at low altitude. Essentially, any scenario the shooters wanted, the drone controllers of the 82d Aerial Targets Squadron at Tyndall could give them.

In 1995 the first replacements for the QF–106 arrived on the ramp at Tyndall. Fittingly, it was a drone version of the venerable Vietnam warhorse, the F–4.

---

1. Source unknown; a common joke among those who control the highly complex world of target drones.

2. History, Tactical Air Warfare Center, Combat Echo, WSEP Profile report, 7 July 1975–19 September 1975, Air Force History Research Agency (AFHRA), Maxwell AFB, Alabama, roll 31584, frame 0004.

3. *Ibid.*, frame 0008.

4. History, Tactical Air Warfare Center, Combat Echo, 1977, AFHRA, Maxwell AFB, Alabama, roll 33413, frame 1274.

5. History, Air Defense Weapons Center, 1 July 1976–30 September 1976, AFHRA, Maxwell AFB, Alabama, roll 32828, frame 0006.

6. History, Air Defense Weapons Center, 1 April 1977–1 July 1977, AFHRA, Maxwell AFB, Alabama, roll 32566, frame 0839.

PART V

RETICLES TO HUDS
THE NEW FIGHTERS

CHAPTER 15

✪

The Eagle

When I checked out in the F–15, I had over 2,000 hours in the F–4, 365 combat hours, and two tours as a fighter weapons school instructor. On my seventh or eighth F–15 flight, I remember thinking, "Damn! I'm just learning how to fly this jet, and I'm already more lethal in it than I ever was in the F–4!"

Although some observers accused the Air Force leadership of being asleep at the switch in terms of fighter training and tactics during the Vietnam War, Pentagon officials were working hard on the new aircraft that would become the next generation of fighters even as the fighting raged in Southeast Asia. The first of the new jets to come off the drawing boards was the F–15 Eagle, followed quickly by the A–10 Thunderbolt II and the F–16 Falcon.

The new jets, especially the F–15, epitomized decades of lessons learned in the bloody skies over Germany, Korea, and Vietnam. Survey after survey of combat pilots in Vietnam revealed broad agreement on what they needed to fight and win in the unforgiving arena of air combat: more thrust, improved maneuverability, perfect cockpit visibility, a powerful radar, long-range missiles, an internal gun, cockpit switches that were easy to find, and the sole mission of air superiority— no bombs. Further, they wanted all this packed into the smallest airframe possible. After years of flying the biggest fighters in the battle, the F–105 and the F–4, they were tired of losing to jets that always saw them first. Oh, by the way, they would add, we want engines that do not leave the Phantom's long, black smoke trails that point directly to our position.

When the first squadron of F–15s was formed in 1974 at Luke Air Force Base, Arizona, fighter pilots throughout the Air Force were amazed to find that the new jet had nearly everything they wanted. Except one thing. It was not small. In fact, it was huge by fighter standards, significantly larger than an F–4. Nonetheless, it was easy, at first, to overlook its size in favor of the many marvelous innovations that the jet incorporated from combat experience.

The pilots wanted more thrust, and more thrust they got. The twin Pratt and Whitney F100 engines produced as much thrust as the airplane weighed. The F–4, which was only ten years old when the first F–15 was delivered from McDonnell Douglas, was a powerful jet for its day, but its engines generated 30 percent less thrust per pound of weight. The F–15 had so much excess thrust that the pilot did not need to use the afterburner for takeoff. One pilot, a former

A row of F–15s reflected in the water epitomizes the strength and beauty of this fighter. *Official USAF photo.*

F–4 pilot who flew 320 combat missions in Vietnam and was in the initial cadre of operational F–15 pilots, described the military power takeoff* as "sheer enjoyment."[1] Thrust while flying was immediate and breathtaking, especially when the pilot threw the twin throttles forward in full afterburner. The jet did not just walk away from other fighters of the day; it sprinted away.

In addition to its terrific speed, the F–15 could turn on a dime and outmaneuver, by a significant margin, every other fighter in the world. The flight controls were silky smooth from the highest speed down to the slowest stall. One pilot described the difference between flying the F–4 and the F–15 as "going from a F–150 pickup truck to a Corvette."[2] Best of all, a modern, computer-controlled flight control system finally beat the adverse yaw problem, long the nemesis of swept-wing fighters. Adverse yaw, the tendency of a fighter to roll opposite the intended direction at slow speeds when the pilot tried to roll with his ailerons, was overcome by the two enormous rudders on the F–15 and a horizontal tail with two halves that could move independently. If the pilot wanted to roll left at slow speeds, he simply moved his stick to the left. The flight control computer, sensing airspeed, angle of attack and other factors, did not move the ailerons. Instead, it neutralized the ailerons, moved the twin rudders to the left, and simultaneously moved the left and right horizontal tail planes opposite each other. The result was a quick, rapid roll left as in a conventional airplane.

The large horizontal tail on the F–15, combined with the twin rudders and flight control computer, also provided an unprecedented degree of control authority for the Eagle pilot. The horizontal tail was as big as the entire main wing surface of the Soviet MiG–21, and one near disaster in Israel highlighted the new jet's phenomenal controllability. After a midair collision between an Israeli F–15 and an A–4 in 1983, the initial report to the Pentagon stated that one wing had been sliced off the Eagle eighteen inches from the fuselage, yet the

---

* Full throttle without the afterburner engaged.

F–15 pilot receiving instructions after landing. *Official USAF photo.*

pilot had successfully landed the aircraft. Air Force pilots who read the report did not believe it. They thought that the observer must have meant that the jet had lost eighteen inches off the end of the wing. Incredibly, photos arrived the next day showing that one wing was almost completely gone from the jet, leaving only a short stub on one side. Essentially, the Israeli pilot had been able to fly the airplane and land it with only one wing. Later analysis revealed that the large rudders and horizontal tail were able to counteract the tremendous rolling force of the remaining wing and provide the pilot enough control to land, albeit at an abnormally high approach speed. A few months later, a major aviation magazine published the photos for its astounded readers. The pilots enjoyed the wonderful handling qualities as well. The F–15 was the first Air Force fighter to reach 5,000 flying hours before one was lost in an accident.[3]

Even with its brute power and agility, the F–15, spawned from the frustrations and limitations of Vietnam, brought other superb qualities to the fighter force. A large, bubble canopy surrounded the pilot, who sat very high in the cockpit. This design might not seem unusual to pilots who had flown the World War II-era P–51s or the Korean War-vintage F–86s, but to the pilots who came from the Vietnam-era fighters like the F–100, F–105, and F–4, the superb view they had from the new Eagle cockpit was sensational. The pilot could turn in his seat and look completely between the twin tails. With his high seat position, he could look over the side of the canopy and see well below him. F–4 pilots, who could barely see behind their wings at all, were almost giddy at the prospect of dogfighting with an unobstructed view of the fight. A fighter pilot touch to the cockpit design had added a small handhold on either side of the canopy rail, so that the pilot could grasp it with his free hand and pull himself even further around in the seat to view the area behind him.

It is impossible to overstate the value of being able to see behind the aircraft in air-to-air combat. To the uninitiated, the value may seem to be the ability to detect an attack from the rear hemisphere, and that is important. However, the main reason is that pilots look out the back and top of their canopies during jet-age dogfights far more than they look out the front. Consider the adversaries who approach head-on. As soon as they pass, both are now looking out the rear of the canopy to maintain their tally as they turn under high-g back toward each other. In another scenario, consider the pilot who sees an enemy level to his left out the side of his canopy. To start his attack, the pilot first rolls his wings to the left so that he can pull directly toward the enemy; now the enemy is directly out the top of the canopy. The bromide, "Speed is life," which was a favorite saying of fighter pilots who stressed having enough airspeed to maneuver against an adversary, gained a new corollary as pilots learned how to fight against small Aggressors. Soon, "Sight is life," became as familiar in mission briefings. In the F–4, the pilot often had to sacrifice maneuvering to maintain a tally; in the F–15, the pilot had to sacrifice nothing.

Of course, the most notable feature of the F–15 cockpit was that there was only one seat. The pilot flew alone without a WSO. The advisability of the single-seat design was a constant source of debate in the Air Force community that was accustomed to a force composed of nearly all two-seat F–4s. Naturally, the WSOs held no small disdain for the single-seat design and were eager to relate the many times they had saved some hapless pilot's bacon by calling a break turn at just the right moment. Even the most staunch single-seat advocate would not argue that an extra set of eyes during the battle was not an asset—sometimes. At other times, however, the pilot and WSO could confuse each other in the heat of battle. Communication between the cockpits had to compete with constant chatter on the radio from other flight members. Nearly every former F–4 pilot who converted to the new F–15 recalls how quiet the cockpit was without the breathing and comments of two people on the intercom.[4] For those who could sever the emotional bonds of a two-place jet, the question was never which was better; the question was whether a single seat was good enough. Obviously, the Air Force—as the Navy would do later with the F–18—decided that one man was enough to do the job and do it well.

Since one pilot had to shoulder the entire workload, the design of cockpit switches and indicators was crucial, and in the F–15 the Air Force fixed all the things that had been wrong with its earlier fighters. As soon as an experienced F–4 pilot sat in the cockpit, he noticed its efficient design. Things that could be preset on the ground and seldom changed in the air were on the right console beside his right hip, whereas things that might be changed in the air were either on the left console or on a panel right below the gunsight. Such placement allowed him to change switches with his left hand while keeping his right hand on the stick. In the F–4, the transponder,* which frequently requires changes to its settings, was on the right console; so the pilot had to release the stick or fly with his left hand and look down while he fumbled for the settings. In the F–15, the settings were on the left console; but even better, the section that required frequent attention was mounted directly in front of his eyes just under the

---

* Black box that tells air traffic control the position, altitude, and speed of the aircraft.

gunsight. Despite the first favorable impression of the cockpit, the best was to come during and after the new pilot started his engines.

The F–15 came equipped with a jet fuel starter (JFS), a very small jet engine mounted between the two big F100 engines. A handle in the cockpit connected to a bottle of compressed air. When the pilot pulled the handle, the stream of highly pressurized air flowed into the JFS, which started to turn the little engine. As soon as the engine started turning from the air, it generated its own electricity and, using fuel from the aircraft main system, ignited and started running on its own. A few seconds after the JFS was "up to speed," the pilot merely lifted a switch on the throttle that engaged a clutch between the JFS and the main engine. The little JFS then spun the main engine until its generator produced enough electricity for ignition. As the main engine spun up to idle speed, the JFS disengaged automatically, ready for the pilot to engage it to the other engine and start it in the same manner. Of course, the beauty of the JFS scheme was that no external compressed air or electrical sources were needed to start the Eagle since everything was self-contained.

As soon as the engine start sequence was complete, the F–15 pilot could do something very simple but very good: close the canopy. Earlier fighter cockpits had been air conditioned, but the systems never worked well on the ground. In the air they worked poorly at low altitude. After engine start, it was impossible to close the canopy until just before takeoff—usually twenty to thirty minutes later—unless it was a very cold day. On a normal day, the crew would bake under the Plexiglas canopies, and at the hot Southern bases in the United States or in Southeast Asia, many crews did not close the canopy until they were actually on the runway and only seconds from takeoff. The F–15, though, had a superb air conditioner, so the pilot sat in cool comfort as he ran his ground checks and taxied, while his brethren in older jets sweltered in Nomex* flight gear surrounded by heat-generating electrical equipment.

Once airborne, the Eagle's combat systems were nothing short of sensational. Most useful was the heads up display (HUD), which was projected on a set of combining glass plates directly in the pilot's line of vision like the gunsight reticle in earlier fighters. However, the HUD was far more than just a gun reticle; it was a total performance display of green lines and symbols. A scale across the top indicated the magnetic heading of the aircraft, while scales on the left and right sides of the HUD indicated airspeed and altitude. In the center of the HUD was a miniature aircraft symbol that displayed the flight path, which worked with a pitch ladder to show degrees of climb and dive.† Pilots no longer needed to look into the cockpit to check their altitudes, a glance that might result in a loss of

---

* Fire retardant material used to make flight suits, jackets, and gloves.

† Little has been said in this book about the A–7, a superb attack aircraft the Air Force purchased in small numbers. The A–7 had a similar display many years before it came

tally—No Joy! Of course, video and computer games of the 1990s used those kinds of displays as a matter of course, but when new F–15 pilots saw the HUD in the mid-1970s, oxygen masks around the world had to be ordered in wider sizes to contain the smiles underneath.

There was one innovation in the HUD that every F–15 pilot remembers seeing for the first time—the target designator (TD) box. When the F–15 radar was tracking a target, the computer displayed the small green box on the HUD around the target. To get a tally, all the pilot had to do was point in the general direction of the target, look through the TD box, and there was the adversary! Suddenly, in one swoop of technology, Eagle pilots saw the Aggressor at long ranges, often before he could see the Eagle. One pilot called the TD box the greatest thing since sliced bread.[5]

F–15 pilots did not need to cut plastic oil sample tubes and jam them onto switches as they used to in the Phantom. In the Eagle, every switch the pilot needed to move during dogfighting was mounted on either the stick or the throttles. Central to the F–15's capabilities was the large radar in its nose. It was a pulse doppler (PD) radar that could look down and see targets against the ground clutter because the radar eliminated anything not moving, the ground, and only displayed things that were moving above a certain speed. In the F–4, the WSO controlled the radar by means of several control panels and the radar control handle. In the F–15, the pilot preset switches on one panel before takeoff. Once in the air, he controlled the radar through a few switches located on the stick and throttles. For instance, a small wheel on the outside of the left throttle controlled elevation. The pilot could roll the wheel forward with his left pinkie finger and the radar searched lower. Further, the F–4 crew had only an elevation mark on the radar scope to tell them generally where the radar was looking. The F–15 radar computed its search volume and displayed on the radar scope that the pilot was looking from 10,000 feet to 30,000 feet or wherever he had the elevation set. As icing on the cake, the radar displayed the exact altitude of the target it was tracking, another function that had to be done mentally by the F–4 WSO, then passed verbally to the front-seater. Such computerization quickly turned the single-seat versus two-seat arguments toward the side of a single crew member. A pilot had information at a glance that the F–4 pilot had to ask for, sometimes without an answer if the busy WSO was doing something else.

Computerization in the F–15 not only made the radar more effective and easier to use, but also gave developers the opportunity to help fix perhaps the biggest problem experienced in aerial combat during Vietnam: the proclivity of Air Force pilots to shoot missiles out of proper parameters. While gun cameras and strictly regimented evaluation programs made a big improvement in the F–4 community, the computers and HUD of the F–15 made the largest strides in performance.

---

out in an improved form in the F–15. Nonetheless, since nearly all pilots who transitioned to the F–15 were from the F–4, the HUD was a revelation.

The F–15, just like the F–4, was capable of carrying four Sparrow, radar-guided missiles, four Sidewinder heat-seeker missiles, and an internal 20-mm cannon.* As in the newer F–4s with the 556 modification, the F–15 had a single switch to select radar, heat, or gun. Unlike the F–4, though, the new F–15 HUD displayed the proper weapons envelope to help the pilot shoot at the correct range and angle.

If the pilot selected radar missiles with his left thumb switch, the HUD displayed the maximum and minimum range of the missile based on every imaginable factor like F–15 altitude and speed, target altitude and speed, and missile range to arm. The pilot could interpret the information at a glance because a small marker moved on the range scale as he closed on the target. It was "a piece of cake" to see when the range marker moved to "in range" and to judge how long it would be there before it came inside minimum range. Further, when the target was in range, a small triangle, called a shoot cue, appeared on the TD box. Of course the same information was there for a Sidewinder shot. If the pilot had a radar lock on, the fire control computer displayed the same sort of information for the pilot.

During the late 1970s, the 422d Test Squadron at Nellis modified a few F–4s to test a similar system for the F–4, minus the HUD. Technicians mounted a series of lights on the F–4 canopy bow nearly in front of the pilot's line of sight. When the computer said that the target was in range, the lights came on and flashed furiously. The modification was called the SYDS mod, an acronym for "shoot, you dumb shit." Although a good idea, it never worked well in the F–4 because of its slow computer and the inability to transfer flight data from the old F–4 into its black boxes. Nonetheless, the fighter developers had the right idea in the F–4. If flashing lights were the answer, then so be it. However, it was not until the F–15 arrived that the pilots had an accurate display of missile parameters from which to plan and execute their shots. The HUD also contained an extremely accurate gunsight to aim the 20-mm cannon that was embedded in the right wing root. One instructor recalled flying in the back seat of a tub[†] while his student, Ron Fogleman[‡], was the flight leader for a four-ship of new pilots tabbed for duty at Bitburg Air Base, Germany. The mission was aerial gunnery, where each pilot had the opportunity to shoot the gun at a target towed by an F–4. The silver target, made of honeycomb about ten feet long by four feet wide, was shaped like a dart. Although it was their first time to shoot the dart from the F–15, Fogleman and all three of his wingmen hit the target on their first pass.[6]

---

* The six-barrel, 20-mm, electric Gatling gun was developed in the 1950s and installed on nearly every USAF fighter thereafter. It is a classic design that has seen little change in nearly fifty years of operation.

† A two-seat version designated the F–15B. Normally an operational squadron was equipped with twenty-two single-seaters, the F–15A, and two two-seat F–15Bs. Training squadrons had several more tubs, so instructor pilots could monitor the front seat student during his first experience with more difficult tasks such as air refueling.

‡ Fogleman later became the chief of staff of the USAF.

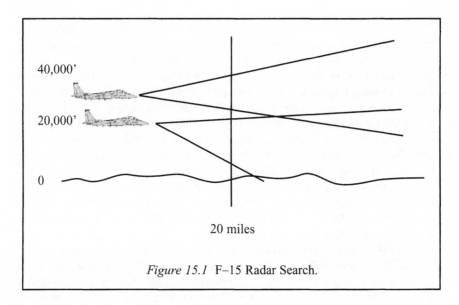

Figure 15.1 F–15 Radar Search.

The radar inputs to the HUD were only a part of the radar's phenomenal capability. No Air Force fighter pilot had ever flown with a radar so capable and so easy to use. The F–4 radar displayed everything reflected back to it, and the WSO had to adjust his electronic gain controls manually to find the target. The F–15 computers did all that automatically. Further, they displayed only the target on the scope without the distractions of altitude reflections and noise. The screen was "clean" until the radar computers saw, processed, and displayed a small bright rectangle that represented the target. The pilot then moved the acquisition gate, represented by two small vertical, parallel lines over the target and command lock-on. He did this by pressing a small button under his left middle finger on the throttle. The button was actually a miniature joystick that moved the acquisition symbol around the radar screen.

The search volume of the radar was huge, and two Eagles in tactical formation could search from ground level to 40,000 feet merely by overlapping their coverage. (Fig. 15.1)

The radar search shown above is only representative of what the F–15 could do; the pilots could easily roll the elevation wheels under their left pinkie finger and change the altitudes, ranges, and volumes of the search areas. The figure also shows a capability of the F–15 radar that dramatically impacted tactics in the new jet—the ability to easily spot targets flying lower than the fighters. Not only could the Eagle fly high and fast, but it could "look down-shoot down" as well. F–4 pilots always needed to get below the adversary, but the advent of the F–15 effectively doubled the airspace in which to fight. Eagle pilots could plan, if the situation demanded, to pounce on their intended victims from the high altitudes denied the F–4 because of its weaker engines and poor radar.

The ability to "shoot down" came to the F–15 in the form of the newest missile in the AIM–7 Sparrow family, the AIM–7F. Externally, the new Sparrow looked the same as the earlier versions used in Vietnam, but inside were all new digital computers and processors that gave the missile more reliable and accurate guidance, especially against targets below the shooter's altitude.

Air Force pilots had discovered in the skies over North Vietnam that it was not always possible to shoot at long range, so the radar computer in the F–15 gave the pilot several short-range acquisition modes to use in the turning, swirling dogfights known as furballs. The most basic of these modes was the auto-guns option. Whenever the pilot pulled the radar-heat-guns switch under his left thumb back into the guns position, the radar, if it was not already tracking a target, went into a very quick scan of the area directly in front of the jet, out to ten miles. The first target it saw it locked on to. The pilot could move the search field around with his radar joystick button. So, if the F–15 pilot saw an adversary high to his left, he could pull the thumb switch back to guns and move his joystick button up and to the left as he pulled the nose of the jet up and left. By the time he got his nose on the target, or even close to it, the radar would have already locked on, so that he could use the HUD information and shoot cues to take a shot the instant it was available. Another useful automatic acquisition mode was the vertical scan option. On the stick, below the pilot's right thumb, was a button that pivoted fore and aft. If the pilot pulled it aft, the radar started a rapid scan in the air out to ten miles from level to 60 degrees high. Often, in a visual engagement, the pilot looked out the top of his canopy as he turned toward the adversary. In this case, the pilot wanted to put his lift vector—an imaginary line perpendicular to his wings—directly at the target as he pulled hard towards it. The vertical scan was aligned along that same lift vector, so that as the pilot pulled toward the target, all he had to do was thumb the switch back, and the radar would lock onto the target well before he actually got his nose to it. Where split seconds meant the difference between being the hunter or the prey, the quick lock ons from the auto acquisition modes gave the Eagle pilot a vital edge.

Learning how to use all these switches in concert required much practice and a certain dexterity. Some called the constant movement of switches on the stick and throttle "playing the piccolo." Others joked that before one could become an Eagle pilot, one had to take piccolo lessons. Such joshing was in good humor, though, for no one doubted that the ease of employing the F–15's awesome radar was a joy, especially to those Vietnam combat veterans who had seen themselves and their buddies miss MiG kills because of poor cockpit design. One combat veteran recalled, "What a travesty that we didn't have [the F–15] in Vietnam. We didn't have a…clue. When I saw what we could do in later years, that's when the travesty of Vietnam came home to me."[7]

If the Eagle had one important weakness as an air superiority fighter, it was its heat-seeking Sidewinder, the AIM–9J. The J was the final version of the AIM–9 family to see combat in Vietnam, and when the F–15 was delivered to the

F–15 aircraft flying in steep bank, with four AIM–7s on the fuselage and two AIM–9s on each wing. *Official USAF photo.*

555th Tactical Fighter Squadron at Luke Air Force Base in 1974, the J was still the frontline Air Force heat-seeker.* In order to shoot the J, the pilot had to maneuver to a restricted cone behind the target. With its great maneuverability and tremendous power, though, the F–15 in a one-against-one (1 v 1) fight could meet an F–4 head-on and get behind it into J parameters very quickly. However, in a battle of many fighters and adversaries, such maneuvering made the Eagle vulnerable to attacks from unseen directions as it maneuvered for the kill. An "improved" AIM–9, the P, came soon afterward, but it had nearly the same limitations as the J.

AIMVAL-ACEVAL

The solution to the Sidewinder problem emerged from a joint USAF-USN test conducted at Nellis Air Force Base in 1977, three years after Eagles started coming off the McDonnell Douglas production line in St. Louis, Missouri. The test was the air intercept missile evaluation, or AIMVAL. One purpose of the test was to compare effectiveness of several contending missile designs, all of which claimed the ability to be fired from any target aspect—front, side, or rear. The Air Force dedicated F–15s to fly solely test sorties, and the USN contributed its newest fighter, the F–14 Tomcat, as well. Nellis provided a cadre of its Aggressor F–5 aircraft and pilots to fly as Red Air. The Blue Air Eagles and Tomcats flew all the test sorties against the Aggressors on the new Nellis ACMI range, so that every detail of the missions could be thoroughly documented and studied. The test lasted many months, and when the results were studied, one of the Air Force candidate missiles emerged as the selection to provide a common missile for both services. The winner was a version of the Sidewinder, the AIM–9L, or Lima, as it came to be known.

---

* The Triple Nickel was the leading MiG-killer squadron of the Vietnam War, so its designation was moved to Luke to become the Air Force's first Eagle squadron.

The Lima had a supercooled guidance head that was much more sensitive than the older Sidewinders, allowing the seeker to discriminate the target location very accurately. The missile also had a new fuzing system that could predict the high closure rates of a head-on approach and detonate the warhead in enough time to "lead" the target. It was a very fast missile as well, much faster than the Sparrow, and because it did not need a radar to guide it, the new Sidewinder was literally a point-and-shoot weapon.

The Lima revolutionized tactical thinking. No longer did the pilot have to maneuver to get behind the adversary in a restricted cone; he could shoot him in the face. Some called it shooting him in the lips; others called the missile the "Lip-winder."

Whatever they called it, the effect was devastating to the side that did not have Limas. One engagement during the test vividly pointed out the differences. Four Eagles fought four Red Air F–5s equipped with Limas. As the battle neared its conclusion, all of the combatants had "died," except for one Eagle and a single F–5. The Eagle was a few miles behind the F–5 and launched a Sparrow. Simultaneously, the F–5, which knew the Eagle's position, came around in a very tight turn, saw the Eagle, and launched a Lima at it. A split second later, the ACMI put a coffin around the F–5, signaling that it was killed from the Sparrow. However, the Lima, already unleashed, continued to streak head-on at the F–15 and killed it as well. The AIM-ACE pilots saved the ACMI tape to show visitors the impact the Lima had in a fight. They called the mission "The Towering Inferno" because all eight of the players died—the last one the victim of a dead man.

As soon as the new missiles arrived in the field, they were allocated to the F–15s.* Some proclaimed that the days of basic fighter maneuvers were over. There was no reason to do quarter-planes, high and low yoyos, and barrel rolls to the other guy's six o'clock, they said. All one had to do was point and shoot. What they discovered was that BFM was not dead; the maneuvers just got bigger and started further away. They also found out that there was no such thing as an I-wish-you-were-dead weapon. For every new weapon there were counters—white spy vs. black spy with the counter to the counter to the counter.[8]

Many countertactics came from the other part of AIMVAL, the air combat evaluation (ACEVAL). One purpose of the ACEVAL test was to determine the effect of numbers in an aerial battle. If one Eagle can defeat one F–5, can it defeat two, or three, or four? During this tactics evaluation that pitted countless combinations of aircraft against one another, the pilots were given free rein to devise whatever tactics they could to defeat their adversaries.[9] The innovations they devised were imaginative and affected fighter tactics for the next twenty years.

---

* Some halfhearted efforts were made to modify the F–4 fleet to carry the face-shooters, and a few got the new capability, but the vast majority went to the Eagles.

Sometimes, the test plan permitted the players to use ground radar to help them find their adversaries. When they did not have ground radar to serve as their long-range eyes, the F–5s were at a great disadvantage to the F–15 and its powerful radar that could find them at any altitude. The F–5s, though, were allowed on some missions to know if an F–15 radar was locked on to them, thus simulating a fighter that had radar warning receiver equipment. The F–5 pilots quickly learned that if they had an F–15 radar on them, they could turn and run before a missile could get to them, a maneuver they called a "drag." A fighter that drags might not get a kill on that mission, but he would not die either. They also figured out that if they could get one of their Red fighters past the F–15 radar coverage, he had a chance to use his small size to sneak up on the F–15s and kill one or more of them. Occasionally, the F–5s would fly very close together so they looked like one target on the F–15 radar. When the F–15 would lock on, one of the F–5s would drag, and the other would press ahead. If the radar stayed on the dragger, the unseen F–5 might get to the F–15 unobserved and get a kill, or "bag," an Eagle.

Of course, these drag and bag tactics had countless variations that depended on who had GCI, who had or did not have RWR, who had Limas, and myriad other factors. The impact on fighter tactics, though, came in how the F–15 pilots learned to cope with the wily, imaginative, and obsessively competitive Aggressor pilots who would do anything within the rules to win. The Eagle pilots learned, often the hard way, that there were three keys to surviving and winning: discipline, discipline, and discipline.

Perhaps the most important task that required strong discipline to succeed was in the use of their fighters' radars. When the radar was tracking a target, it could see only that target and no others. So, pilots had to learn not to get more than one radar locked on to the same F–5. If there were two F–5s and two F–15s, the Eagle pilots had to get one radar on each F–5. They did this by strict adherence to a plan to "sort" the targets. The sort plan in use by F–15 pilots everywhere was simple to remember. If the targets were side by side, the F–15 leader took the left one; if they were stacked in altitude, he took the low one; if they were in trail, he took the lead one. It was easy to remember; lead took left, low, lead—all started with the letter L. The wingman took the opposite. Easy to say and remember, but harder to do. In order for the system to work, the F–15 pilots had to resist the temptation to lock on and call over the radio, "I've got mine; you find another one."*

As long as the Eagle pilots maintained strict adherence to the battle plan, detailed in the mission briefing, they could succeed, but they could not muscle their way into the fight and clean house on Red Air just because they had a vastly

---

* Sometimes called the "field-grade sort," because senior officers have a reputation for being unable to work the radar as well as the young studs. That happens when the old man grabs a target and stays with it, hoping the younger, more proficient pilots in his flight will sort, or find, another target near his.

superior airplane. Both forces were manned by some of the best fighter pilots in the Air Force. They were good, and they were always looking for ways to win.

The Red Force pilots did not have a real RWR in their cockpits to warn them when the Blue Force radars were tracking them. The only warning they got of a lock on was through an artificial system in the ACMI that was not always accurate, and sometimes the information was slow to be passed to them. Since the Air Force was not interested in modifying the F–5s, one of the pilots went to the local Radio Shack and bought a battery-powered radar detector of the type speeders use to protect themselves from radar speed traps. He found that the F–15 radar would trigger the device if he carried it mounted inside his F–5 cockpit. When the Blue Forces discovered that the Reds were using the devices, they yelled "Foul!" loud and clear. When umpires refused to force Red Air to discontinue using the fuzz-busters, the Blue team worked on their own tactics to find ways to counter the new equipment."[10]

The Red pilots did not have the market on innovation cornered, however, as Blue pilots devised some tricks of their own. The F–15, surprisingly to some, did not have the powerfully magnified telescope, TISEO*, that the F–4 carried. TISEO allowed the F–4 crew to see what the radar was locked to and identify targets from many miles away. The idea of TISEO was to give the crew enough time to identify the target visually in order to fire a Sparrow before the target could shoot at them. Since they had no such system, the F–15 pilots were hard-pressed to get a Sparrow shot off before minimum range when the rules of engagement required a visual identification. Often, they could see the F–5 in the TD box as a black dot, yet still not positively identify it until it was too late to shoot. Blue Force pilots rigged a simple piece of equipment that made their problem much easier to solve. They purchased a standard telescope of the type used on hunting rifles and manufactured a bracket to attach the scope to the side of the HUD glass. On the HUD was a "W" symbol that always showed exactly where the nose of the airplane was pointed during flight. Before takeoff, the pilot would note where the W was projected on the ground in front of his aircraft. He then leaned forward and used two small adjusting screws on the scope bracket to tweak the scope to exactly that same place. Then, in the air, when the radar was locked to a target, he had only to fly the W so that it was exactly over the TD box, then look through his rifle scope. If he did those things carefully, the target would be in the scope field of view, and he could identify it in plenty of time to fire his Sparrow. The Blue pilots nicknamed this clever modification Eagle Eye, and it quickly swept throughout the growing F–15 community. It was not long before every F–15 awaiting takeoff at the end of the runway at Langley or Bitburg had a rifle scope attached to the side of the HUD.

---

* Target identification system electro-optical.

Da Nang Air Base, Vietnam: Lt. Clyde Phillips before he became known as Joe Bob. *Courtesy of Joe Bob Phillips.*

Changes in Attitudes

Perhaps the biggest impact of the tests, though, was a cultural change in the fighter pilots' attitudes toward aerial warfare with long-range missiles. Before the F–15 with its AIM–7F and AIM–9L, fighter pilots had always focused on getting behind their opponent. Granted, F–4 crews often started their engagements from twenty to thirty miles away, found their targets on radar, and called Sparrow shots as they closed with their adversaries. However, the scenarios they used seldom allowed them to call a kill on the adversary pre-merge.* Their focus was getting to the merge in a position from which they could convert their intercept into a positional advantage behind the adversary, where they could employ the Sidewinder and, best of all, the gun. Such attitudes are not surprising when viewed in the context of combat experience. In Korea, pilots on both sides had only guns. Although the long-range Sparrow was used in Vietnam, crews were seldom given the option to fire it beyond visual range because there were few times when they could be assured that they were not firing at a friendly jet. Besides, in training, it was just plain fun to get into a swirling, twirling dogfight with afterburners cooking, sweat pouring, adrenaline rushing, and heart pounding. In the furball, only one thing mattered—who had the best hands.

---

* Generally, a fight was broken into two segments defined by the point at which the adversaries passed each other the first time—the merge. The first segment of the fight, pre-merge, was characterized by jockeying for a good position; the second portion was post-merge.

At the F–4 Fighter Weapons School, Larry Keith and his band of radical, firebrand tactical thinkers—led by Joe Bob Phillips, Ron Keys, John Jumper, Dick Myers, Buzz Buzze, Tom Dyches, Jack Sornberger, Dave Dellwardt, and others—pressed hard to devise scenarios that honored the threat of a Sparrow streaking out at long range. Theirs was a losing battle, though, because the Sparrow's record was dismal on the F–4. In the early 1970s, if an F–4 pilot briefed his adversary that a Sparrow shot from ten miles would be counted as a kill, he would be laughed out of the briefing room with hoots of "Get a grip," or "You need a tally on reality."

Gradually, though, the impact of the F–15's combat capabilities started to sink in across the fighter forces. When F–15s from Langley went to Eglin to shoot missiles in WSEP over the Gulf, the AIM–7F success rate was four to five times higher than it had been on the F–4. Even more astounding was the success rate for the AIM–9L, which confirmed the engineers' hopes for a one-shot-one-kill weapon.

It was a good thing the F–15 systems proved to be reliable at long range, because the aircraft sometimes did not do well in the classic, roiling dogfights. The F–15 was more powerful and more agile than any other fighter in the world. However, it was also the biggest fighter and very easy to see. When nose on, it had a relatively low visual profile, but as soon as it began turning, its enormous wing could be seen for miles. Some called it the "flying tennis court;" others called it "Big Bird." F–4 pilots and WSOs licked their chops at the opportunity to get in a fight with Eagles before the F–15 got the Lima. The WSOs especially made no effort to hide their disdain for the new, single-seat jet. One Langley F–15 pilot went on a tour of F–4 bases to brief crews on what the new Eagle could do. He was stunned to find that F–4 back-seaters at every stop could only focus on how the new jet would die wholesale in combat because it did not have that extra set of eyes to watch for threats.[11]

Ultimately, the Eagle pilots could not be denied. They started walking into briefing rooms and telling their adversaries, "If you come straight down the snot locker today, I will shoot two Sparrows at you and call you dead. If I am out of Sparrows, I will rip your lips off with a Lima before you can get to the merge. Questions?"

In response, adversaries studied the lessons learned by AIMVAL-ACEVAL pilots on how to survive in an all-aspect missile environment. As the reliability of the missiles improved, the culture of long-range missiles slowly spread throughout the fighter force. Of course, clever pilots developed ways to defeat some of the long-range shots, but as they devised one counter, the F–15s developed new techniques based on the lessons of formation discipline, radio discipline, radar discipline, and shot discipline learned in the weapons schools and at ACEVAL-AIMVAL. The cycle of counter vs. counter vs. counter continued, but the fight did not start at 1,000 feet range as in the days of "40-second Boyd." The struggle was starting while the adversaries were thirty miles apart, and the F–15 pilots were seriously intent on killing every adversary pre-merge.

Despite its ability to dominate the aerial arena, the F–15 attracted a vocal and influential group of detractors who continued to fight a battle for small, cheap dogfighters. Gathering advocates from several walks of life, a splinter group of congressmen, journalists, aircraft designers, former fighter pilots, and military analysts marched under the banner of the Military Reform Caucus to demonstrate the folly of the F–15. James Fallows eloquently expressed their credo in his best-selling book, *National Defense*. The reformers who focused on money saw the F–15 as too expensive at $20 million, seven times the cost of an F–4 and twenty times the cost of an F–5. They further argued that the airplane was so big and easy to see that the pilot of a small F–5-sized fighter could easily get inside the F–15 pilot's OODA loop and wreak havoc. Ironically, the very argument the reformers used proved the case against them. The Eagle was big, but its radar and superb missiles not only gave the F–15 pilot the first chance to observe, orient, and decide, they also gave him the first chance to act. The reformers had good arguments, but they were based on old information. A new paradigm was emerging, and it was the paradigm of a very large battlefield, with reliable missiles that could truly "reach out and touch someone."

This did not mean that the day of the dogfight was over—far from it. Aggressors often found a way to deceive and befuddle Eagle pilots, and the huge F–15s could end up in a tiny furball with the little F–5s. Nonetheless, the battle arena was getting larger, and the training was improving as dissimilar air combat training spread to every Air Force fighter unit. To many, the issue was starting to change from who had the best hands to who had the best head. A new fighter force with new jets, new missiles, and new ideas was starting to define the parameters for aerial combat at the end of the twentieth century.

---

1. Thomas A. Owens, interview with author, Rosslyn, Virginia, June 2, 1999.

2. *Ibid.*

3. Walter J. Boyne, *Silver Wings, A History of the United States Air Force* (New York: Simon and Schuster, 1993), p. 302.

4. Owens interview.

5. *Ibid.*

6. *Ibid.*

7. *Ibid.*

8. Joel T. Hall, interview with author, Las Vegas, Nevada, April 12, 1999.

9. *Ibid.*

10.*Ibid.*

11.Owens interview.

CHAPTER 16

✪

Down 'n' Dirty: The A–10

When we started teaching weapons delivery at Nellis, we began with the F–4 textbooks. Every place the book said 500 knots, we scratched it out and wrote in 350 knots.[1]

Purists will argue that close air support* is a mission, not an airplane, but if ever the Air Force produced an airplane with a specific mission in mind, it was the A–10. Its official name is the Thunderbolt II, in honor of the sturdy P–47 Thunderbolt of World War II fame. But the A–10 pilots called it the Warthog—a beast with a face only a mother, or pilot, could love.

A constant source of frustration to the combat veterans of Vietnam, especially the F–4 crews, was the multiple mission areas in which they were supposed to maintain proficiency. One day they might be dropping bombs on interdiction targets in Laos, hunting MiGs the next, and supporting Army troops in contact with the enemy on the third. Most considered themselves jacks-of-all-trades and masters of none. However, as the fighter culture changed during the war and immediately afterwards, an era of specialization emerged. The F–15 had the air superiority mission alone. Whenever someone had an idea to modify it with heavy extra racks or equipment to carry bombs, they were usually met with the retort, "Not a pound for air-to-ground!"

Yet the Air Force still had the mission of supporting ground troops in action. The F–4 and the F–100—and other jets—had flown countless CAS missions during Vietnam and usually did them well, but both aircraft had some significant disadvantages in terms of loiter time available, distinguishing friendly troops from enemy, and dropping ordnance on the bad guys without hurting the good ones. It might be true that speed is life when engaged with a MiG or dashing through a flak blanket, but that same speed made it very difficult, sometimes impossible, to sort out who was who among troops in close battle. When planners for the next war, who were focused on the Fulda Gap and the hordes of the Warsaw Pact, considered the next conflict, what they mostly saw was armor, rivers of tanks and armored personnel carriers, slamming into NATO defenses. An airplane designed for CAS in the future had to be able to contend with armor if it were to succeed, and the pilots had to be highly proficient at killing armor and working with

---

* Air missions that directly support ground troops who are in contact with the enemy.

The A–10 Thunderbolt II was designed for the close air support mission. *Official USAF photo.*

ground commanders. Said another way, the Air Force had to commit to a specialized aircraft with specialized training for CAS in the same way it had committed to air supremacy with the F–15 Eagle.

In 1967, early in the Vietnam War, the Air Force conducted several studies to determine the requirements for a new CAS aircraft. Their basic considerations were that the new jet had to be able to carry a large payload, stay overhead the troops for a long time, operate under low ceilings, and have ordnance delivery accuracy good enough to support the troops. In April 1970 the Department of Defense approved the attack experimental (AX) concept for prototype development, and by December they had selected two candidates for competition: the A–9, built by Northrop, and the A–10, built by Fairchild Industries. In January 1973, after 625 competition sorties, the Secretary of the Air Force awarded a full-scale development contract to Fairchild for its A–10 design.[2]

The new airplane was big—53 feet long with a thick, straight wing that spanned nearly 60 feet. The engines were mounted on nacelles—some called them warts—between its large double rudders. The engines produced a thrust-to-weight ratio less than half that of the F–15, making the A–10 very low power for a jet of the time. However, the engines also had some strong advantages. They were mounted apart, so that if one came apart in combat, pieces flying off its rotors were unlikely to damage the other engine. Also, they were high-bypass fan engines, which meant that their exhaust heat signature was very low. Since the engines were mounted between the tails that acted as shields, the aircraft was considered to be less vulnerable to heat-seeking missile attacks from either the ground or the air. Even with its low-power engines, the A–10 could take off with an impressive combat load in 4,000 feet of runway, thanks to the large, straight wing that produced exceptional lift. Perhaps the strongest point about the engines, though, was their low fuel consumption rates. Without external fuel tanks, the A–10 could stay airborne five hours while carrying eighteen

500-pound bombs, more than twice the capability of the F–4. One A–10 pilot recalls a mission where he and his wingman were training to defeat air attacks. They fought against two F–4s until the F–4s had to return to base (RTB) because of low fuel. Then they took on two F–15s until the Eagles had to RTB. Then instead of landing at Nellis, the two A–10s flew a long hop to a base outside Denver, Colorado, and landed there to spend the night on other business.[3]

The A–10 was also built to survive the hail of fire that would greet any aircraft attempting to attack the Warsaw Pact forces. The pilot and cockpit were surrounded by a titanium armor "bathtub" capable of defeating antiaircraft fire up to 23-mm caliber.* The bathtub also protected vital flight control components and junctions. The front windscreen was bulletproof to small arms fire. The fuel tanks were filled with fire-resistant foam that resembled a very coarse sponge. It performed so well in tests that many jets, the F–4 among them, were modified with the foam to prevent fires if antiaircraft bullets penetrated the tanks.[4] Some wags joked that the A–10 was the only Air Force aircraft that could do what it was designed to do—take hits.

Taking and surviving battle damage was not the only thing the unattractive jet could do. Its entire design centered on its most important feature, a 30-mm Gatling gun that could spew out up to 4,200 rounds per minute (70 per second). The entire gun assembly was as long as a Cessna 172 and weighed as much as a Volkswagen bug. The 30-mm ammo used a depleted uranium bullet that weighed over three-fourths of a pound and came out of the barrel at nearly 3,400 feet per second. The small, dense mass of the bullet traveling at such high velocity could penetrate the armor of a Soviet tank. With even a short burst, the A–10 pilot could lay twenty or thirty of these bullets dead-on from nearly a mile away. Because of the size and enormous recoil of its gun, the airplane had to be large and very sturdy.

Even though the A–10 was the clear choice of the Air Force for the future close air support aircraft, there was another candidate already flying. The A–7, nicknamed the SLUF, or short, little, ugly fellow, was still in the Air Force inventory, although in small numbers. Originally a Navy design, the A–7 was a single-engine, single-seat attack jet known for its superb bombing accuracy, the result of a computerized HUD and an exceptional computer delivery system. The A–7, which did not have an afterburner, did not have a high top-end, supersonic speed like the F–4; but when it carried bombs, it flew at about the same speed as the F–4. Unlike the F–4, which gulped fuel at great rates, the SLUF sipped at its fuel tanks.

In September 1973 the Senate Armed Services Committee directed the Air Force to conduct another fly-off, this time between the A–10 and the A–7. In order to keep personal biases out of the competition, the committee ordered the

---

* The most feared Soviet gun system of the time was the ZSU–23-4, a four-barrel, 23-mm, radar-aimed, antiaircraft gun with exceptional accuracy and a very high rate of fire.

Air Force to select four pilots who had extensive fighter and CAS experience but had never before flown either the A–10 or the A–7. The fly-off took place from April 15 to May 9, 1974, as the four pilots flew representative CAS missions, first in one jet, then in the other. The consensus was that the A–10 was the better airplane. The A–10's slower speeds made it easier to keep the target area in sight, while its excellent maneuverability allowed it to stay close to the target area and attack several times quickly. Nevertheless, to a man, the pilots expressed concern about the A–10's inability to sustain its airspeed while maneuvering. They thought that the jet was underpowered. Officials dismissed their complaint by pointing out that the test aircraft were heavier than the production models would be, so the operational airplanes would be able to sustain their speed better.[5] Despite those assurances, the pilots who flew the first production models complained about the poor sustained turning capability, and many are still dissatisfied with it today.[6]

After it won the competition against the A–7, the A–10 underwent serious operational testing at Edwards Air Force Base, California. The airplane took some getting used to, since its slow speed and high-lift wing enabled it to turn quickly. Of course, accuracy was very important during CAS, and the A–10, in order to be simple, maintainable, and cheaper, did not have a bombing computer. All the bombs had to be dropped manually, just as they were in the earlier dis-cussion on dive bombing. F–4 pilots dropped their 45-degree dive bombs on the practice range at 4,000–4,500 feet in order to recover above 1,000 feet and avoid the frag from their own bombs. A–10 pilots could do the same from 2,000 feet and still recover above 1,000. Bombing accuracy from half the distance from the target was significantly better, but for the former fast-mover pilots it was at first disconcerting to be so steep so low to the ground.[7]

For many, learning to use the phenomenal gun was the true joy of flying the A–10. From 6,000 feet the pilot could open fire and be assured that the bullets would hit exactly where he placed the pipper. Capt. Wally Moorhead, who, along with Capt. Al Whitley, brought the first A–10s to Nellis to start the A–10 Fighter Weapons School, demonstrated the stunning firepower of the gun to a startled F–4 pilot who was chasing Moorhead on a test mission. With some time to kill, the two aircraft were circling the range when the F–4 pilot asked Moorhead how the gun worked. Moorhead volunteered to show him, rolled over, and pulled down toward a convoy of tank hulks sitting on the ranges below them. On his first pass, Moorhead obliterated the first tank and the last tank in the column. Then, on a second pass, he smashed the three in the middle of the column. On neither of the passes did he come within half a mile of the column. After a moment of stunned silence, the F–4 pilot transmitted, "Nice."[8]

Starting the A–10 Fighter Weapons School was no "walk in the park" in 1978. The ranges were jammed with the F–4 school, the F–15 school, Red Flag, Aggressor training, and countless tests conducted by the 422d Test Squadron. Moorhead recalled, "You had to fight your way onto Nellis."[9] The only range times available to the "new kids on the block" were very early in the morning or very late in the afternoon. Fighter squadrons usually schedule a certain number of jets to fly two or three times a day. The early and late range periods meant that the A-10s had to fly early, then wait all day and fly again late. It was a brutal schedule, but no slack was given, and none was requested. Not only did the A-10 have to fight its way into the range scheduling; it had to fight for respect from the solidly established F-4 weapons school that had been the premier unit at Nellis for over a decade. The F-15 school was not as senior as the F-4 school, but its pilots were flying the glamor jets. After the A-10 school had knocked around the base for a few months, the colonel in charge of all the weapons school operations found a place for the A-10, designated the 66th FWSq, in the same building as the F-15 school, the 433d FWSq. Moorhead remembers this as an excellent set up. The two new jets were in the same building, which forged strong associations among the pilots of the two vastly different jets with totally different missions: one sleek and swift, the other neither. After a day's flying was complete, the pilots often swapped tactical ideas over cold beer. Warthogs learned about air-to-air, and Eagle pilots learned about beating mud.[10] Although their missions were different, their jets were similar in that they both had twin vertical stabilizers. Soon the pilots started calling the common squadron radio station they shared, "Split-tail Ops."

The first order of business for Moorhead, Whitley, and the others was to develop a syllabus of instruction, flying and academics, for the A-10 school. They used the F-4 course as a template and modified it to fit the mission areas assigned to the A-10. The academic courses were relatively easy to construct. All of the weaponry the airplane could carry was already being carried by the F-4. As Moorhead said, "a bomb is a bomb; a fuze is a fuze."[11] Ultimately, the A-10 and F-4 schools combined their academic courses, and a little later all the fighter weapons schools changed their schedules, so that all students started and graduated at the same time, allowing airmen from different aircraft to share the same classroom space and, more importantly, their ideas.

Compared with the ease of setting up the academic program, the development of the A-10 flying program proved more difficult. Besides CAS, the Warthog was given the role of search and rescue support. During the Vietnam War, Air Force helicopters were active in rescuing downed U.S. airmen. When a SAR was active, firepower to support the helicopters directly came from old A-1E Skyraiders, a Korea-vintage, propeller-driven attack airplane. The A-1 was slow, perfect for finding the survivor as well as escorting the vulnerable helicopters to and from the pickup area. The A-1 was big for its day and carried a wide variety of ordnance, along with a generous fuel load. All the A-1s went to the boneyard after Vietnam, so it seemed logical for the new A-10 to pick up a mission that had lain dormant for several years. The new A-10 pilots at Nellis got plenty of practice at SAR operations because they were the only A-10s available to support Red Flag missions that were happening back-to-back by 1978. Every Red Flag put a pilot out in the desert as part of the exercise to coordinate rescue forces, and usually the helicopter escorts were Nellis A–10s flying with the familiar "Sandy" call sign.[12]

When the A–10s were free from Nellis duties in the weapons school and Red Flag, they often traveled to Army posts to work closely with the "grunts" in the primary role of supporting troops in combat. The Warthogs' radios were designed to talk to ground troops, and the jets had three different types to communicate with the ground commander. The A–10 also was equipped with a laser spot detector called Pave Penny. A soldier could fire a handheld, portable laser on a target, for example the lead tank in a threatening group. The A–10 pilot's HUD then displayed steering to that spot that the pilot could follow until he got close enough to see the target himself.[13] The laser system also gave the air-ground team the ability to hit targets on the ground without using the radios, a great capability, especially if the enemy was jamming the radios. Each time the A–10 attacked, the ground commander could have the spot moved to the target he wanted hit next.

These exercises with the Army were invaluable as the A–10 pilots learned more and more about how their sister service operated. The plan to defeat Soviet forces at the Fulda Gap and other fronts in Europe was simple to say, harder to execute. A–10s* would be based at large host bases in England and Germany. Each host base would have a few forward operating locations (FOL) closer to the NATO/Warsaw Pact border. During normal peacetime training, small numbers of A–10s would operate from the FOLs on a rotational basis, exercising frequently with the ground unit that they would support in wartime. If war started, the whole host base of A–10s would deploy to the scattered FOLs and work hand-in-hand with the ground forces. The tactics, coordination, and communication were issues the Nellis instructors worked on every day.

The A–10 fought its way into the fighter community the way it flew—slowly. But, just as surely, it earned the respect of those who watched it bust tanks, cover ground troops, and escort rescue helicopters. During a party celebrating the graduation of their first A–10 Fighter Weapons School class, the students showed a film clip pirated from a wildlife movie. In the short clip, two warthogs root around the ground, lazily snuffling up bits of fodder. They are ugly but seem at peace with the world. A voice-over, made by the A–10 pilots, adds a sound track of two A–10 pilots in casual conversation on the radio. Suddenly, seemingly from nowhere, a leopard streaks toward one warthog. The radio voice calls, "Hog 2, break left! Bogey 6 o'clock, 20 feet!" The warthog on the screen jumps left, and the speeding leopard overshoots, his extended claws barely missing the startled hog. A series of radio calls about the bogey's (leopard's) position ensue as both hogs try to run away (extend) from the leopard. The leopard is faster and closes as more radio calls are made, including a final one of "circle the hogs," a common

---

* Seven hundred thirteen A–10s were built for worldwide deployment. (Boyne, p. 288)

tactic used by A–10s under an air attack. Both hogs form a circle until the leopard is between them, and suddenly the hunter is the hunted. The ungainly, ugly hogs are now on the offensive, and they are very angry. Tusks flash at the leopard's haunches, and in an instant he sprints out of the picture to a radio call of "knock it off, knock it off," the common phrase for all players to discontinue the fight. The warthogs settle back into their rooting and snuffling.

The lesson was clear. They might be ugly, but they were proud ugly, and they could do their job. Approach with extreme caution.

---

1. Maj. Gen. Wally Moorhead, interview with author, April 14, 1999.

2. Harlan E. Branby, "A–10 Tank Killer," *USAF Fighter Weapons Review*, Winter '75, Nellis AFB, Nevada, pp. 5–6.

3. Moorhead interview.

4. Branby, pp. 3–5.

5. History, Air Force Systems Command, 1 July 1973–30 June 1974, Air Force Historical Research Agency, Maxwell AFB, Alabama, index number 1164, frame 1238–1251.

6. Moorhead interview.

7. Branby, p. 6.

8. Moorhead interview.

9. *Ibid.*

10. *Ibid.*

11. *Ibid.*

12. *Ibid.*

13. Branby, p. 3.

CHAPTER 17

✪

The F–16: The Fighter Pilot's Fighter

The whole thrill of flying single-seat got to me...one of those hidden lusts.[1]

Many fighter pilots, including a significant number of the Pentagon's Fighter Mafia, were not pleased with the way the F–15 came off the drawing boards and into production—big and expensive. Never mind that the Eagle was designed to outfly and outshoot the newest Soviet fighter, the Foxbat. Instead, the Eagle's critics continued to press within Air Force channels and the U.S. Congress for another fighter. They wanted one that was small, agile, and cheap. While debate raged inside the Washington Beltway, two prototypes emerged and competed. The winner was the General Dynamics F–16.

Less than five years after the Eagle and Warthog entered the inventory, they were followed by the F–16. Lord Byron said that a thing of beauty is a joy forever, and the newest jet to join the Air Force was indeed a thing of beauty. The sleek design wrapped around a single, powerful F100* engine in smooth sleekness said, "This is one hot jet." A one-piece bubble canopy surrounded the single cockpit and gave the pilot a perfect view of his surroundings; there was not even a canopy bow† to clutter his vision. Inside the small, tight cockpit were several innovations. The most startling was the absence of a stick between the pilot's knees. Replacing the age-old stick was a small hand controller, like a video game joystick, on the right console. Called the sidestick controller, it was designed to fit perfectly in the pilot's right hand and command flight control movement by feeling the pressure from the pilot.‡ The pilot's seat was another revelation. It was reclined 30 degrees as a way of lowering the pilot's head relative to his heart, thereby making it easier to maintain better blood flow to the brain under high g. The pilot did not climb into the cockpit; he slid into it. It was a snug fit, and the approved technique was to enter butt first to sit on the seat, then swing the legs in and slide them down narrow channels on either side of the small radar scope between the pilot's knees. After he closed the bubble canopy, the effect was not

---

* The same engine used in the F–15.

† Small metal band that separates the windscreen front from the movable cover of a conventional canopy.

‡ Only the first few airplanes had the immovable controller. The pilots requested and quickly received a controller that moved a small amount, an eighth of an inch or so, to help them feel the proper control pressures more accurately.

An air-to-air close-up view of the cockpit of an F–16 Fighting Falcon during refueling.
Official USAF photo.

being *in* the jet, but of *wearing* it—an aluminum and titanium glove made just for him and him alone.

Ernest Hemingway said that no man loves any airplane more than his first, but the F–4 and A–7 pilots who converted to the F–16 were hard-pressed to love this beautiful new jet less. Every generation has an airplane for which pilots unabashedly carry a flaming torch. In World War II, it was the P–51 Mustang; in Korea, the F–86 Sabre. After Korea and the F–86, a few might argue, but most would point to the F–104 Starfighter—the "Last of the Sport Models." All had common features—small, powerful, single-seat, single-engine, and a joy to fly.

The F–16 epitomized its little predecessors in every way, especially the joy of flight. The sidestick controller was easy to get used to, and it took virtually no time for the pilot to adjust to not having a conventional, push-pull stick between his knees. One pilot, when asked how long it took to acclimate to the new controller, responded, "About three hundred feet down the first takeoff roll."[2] The feeling of takeoff, however, was entirely different from the blasting, snorting, and thundering roll of the old Phantom. The F–16, like the F–15, needed no afterburner for a normal takeoff; acceleration was smooth and rapid in the airconditioned comfort of a chilled cockpit, and the little jet fairly danced off the concrete.

The original F–16 design called for a lightweight fighter, small and agile, that could polish off those adversaries in close-in dogfighting that survived the Eagle's attacks with long-range Sparrow shots. The F–16 had no radar missile; its armament consisted of an internal gun, the same one carried by every other Air

Capt. Steve Hanes in a Fighter
Weapons School F–16A at
Nellis Air Force Base.
Courtesy of Nancy Hanes.

Force fighter,* and Sidewinders. This ordnance could be used only in visual conditions where the F–16 pilot could see his adversary and close on him for the kill. The jet had a small radar that could search and track targets, but it was not nearly as powerful as the Eagle's. Nonetheless, it was good enough to get the F–16 pilot to the merge, and once he was there, his jet was the best dogfighter in the world.

The first pilots to fly the jet soon started to call it the Viper, despite the Falcon appellation given it by the Air Force. The official name never stuck with the pilots, just as the Thunderbolt name never stuck with the Warthog drivers. Whatever its name, the F–16 in a fight was incredibly agile, thanks to its design and a computerized flight control system. When the pilot put aft pressure on the controller, the flight control computer responded by positioning the elevator to increase g loading. If the pilot wanted maximum g, all he had to do was pull back against the controller as hard as possible, and the little jet would respond immediately with the maximum g it could pull. It could then hold that g as long as the pilot wanted it or the airspeed would allow. No other jet could pull as many gs as the Viper. The pilot could snatch into an immediate 9-g turn without fear of overstressing the little jet or pulling off its wings. Pilots of older fighters, including the F–15, had to smoothly blend in the g up to a maximum rate turn by feel.† Thus, the Viper had an advantage in a maneuvering fight.

The F–16's small size was a clear advantage in a daytime, visual dogfight, and the pilots loved it. Steve Hanes said that the F–4 had been a great airplane, and, in the hands of a very good pilot, it could survive against the new jets if the F–4 pilot

---

* Except the A–10, which carried the tank-buster 30-mm cannon.

† There was a g-meter that showed the pilots how hard they were pulling on the pole, and the F–15 had a digital g-readout in the HUD. However, since most turning was done as the pilot looked out the top and back of the canopy, the readouts were useless. Pilots were trained to learn the feel or pressure of g-loads so they did not damage or even destroy the jet by pulling too hard. A modification to the F–15 in the early 1980s gave the pilot a tone in his headset that warned him of an impending over-g.

Capt. Kevin McElvain in the cockpit of an F–4 at MacDill Air Force Base, Florida.
Courtesy of Mary McElvain.

had a lot of "moxie."[3] However, the agile, powerful, and diminutive F–16 was overwhelming, even in the hands of a mediocre aviator. Joe Bob Phillips said that the F–16 was the airplane he had always been looking for, "an F–4 writ small, not writ large like the F–15."[4] Adding to the little jet's lethality was the AIM–9L, which could be shot from any direction, or aspect, at the target. A close-in, maneuvering fight against the deadly Viper was not where other pilots wanted to be, especially the F–15 "Flying Tennis Court," which could be easily seen from several miles away.

Yet the Viper was not just a dogfighter; it was also intended to replace the bombing capability of the aging F–4. Included in the F–16 computer software were some very accurate delivery modes. The gunsight, as it was projected on the HUD, constantly predicted where the bombs would hit when it was in the A/G mode. All the pilot had to do was fly the pipper to the target and press the pickle button with his right thumb on the sidestick. The system was so accurate that the pilots soon began calling the pipper the "death dot." Despite its accuracy, bombs and the F–16 were not an ideal mix. The little jet, like most of its small predecessors, was extremely sensitive to the drag produced by bombs hanging in the slipstream. When the small fighter was loaded down with two external fuel tanks, a jamming pod, a couple of Sidewinders, and bombs, it was like flying with the barn door open in the breeze. Phillips and others believed that the Viper was not as good a mud beater as the F–4 because the venerable Phantom carried a much larger payload to the target.[5] Others argued that the F–16's lethal death dot overcame its inability to carry a large payload.

In the midst of the controversy about how the F–16 should be used in the ground attack mission, the Tactical Fighter Weapons Center activated the F–16 weapons school at Nellis Air Force Base, Nevada, in October 1981.[6] Maj. Kevin McElvain, an instructor pilot in the F–4 weapons school, was the base project officer in charge of organizing the new flying and academic syllabi for the fledgling fighter.[7] Like Wally Moorhead and the A–10 weapons school, the new

Viper drivers had to "fight their way onto Nellis." However, this time the new guys on the block were competing for space and dollars against all the same adversaries, as well as the F–4, F–15, and A–10 schools. The new F–16 pilots started by being jammed into a small office at the headquarters building: three desks in a small room shared with another office. They had a blank notebook from which to start, but their direction from TAC headquarters was clear. The F–16 was replacing the F–4, so the breakdown of missions should look very similar. McElvain, who was a former F–100 and F–4 pilot, knew the F–4 course well. He and his helpers, Captains Steve Hanes and Kees Rietsema, used the F–4 course as a template and modified it slightly to add a little more A/A to it. They immediately ran into a stone wall of disapproval from TAC. Officers there had determined that the mix of A/A and A/G sorties would be exactly what it was in the F–4 and exactly what the operational units were flying: 35 percent for A/A and 65 percent for dirt beating. McElvain arranged a trip to the TAC headquarters at Langley Air Force Base, Virginia, to explain their rationale. The pilots argued that the purpose of the weapons school was to train instructors, and A/A was the hardest thing to teach; therefore, more sorties should be devoted to it. They did not even finish the briefing before the TAC general in charge of operations summarily dismissed them.[8]

As the F–16 weapons school labored to get started, another squadron at Nellis, the 422d Test Squadron, was conducting a test that was a fighter pilot's dream. The main purpose of the test was to investigate ways to reduce the radar cross section of the F–16. Radar cross section, or RCS, is the amount of radar energy an airplane reflects to a tracking radar. The more it reflects, the larger its RCS. An airplane with a large RCS can be tracked from farther away, and more accurately, than one with a smaller RCS. The test would compare different techniques for reducing the F–16's RCS against a variety of radar systems. This meant that the F–16 pilots would fly against the pulse radar of the F–4 and the pulse doppler radar on the F–15, over some 200 test missions. For the Eagle, Phantom, and Viper pilots in the 422d, it was heaven. It was a license to fly unlimited A/A against one another in every conceivable scenario: two Eagles against two Vipers, four against two, four against four, two F–16s against four F–4s, and so on. Every mission was flown on ACMI to document performance, or lack of it. The F–16s always had to fight against an equal or greater number of adversaries; they were never allowed to outnumber the opponents.

Although the test parameters were set, the pilots, like the AIMVAL-ACEVAL pilots, had considerable latitude in selecting and devising tactics. The considerations boiled down to a few key facts. The F–4s and F–15s could shoot their radar-guided Sparrows well beyond visual range. The F–16 had neither a radar missile, nor a radar as powerful as the others did. Therefore, the F–4 and F–15 could not only see the Vipers first, they could also shoot at them first. Also, the new Sparrows, the AIM–7F, on the F–15 were proving to be very accurate and reliable in shots against drones. In effect, "the F–15 was playing a whole new ball game, and they got to write the rules."[9]

Without doubt, the pilots who would fly in the test were some of the best in the Air Force. The 422d commander, Lt. Col. Joe Merrick, had commanded the Multinational Operational Test and Evaluation of the F–16 at Hill Air Force Base before taking over leadership of the 422d, and he immediately surrounded himself with the best pilots he could find. Most, if not all, were combat veterans, and all were weapons school graduates.[10]

The F–16 pilots immediately started to look for ways to survive to the merge. They drew on the lessons learned a few years earlier by the AIMVAL-ACEVAL Air Force pilots who had found themselves in the same situation. They studied the F–15 radar and the Sparrow missile and found some small vulnerabilities, which they exploited. It took perfect timing and pilotage, but if they could confuse the Eagle and Phantom pilots and get one or two Vipers to the merge, they could fight on F–16 terms. Of course, the Eagle and Phantom pilots immediately developed techniques that countered the tactics of the F–16s, and another cycle of countering the counter to the counter began. The stakes were high. Everyone knew that the Soviets were equipping their fighters with missiles similar to the Sparrow and Sidewinder. The days of U.S. pilots having the only effective radar missile in the battle were long gone, and the F–16 pilots had no radar missile at all. Blithely flying straight into the merge from twenty miles away was a sure recipe for disaster.

The competition was intense. One day a pilot brought a rubber chicken, the kind used in slapstick comedy, to the squadron, and he and his buddies stuck into the silly, limp carcass a host of small plastic models of A/A missiles. The next day they hung the bird over the entrance door to the flight room of the guys who had lost the fight. The day after that it reappeared over the door of that day's losers. No one wanted it, and the pilots studied hard, flew hard, and schemed hard to avoid seeing it show up at their door. From this atmosphere of intense competition in Merrick's squadron emerged a new tactical term: all-aspect missile defense (AAMD). As pilots of each of the fighter models learned ways to survive—and kill—in the all-aspect missile environment of the Sparrows and Sidewinders, they spread the word throughout the weapons school. Students then took the new tactics back to their home units. Within five years, all Air Force fighter squadrons were using AAMD as part of their daily training routine. As they honed their skills to employ their own "face shooters," they also learned how to survive ones fired at them.[11]

Work done in the 422d Test Squadron was not totally original. Those who were there are the first to say that AAMD developed over several years and carried the fingerprints of dozens of great fighter pilots.[12] Aggressors had been defending themselves against all-aspect missiles for years, and the AIMVAL-ACEVAL pilots brought the tactics to an even higher level. Yet several factors converged in the early 1980s that made AAMD vital to the newest generation of fighter pilots. First, the missiles were becoming more credible every day as the WSEP results revealed superb missile accuracy and reliability. Second, the new HUDs and fire control computers showed exact launch parameters, helping pilots know exactly where they were within the missile's capability to hit the target. Additionally, the Soviets were fielding a new generation of missiles as good as—some thought better than—the Americans, giving the development of an effective AAMD added urgency. Finally, dissimilar air combat training, testing, and evaluation had matured to the point that every pilot had the opportunity to fight often against different aircraft. A feeling started to grow within the Air Force fighter community that if an F–16 pilot could beat an F–15, or an F–15 could beat a Navy Tomcat, then when the next war came, the enemy would be dead meat.

By 1984 the most striking change in the battle arena was how much technological changes had expanded the air-to-air battle space. Ten years earlier, F–4 pilots had struggled mightily to get radar contacts and tried to take the first shot with a questionable radar missile. The main focus for the Phantom drivers, however, was to get to position from which they could visually engage and kill the bulk of the targets. In the mid-1980s, the F–15 could see fighter-size targets over fifty miles away and start to jockey for the first shot. Even the small radar on the Viper could see targets beyond twenty miles. The new jets were maneuvering at vastly extended ranges based on the information from their radars.[13] "The tactics development from all that shucking and jiving made everybody learn."[14]

The pure joy of the F–16, though, was in the furball, where the aircraft had the edge over the F–15 and a significant advantage over everything else. With the F–16's incredible agility and power, the pilot could get close and stay close. He was less a viper than a python gradually squeezing the fight closer while beating down his victim's energy and resistance until the time came for a mortal blow. Chaff might spoof a radar missile or flares might decoy a heat-seeker, but as one pilot said, "The gun is stupid. You can't jam it and you can't fool it."[15] The F–16 was a superb gunfighter, and in the furball it was the top cat.

1. Stephen W. Hanes, interview with author, Peachtree City, Georgia, July 7, 1999.
2. Joe Bob Phillips, telephone interview with author, July 7, 1999.
3. Hanes interview.
4. Phillips interview.
5. *Ibid.*
6. Briefing given at 50th Anniversary celebration of the USAF Weapons School, Flamingo Hilton Hotel, Las Vegas, Nevada, June 19, 1999.
7. Kevin L. McElvain, telephone interview with author, July 8, 1999.
8. *Ibid.*
9. Hanes interview.
10. Phillips interview.
11. *Ibid.*
12. *Ibid.*
13. Hanes interview; Phillips interview.
14. Phillips interview.
15. *Ibid.*

CONCLUSION

○

Volumes have been written about bitter veterans returning from Vietnam, and more has yet to be written. Certainly the cynical soldier's story reinforces a certain perception of the military establishment as inept at best. There is no denying that the military bureaucracy is ponderous and sometimes inefficient. However, there is a core of officers and sergeants who always seem to make things happen despite the odds. They are military, too, and after every war they stick around to make things better. While others leave the service for greener pastures—or at least pastures that are perceived to be greener— the hard core hangs on, willing to face the challenge.

Fighter pilots returning from Vietnam to the peacetime Air Force did not come home with their tails between their legs. Many had more than one tour and would have gone back again if the service had let them. They were proud of the effort they put forth under difficult circumstances, and most would echo the line, "I don't know what went wrong; we were winning when I left." If nothing else, fighter pilots are pragmatists; they knew the difference between what went well and what went badly. They also knew that the things that were wrong needed repair, and that the things that had gone right probably would not work in the next war anyhow. For creative tacticians like John Jumper, Ron Keys, Joe Bob Phillips, and Earl Henderson there was only one direction to go—forward.

Training for combat in Vietnam was abysmal. The RTUs did their best, but the steady flow of pilots in the pipeline was overwhelming. Commanders were graded by how well they could grind out new crews for the war, while not losing airplanes in crashes. Therefore, they seldom washed out anyone, and they went through the motions of providing training in events perceived to be more dangerous, such as air combat training. John Madden, who shot down three MiGs, recalls pilots flying air combat patrol over North Vietnam who did not know how to do even the most basic defensive turn.

The veterans who stayed worked hard, often under worse, though safer, conditions than they had seen in the war. The Air Force had been declining in manpower since the end of the Korean War, and after Vietnam the drawdown accelerated. Flying hours declined dramatically as budget cuts ripped into funds for spare parts and supplies. Frustrated pilots described their disgust by saying, "Brief four, start three, taxi two, takeoff alone." Their meaning was that they would be assigned four aircraft for a mission, but only three would be operational, another would break after engine start, and a third would abort right before takeoff, leaving a single jet to fly the mission planned for four.

At the end of the war, though, there were some very bright lights at the end of the tunnel. Laser-guided bombs showed that precision bombing, or surgical strike in Washington-speak, was the wave of the future. Therefore, the Air Force dove headlong into laser development and produced five generations of laser designators

F–16 in flight from
Hill Air Force Base, Utah.
Official USAF painting.

and three generations of laser bombs in fifteen years. New jets were on the agenda as well, and the first F–15 Eagles were sitting on the ramp at Luke Air Force Base with the tips of their tails painted with the green stripe of the Triple Nickel barely a year after the war ended.

The brightest lights, though, were the great minds and selfless leaders who put hardware to work by finding more efficient and useful ways to train fighter pilots to do their job—intimidate the enemy into inaction, or, failing that, crush him without mercy. Much of the work was done at Nellis in the 57th Fighter Weapons Wing, and what an ideal place to do it—nearly perfect weather, vast chunks of airspace, targets that looked like enemy equipment, and a charter to develop weapons and tactics. The icing on the cake, though, were the pilots and WSOs, handpicked from the best of the best. There was no shortage of opinions on how to do things, and Moody Suter was not the only one to have 1,000 ideas a week, or a day. There was no shortage of egos either, and many throughout the Air Force looked at the weapons school graduate "target arms" as prima donnas in an ivory tower. Some Nellis commanders cultivated that view until commanders like Larry Keith made some attitude adjustments. However, Keith and others knew that the way to make change was by changing the institution, not by giving orders; so he greatly increased the number of trips his Nellis instructors made to other bases. There, they were reminded of what it was like down in the trenches with no ranges to drop live bombs and the nearest air combat airspace so far away there was only enough fuel for one quick setup. He also made sure that his instructors learned how to be teachers and learned how to teach how to teach.

Measurements of combat capability sprang from the fertile minds of several aviators. Tired of seeing pilots get by without knowing really how good or bad they were, Joe Bob Phillips, Dave Dellwardt, Tommy Dyches, Ron Keys, Bob Tone, Dick Myers, and many more drew up specific training objectives that fit within Jumper's building block approach. As gun cameras, video recorders, ACMI, bomb scoring with TV, and other documentation devices became available, fighter crews learned who really had the good hands. More importantly, though, they learned why. For many it was the first time their fighter pilot ego had to face the cold reality of counting every flickering frame of a tracking gun shot. At first some pilots faced the humiliation of throwing five dollars in the kitty, but with discipline came success, and the kitty got smaller and smaller.

Even though the 414th FWSq and the F–4 weapons school were calling the tactical shots at Nellis, the two biggest strides in tactical aviation came from earlier graduates in the form of the Aggressors and Red Flag. The Aggressor charter was to fly a MiG-sized aircraft, using MiG tactics, and to replicate the enemy as closely as possible. Seemingly overnight the tactical fighter forces had an enemy to practice against, and a realistic one at that. An entire generation of fighter pilots suddenly learned, sometimes in embarrassing ways, that what worked against their squadron buddy in an identical airplane was useless against an Aggressor. Check left and extend went out the window quickly, as did fighting wing, a formation/tactic that had not changed in over twenty years.

Most important, though, was the cultural impact of the Aggressors. Before the Aggressors, there was little dissimilar air combat training in the Air Force, and often it was prohibited altogether. Less than five years after the Aggressors started, regulations encouraged squadrons around the world to pick up the phone to call a Navy or Marine unit nearby and say, "How about a four on four in the restricted area tomorrow at 10:00 hours?" The impact of Red Flag on combat training is nearly immeasurable. Tens of thousands of aviators from the USAF, Navy, Marines, Army, Canada, NATO, Air National Guard, Air Force Reserve, and countless allies have participated to get those all important first ten combat missions under their belts before the shooting started for real. It was at Red Flag that fighter pilots like then-Lt. Col. Chuck Horner decided that low altitude was for the birds and that there had to be a better way. Clearly, for Desert Storm, he was right because he fought a successful medium-altitude war over Iraq, using electronic equipment, weapons, and stealth aircraft that could disable or destroy the enemy radars that so preoccupied aviators in the 1970s. But that's another story.

The addition of the F–15, A–10, and F–16 to the fighter inventory helped keep the USAF the strongest air force in the world. The F–15 and A–10 returned mission specialization to former F–4 pilots, who had suffered for years with the jack-of-all-trades millstone hanging on the fronts of their flight suits. The F–16 was such a sweet jet to fly that even though it had to do both air combat and dirt beating, the pilots fell in love with it at first sight. Two of the new jets were sleek and powerful, the other slow and not so pretty. Nonetheless, those who flew any of them couldn't wait for the next sortie because they were designed so well. Bubble canopies, switches under the fingers, HUDs, and reliable firepower made them a joy to fly. They were born from the lessons of combat, and their pilots had total confidence that the next war would see them equipped to handle any contingency.

The decade after the end of the war in Vietnam was at once exasperating and exhilarating. However, the changes were incredible. Perhaps a short narrative will show just how incredible. In 1974 the Air Force reassigned me from an overseas assignment in England to Nellis. When I arrived, I had over 1,200 hours in the F–4, including 365 combat hours. I had never flown a dissimilar air combat sortie. I had never carried a training AIM–9 and had not even seen one since my combat tour four years earlier. I had never used a gun camera. The only tactical formation I had flown was Fluid Four/Fighting Wing. I had never intercepted a target at low altitude. In other words, I was a typical F–4 pilot with a combat tour. Ten years later, on my second tour of duty in Europe, I took off from Bitburg Air Base, Germany, in an F–15C with my wingman. At 500 feet I leveled off and gave him a visual signal to go to tactical formation—line-abreast, one mile apart. We flew east fast and low, making silent comm-out turns until we reached a special piece of airspace in eastern West Germany, called Low Fly Area 7, where we set up a combat air patrol. Over the next thirty minutes we intercepted fighters from the German air force and others from the USAF at low altitude using the F–15 radar. Most of our shots were in-the-face Sidewinders. After our patrol time was up, we flew, still at low altitude, and still silently, back to Bitburg, where I turned us onto the initial approach and called the tower for landing, the first radio call I had made since asking for takeoff clearance an hour earlier. When we got back into the squadron building, my wingman and I reviewed our videocassettes to assess every shot each of us had taken. Every one of his shots was valid; mine were nearly as good. My wingman had less than 100 hours of fighter time. To him, it was just another day in the 525th Tactical Fighter Squadron; to me it was a revelation. *Sierra Hotel!*

APPENDICES

The True Story of Jeremiah Weed

Every USAF fighter squadron has a lounge where the pilots sometimes gather for a cold beer after the flying day is over. Every refrigerator in each of those lounges contains a chilled bottle of a 100-proof product called Jeremiah Weed. For special occasions, and sometimes for no reason at all, someone will bring out the Weed, fill a shot glass for each person present, and propose a toast. At the conclusion of the toast, all down their Weed in a single gulp. It is not tasty. To many it seems like drinking kerosene, and it leaves a very strong after-taste. Be that as it may, few refuse because the downing of a Weed is a ritual deeply imbedded in the fighter pilot culture. That ritual started long before today's squadron commanders were even in college, and stories abound as to how the custom started. A famous newsman once said, "When there is disagreement between the legend and the truth, always print the legend." Since I disagree, here is the true story of Jeremiah Weed, and I know it's true because I was part of it.

On December 1, 1978, I was flying as an instructor in the back seat of a F–4E, tail number 649, on a BFM hop out of the 414th FWSq at Nellis Air Force Base, Nevada. The student in my front seat, Maj. Nort Nelson, was a highly experienced F–4 pilot with hundreds of combat hours. Leading the flight was Capt. Joe Bob Phillips, who had in his back seat Capt. Larry Ernst, an instructor who was just along for the ride. The mission called for Joe Bob to attack Nort in a scripted scenario that gave Nort the opportunity to use his best defensive BFM to defeat Joe Bob's attacks. The mission did not last long. On the first engagement, Nort managed to put the airplane into a position from which I judged that recovery was impossible.* I ejected both of us from the jet. Neither of us was injured, and within an hour we were picked up by a helicopter that returned us to Nellis. It probably goes without saying that Nort and I had different views: he thought he could miss the ground; I did not. It was too close to bet my life on. The accident investigators agreed with me. They determined that ejection was the only possibility for survival. Further, they believed that if I had delayed more than a second, one or both of us would have died in the desert seventy miles north of Las Vegas.

A year later, both Joe Bob and Nort were members of the F–16 Multinational Operational Test and Evaluation squadron at Hill Air Force Base, Utah. On the first anniversary of the accident, they were flying to Nellis to participate in Red Flag. As they passed over the crash site, which Joe Bob easily found since he had circled our downed position many times, they sketched some brief road maps on cards in their cockpits and decided to return to the site by car.

---

* The details are for another story, which I will tell in a future book.

The next day, a Friday, they drove out of Las Vegas with a friend, Pete Mock, intending to find the site and camp out in the crater that the crashing airplane had gouged in the high desert. However, it was dark by the time they got to the dirt road they thought would lead them to the site. After a couple of aborted attempts to drive up dirt roads to nowhere, they decided to go back to a roadside café they had passed to ask directions.

They entered the Paranaghat Bar and found no customers, only a bearded bartender who looked a lot like Grizzly Adams. When they told the bartender what they were up to, he was delighted to tell them he had seen the fire from the crashing airplane the day of the accident. Further, he was very pleased that he had three real fighter pilots in his bar. He had heard that fighter pilots knew many bar games (true), and he wanted to play games for drinks. When they balked at the idea, he persisted, and after much cajoling asked them if they knew the game "horses." They shook their heads no (not true). Over the next several minutes, the bartender "taught" them horses, finally saying that whoever lost had to buy a round of drinks. After three games of horses, the bartender had bought all three rounds. And after three rounds the pilots were a little less stressed to get to the crash site.

Joe Bob asked the bartender if he knew how to do afterburners. No, the bartender said, he had never heard of that game. So, Joe Bob explained to him how a shot of brandy in a shot glass is ignited so that the alcohol on top burns, and then the drinker throws down the flaming shot. If done correctly, all the brandy is emptied from the shot glass, so that when the drinker puts the glass down, a small, blue flame still burns in the bottom. The bartender was eager to play but said he had no brandy. Nort suggested that any high-proof booze might work, and the bartender fumbled around under the bar for a moment. He straightened up and plopped a tall, brown bottle with a brown and green label on the bar, and said, "I've got this here stuff—it's 100 proof." The brand name on the green label proclaimed that it was Jeremiah Weed. The three fighter pilots filled their shot glasses and demonstrated, all three glasses returning to the bar empty except for a small blue flame flickering at the bottom.

The bartender immediately poured one for himself and lit the top. Now, these were no ordinary twentieth-century shot glasses. Joe Bob thought they might be from the 1800s because the glass was very thick, and the bottom was probably an inch of heavy glass. When the bartender picked his up, he held it by the bottom while he licked and smoothed the mustache of his thick beard out of the line of fire. He took several moments on his grooming, not realizing that as he held the thick glass at the bottom, the top near the fire was heating quickly. By the time he tilted his head back and put the glass to his lips.....well, Joe Bob says you could probably hear the s-s-s-s-sizzle of the hot glass barbecuing the bartender's lips halfway to Las Vegas. Then the bartender made his second mistake and flinched. The flaming Weed went all over his beard, and by the time Joe Bob, Nort, and Pete could beat out the flames, the bar was filled with the smell of cooked lips and singed hair.

As soon as things calmed down a bit, the trio, feeling badly that they had not paid for a drink all night and greatly embarrassed that they had nearly immolated their new friend, bought another bottle of Weed from him and left again for the crash site, this time guided by one of the bartender's friends who had entered the bar just in time to witness and smell the blistering. The friend showed them the correct dirt road, and the trio found the crash crater, where they spent the rest of the night camped out and drinking the entire bottle of Weed.

The next morning they dragged themselves out of the crater, gathered a few souvenirs from the parts still lying around, and headed straight for the Nellis Air Force Base Officers' Club. There they found the manager, showed her the empty bottle, and strongly suggested she add it to the bar stock. She did. Soon, the Nellis fighter pilots were downing shots of Weed (nonflaming) for no good reason except it was different, and it was a good excuse to toast "fallen comrades." As Red Flags came through the Nellis club, they saw the weapons school guys doing it, so they did it, too.

And that is the true story of how Jeremiah Weed started. I have a bottle in my freezer.

The Dear Boss Letter*

Dear Boss,

Well, I quit. I've finally run out of drive or devotion or rationalizations or whatever it was that kept me in the Air Force this long. I used to believe in, "Why not the best," but I can't keep the faith any longer. I used to fervently maintain that this was "My Air Force," as much or more than any senior officer's... but I can't believe any more; the light at the end of my tunnel went out. "Why?" you ask. Why leave flying fighters and a promising career? Funny you should ask—mainly I'm resigning because I'm tired. Ten years and 2,000 hours in a great fighter, and all the time I've been doing more with less—and I'm tired of it. CBPO [Central Base Personnel Office] doesn't do more with less; they cut hours. I can't even entrust CBPO to have my records accurately transcribed to MPC [Military Personnel Center]. I have to go to Randolph to make sure my records aren't botched. Finance doesn't do more with less; they close at 15:00. The hospital doesn't do more with less. They cut hours, cut services, and are rude to my dependents to boot. Maintenance doesn't do more with less; they MND [maintenance non delivery] and SUD [supply delete] and take 2.5 to turn a clean F–4. Everybody but the fighter pilot has figured out the fundamental fact that you can't do more with less—you do less. (And everybody but the fighter pilot gets away with it... when's the last time the head of CBPO was fired because a man's records were a complete disaster?) But on the other hand, when was the last time anyone in the fighter game told higher headquarters, "We can't hack 32 DOCs [designated operational capability] because we can't generate the sorties?" Anyway—I thought I could do it just like all the rest thought they could... and we did it for a while... but now it's too much less to do too much more, and a lot of us are tired. And it's not the job. I've been TDY [on temporary duty] to every dirty little outpost on democracy's frontier that had a 6,000-foot strip. I've been gone longer than most young jocks have been in—and I don't mind the duty or the hours. That's what I signed up for. I've been downtown and seen the elephant, and I've watched my buddies roll up in fireballs—I understand—it comes with the territory. I can do it. I did it. I can still do it—but I won't. I'm too tired, not of the job, just the Air Force. Tired of the extremely poor leadership and motivational ability of our senior staffers and commanders. (All those Masters and PMEs [professional military educators] and not a leadership trait in sight!) Once you get past your squadron CO [Commanding Officer], people can't even

---

* This letter was written a few years after the end of the Vietnam War by Capt. Ron Keys to Gen. Wilbur Creech, then commander of TAC. See p. 65 for historical context.

pronounce esprit de corps. Even a few squadron COs stumble over it. And let me clue you—in the fighter business when you're out of esprit, you're out of corps—to the tune of 22,000 in the next five years, if you follow the airline projections. And why? Why not? Why hang around in an organization that rewards excellence with no punishment? Ten years in the Air Force, and I've never had a DO or Wing Commander ask me what our combat capability is, or how our exposure times are running during ops, or what our air-to-air loss and exchange ratios are—no, a lot of interest in boots, haircuts, scarves, and sleeves rolled down, but zero—well, maybe a query or two on taxi spacing—on my job: not even a passing pat on the ass semiannually. If they're not interested, why should I be so fanatical about it? It ought to be obvious I'm not in it for the money. I used to believe—and now they won't even let me do that.

And what about career? Get serious! A string of nine-fours and ones as long as your arm, and nobody can guarantee anything. No matter that you're the Air Force expert in subject Y... if the computer spits up your name for slot C—you're gone. One man gets 37 days to report remote—really now, did someone slit his wrists or are we that poor at managing? Another gets a face-to-face, no-change-for-six-months-brief from MPC... two weeks later? You got it—orders in his in basket. I'm ripe to PCS—MPC can't hint where or when; I've been in too long to take the luck of the draw—I've worked hard, I've established myself, I can do the job better than anyone else—does that make a difference? Can I count on progression? NO. At 12–15 hours a day on my salary at my age, I don't need that insecurity and aggravation. And then the big picture—the real reasons we're all pulling the handle—it's the organization itself. A noncompetitive training system that allows people in fighters that lack the aptitude or the ability to do the job. Once they're in, you can't get them out... not in EFLIT, not in RTU, and certainly not in an operational squadron. We have a fighter pilot short-fall—didn't you hear? So now we have lower quality people with motivation problems, and the commander won't allow anyone to jettison them. If you haven't noticed, that leaves us with a lot of people in fighters, but very few fighter pilots, and the ranks of both are thinning; the professionals are dissatisfied and most of the masses weren't that motivated to begin with. MPC helps out by moving Lts every 12–15 months or so—that way nobody can get any concentrated training on them before they pull the plug. Result: most operational squadrons aren't worth a damn. They die wholesale every time the Aggressors deploy—anybody keep score? Anybody care? Certainly not the whiz kid commander, who blew in from 6 years in staff, picked up 100 hours in the bird, and was last seen checking the grass in the sidewalk cracks. He told his boys, "Don't talk to me about tactics—my only concern is not losing an aircraft... and meanwhile, get the grass out of the sidewalk cracks!"—and the clincher—integrity. Hide as much as you can... particularly from the higher headquarters that could help you if only they knew. They never will though—staff will see to that: "Don't say that to the general!" or "The general doesn't like to hear that." I didn't know he was paid to like things—I thought he was paid to run things ... how can he when he never hears the problems? Ah well, put it off until it becomes a crisis—maybe it will be overcome by events. Maybe if we ignore it, it won't be a problem. (Shh, don't rock the boat). Meanwhile, lie about the takeoff times, so it isn't an ops or maintenance late. (One more command post to mobile call to ask subtly if I gave the right time because "ahh, that makes him two minutes late," and I will puke!) Lie about your DOC capability because you're afraid to report you don't have the sorties to hack it. "Yes, sir, losing two airplanes won't hurt us at all." The party line. I listened to a three-star general look a room full of us in the face and say that he "Didn't realize that pencil-whipping records was done in the Air Force. Holloman, and dive toss was an isolated case, I'm sure." It was embarrassing— that general looked us in the eye and said, in effect, "Gentlemen, either I'm very stupid or I'm lying to you." I about threw in the towel right there—or the day TAC fixed the experience ratio problem by lowering the number of hours needed to be experienced. And then they insult your intelligence to boot. MPC looks you straight in the eye and tells you how competitive a heart-of-the-envelope three is! ... and what a bad deal the airlines offer! Get a grip—I didn't just step off the bus from Lackland! And then the final blow, the Commander of TAC arrives—does he ask why my outfit goes 5 for 1 against F–5s and F–15s when most of his operational outfits run 1 for 7 on a good day? (Will anybody let us volunteer the information?) Does he express interest in why we can do what we do and not lose an airplane in five years? No—he's impressed with shoe shines and scarves and clean ashtrays. (But then we were graciously allotted only minimum time to present anything—an indication of our own wing's support of the program. Party line, no issues, no controversy—yes, sir; no, sir; three bags full, sir.) ... And that's why I'm resigning ... long hours with little support, entitlements eroded, integrity a mockery, zero visible career progression, and senior commanders evidently totally missing the point (and everyone afraid or forbidden to inform them.) I've had it—life's too short to fight an uphill battle for commanders and staffs who won't listen (remember Corona Ace?) or don't believe or maybe don't even care. So thanks for the memories, it's been a real slice of life .... But I've been to the mountain and looked over and I've seen the big picture—and it wasn't of the Air Force.

"This is your captain speaking ... on your left you should be able to see Denver, Colorado, the mile ..."

Glossary

A/A	air-to-air
AAA	antiaircraft artillery
AAMD	all-aspect missile defense
AB	Air Base
AC	aircraft commander
ACEVAL	air combat evaluation
ACM	air combat maneuver
ACMI	air combat maneuvering and instrumentation (range)
ACMR	air combat maneuvering range (Navy)
ACT	air combat tactics
ADC	Air Defense Command
AFB	Air Force Base
AFROTC	Air Force Reserve Officer Training Corps
A/G	air-to-ground
AGL	above ground level
AIM–7	Sparrow missile
AIM–9	Sidewinder missile
AIMVAL	air intercept missile evaluation
AOA	angle(s) of attack
AOR	assigned area of responsibility
AVTR	audio-visual tape recorder
AX	attack experimental
Bandit	opposing fighter
BBA	building block approach
BFM	basic fighter maneuver
Bull's-eye	direct hit
BVR	beyond visual range
CAS	close air support
CBU	cluster bomb unit
CCC	centralized command and control
CEP	circular error probable
CO	commanding officer
COR	continental operation ranges
DACT	dissimilar air combat training
Dive Toss	computerized weapons delivery
Double Attack	two-ship formation
ECM	electronic countermeasures
EM	energy maneuverability
EW	electronic warfare
FAC	forward air controller

FCS	fire control system
FEBA	forward edge of the battle area
Fluid Attack	two aircraft flying abreast
Fluid Four	four-ship formation
FOL	forward operating location
FWR	*Fighter Weapons Review*
FWS	Fighter Weapons School
FWSq	Fighter Weapons Squadron
g	one force of gravity
GAT	ground attack tactics
GCI	ground control intercept
GIB	guy-in-back
GP	general purpose
GRDCUS	gulf range drone control upgrade system
Have Quick	radio set by atomic clock
HOBOS	homing optical bomb system
HUD	heads up display
IADS	integrated air defense system
IFR	incentive firing plan
IIR	imaging infrared
JFS	jet fuel starter
LGB	laser-guided bomb
Lima	AIM–9L Sidewinder missile
MAC	Military Airlift Command
Maverick	television-guided rocket-powered missile
MER	multiple ejector rack
NATO	North Atlantic Treaty Organization
No Joy	I do not see the bandit
NVAF	North Vietnamese air force
OCS	Officer Candidate School
OODA loop	observe-orient-decide-act loop
OPEC	Organization of Petroleum Exporting Companies
ORI	operational readiness inspection
OTS	Officer Training School
PACAF	Pacific Air Forces
Pave	precision avionics vectoring equipment
Pave Knife	designator for laser-guided bombs
Pave Penny	laser spot detector
Pave Spike	laser designator pod
Pave Tack	pod that utilizes imaging infrared
Pave Way	laser-guided bomb program
PD	pulse doppler
Pickle button	weapons release button on control stick

Pinkie switch	556 modification switch on controls
Pipper	small dot in center of the gunsight
Pod	electronic protective device
RAF	Royal Air Force
RCS	radar cross section
Red Flag	dissimilar air combat training program at Nellis
Rivet Haste	training program against MiGs
ROC	requirement for operational capability
ROE	rules of engagement
RTB	return to base
RTU	replacement training unit
RWR	radar warning receiver
SAC	Strategic Air Command
SAM	surface-to-air missile
SAR	search and rescue
Shack	bull's-eye; direct hit
SLUF	short, little, ugly fellow
Snake Eye	high-drag bomb
TAC	Tactical Air Command
TAF	tactical air forces
Tally-ho/tally	visual sighting
TD	target designator
TDY	temporary duty
TER	triple ejector rack
TFS	Tactical Fighter Squadron
TFWC	Tactical Fighter Weapons Center
TG	terminal guidance
TI	Texas Instruments
TISEO	target identification system electro-optical
TOSS	television optical scoring system
Triple Nickel	555th Tactical Fighter Squadron
UNT	undergraduate navigator training
UPT	undergraduate pilot training
USAF	United States Air Force
USAFA	United States Air Force Academy
USAFE	United States Air Forces in Europe
USMC	United States Marine Corps
USN	United States Navy
VID	visual identification
WRCS	weapons release computer system
WSEP	weapons system evaluation program
WSO	weapons systems operator
Zot	laser aiming system

Bibliographic Notes

USAF Fighter Weapons Review was a quarterly magazine published by the Tactical Fighter Weapons Center, Nellis Air Force Base, Nevada, and is now known as the *USAF Weapons Review*. It is a compilation of articles written by fighter crew members describing the weapons systems and tactics of their various aircraft.

USAF histories are found on microfilm at two locations. The primary location is the Air Force Historical Research Agency, Maxwell Air Force Base, Alabama, where they are filed by reel number. Titles are available in a computerized index with cross-references and search capability by subject, author, or title. Some histories are available through the Air Force History Support Office Library at Bolling Air Force Base, Washington, D.C., but access is limited to those with official business designations.

The author conducted all interviews. Some of them were taped, but most are documented only through the author's notes. Researchers wishing to conduct interviews of those cited in the work may contact the author, who will in turn contact the interviewee to determine the individual's willingness to contribute further.

CPSIA information can be obtained
at www.ICGtesting.com
Printed in the USA
BVHW03s2309150218
508098BV00001B/145/P

9 781931 839044